Doctrines of Salvation

JOSEPH FIELDING SMITH

DOCTRINES

OF

SALVATION

Sermons and Writings of

JOSEPH FIELDING SMITH

Compiled by

BRUCE R. McCONKIE

VOLUME II

B O O K C R A F T
SALT LAKE CITY, UTAH

27th Printing, 1996

ISBN 0-88494-041-1

PREFACE

This second volume in the *Doctrines of Salvation* series has one central theme: Salvation—What it is; How to gain it; and the Laws which pertain to it.

For nearly half a century President Joseph Fielding Smith, true to his apostolic anointing, has travelled in the Church and throughout the world bearing special witness of Christ, raising the warning voice, and teaching the "Doctrines of Salvation" in plainness and simplicity. He is universally esteemed as the chief doctrinal authority of the Church.

No teachings are of greater worth to man than those revealing the truths about salvation, "for there is no gift greater than the gift of salvation";[1] and there is no one better qualified to teach these truths than President Smith.

The selections from his sermons and writings which make up this volume—continuing the pattern set in the first volume—have been arranged by subjects and copiously footnoted.

In *Doctrines of Salvation, Volume II*, the gospel student will find plain and authoritative explanations to virtually every important phase of salvation, the degrees of glory, exaltation, celestial marriage, the Holy Spirit of Promise, salvation for the dead, spiritual life and death, the resurrection, and much more. The devout seeker after salvation will turn to these teachings with an intense desire to master them.

To many I express deep appreciation for help, suggestions, and encouragement: Chiefly, of course, to President Smith, himself, for his scriptural insight, his plain teachings, and his power of expression; to Elder

---

[1]*D. & C.* 6:13.

Oscar W. McConkie, my father, for much counsel and
many helpful suggestions; to Elder Milton R. Hunter of
the First Council of the Seventy, for like assistance; to
Joseph Fielding Smith, Jr., for setting the type and
making many valued suggestions; to Velma Harvey, for
typing the host of documents from which these choice
teachings have been taken; and to Harold Lundstrom,
for a painstaking and careful reading of the proof.

—Bruce R. McConkie

Salt Lake City, Utah
September 25, 1955

CONTENTS

CHAPTER 12. SPIRITUAL LIFE AND DEATH

The Second Death (216). The Sons of Perdition (218). Gospel Brings Spiritual Life (225). Damnation (227). Paradise and Hell (228).

CHAPTER 13. THE LAW OF TEMPLE BUILDING

Temples: Their Nature and Antiquity (231). Kirtland Temple (237). Latter-day Temples (243). Missouri Temple (246). Temple Blessings, Covenants, and Endowments (252).

CHAPTER 14. LAW OF THE RESURRECTION

Christ and the Resurrection (258). Doctrine of the Resurrection (264). Latter-Day Evidence of Resurrection (269). Sons of Perdition and the Resurrection (273). Stillborn Children (280). Resurrection of All Things (281).

CHAPTER 15. SALVATION AND RESURRECTION

Blessings Received Through Resurrection (283). Nature of Resurrected Bodies (284). Physical Perfection in Resurrection (289). First and Second Resurrections (294).

CHAPTER 16. FAITH UNTO SALVATION

The Law of Faith (302). Faith, Works, and Grace (306). Faith and Miracles (311). Faith and the Flood (315).

CHAPTER 17. BAPTISM AND SALVATION

Baptism: A Birth and Resurrection (323). How Baptism Brings Salvation (328). Rebaptism (332).

CHAPTER 18. THE SACRAMENT AND SALVATION

Law of the Sacrament (338). Sacrament Meeting (340). Covenant of the Sacrament (344). Children and the Sacrament (347).

* * * * *

VOLUME I CONTAINS THE FOLLOWING CHAPTERS:

VOLUME III CONTAINS THE FOLLOWING CHAPTERS:

CHAPTER 1

SALVATION

THE PLAN OF SALVATION

TRUTHS OF SALVATION EASILY UNDERSTOOD. *Salvation should be a subject uppermost in the minds of all men.* It is, without question, the most important subject that could possibly be considered, and yet there are so few among the many who pay any attention whatever to this great and important theme, as it may be applied in their lives.[1]

All truth connected with the plan of salvation is reasonable and comprehensible. At least it may be comprehended by those who trust in the Lord and put themselves in an attitude to receive the revelation he may give them. The Lord does not leave man to discover truth without any guidance. Never has he performed any important work for the salvation of the people without first sending among them his specially appointed witnesses who are empowered to speak with authority and with knowledge of the things of which they testify.[2]

LABORS TOWARD SALVATION IN PRE-EXISTENCE. We had an existence before we came to this world. We lived in the spirit, and were in the presence of our Father in heaven, who is the Father of the spirits of all men; and there we walked by sight, for we were in his presence.

It was necessary, in order that we might receive a fulness of blessings and opportunities and become like unto our Father, for us to pass through this mortal probation. Hence, this earth was prepared; and we were sent down here to receive bodies of flesh and bones and to be quickened by blood; and to partake of all the vicissi-

---

[1]*Church News,* Feb. 12, 1938, p. 3.   [2]*Era,* vol. 30, p. 949; Amos 3:7.

tudes of life as we find them here on this earth, that we might, through obedience to the principles of the gospel, know good from evil.

It was necessary that we have the privilege of suffering temptation and experiencing pain and tribulation as well as pleasure; and, if faithful, pass on to our exaltation and become the sons and daughters of God, having gained knowledge, wisdom, and understanding in this mortal life that could not be obtained in any other way. That is why we came here.

We took these mortal bodies; they were granted to us because of our obedience in the world before this, when we dwelt in the spirit and in the presence of God; and we now are suffering the sorrows as well as receiving the pleasures of the flesh.[3]

FREE AGENCY ESSENTIAL TO SALVATION. We are subject to temptation; but the Lord never intended that we should yield to it and thus become subject unto sin, and fall and lose the reward that otherwise would be ours. He knew that on no other terms, only through our free agency and the opportunities which would come to us in this life by knowing good from evil when we no longer walk by sight but by faith, would we be able to come back into his presence and be worthy of exaltation. Without free agency we would amount to very little, and the Lord granted unto us our agency, that we might act for ourselves—to choose the good, or to choose the evil if we desire—with the understanding that we would reap the reward of our labors in this life. Those who do good shall come forth in the resurrection of the just and receive a place of exaltation in his kingdom, while those who do evil shall come forth in the resurrection also, but the resurrection of damnation.[4]

LAWS OF SALVATION REVEALED FROM BEGINNING. We are not ignorant of the things of God, for they have

---

[3]Abra. 3:22-28; Moses 6:33, 48; 2 Ne. 2:24-25.　　[4]Gen. & Hist. Mag., vol. 9, p. 16; 2 Ne. 2:11-16, 27-30; John 5:28-29.

been made known to us from the days of Adam until now and are recorded in the holy scriptures. Messengers from the presence of God have been sent to the earth from the beginning to establish in the hearts of men, and to reveal to them, all that is essential for man's salvation. If any among us is ignorant of these things, it is due to wilful rebellion.

The Son of God came to earth himself to show us by example the way to eternal life, and was himself free from all sin. *We cannot excuse ourselves for the violation of the laws of God on the ground of ignorance.* With all of these commandments before us, we are moral agents responsible to the Most High and under obligation to be obedient.[5]

TERMS AND CONDITIONS OF PLAN OF SALVATION. The primary and fundamental principles of this plan of salvation are:

1—Faith in God the Father, in his Son Jesus Christ, and in the Holy Ghost. We must accept them as the presiding authority in the heavens, who govern and control all things, who are omnipotent, just, and true.

2—We must accept the infinite atonement of Christ, believing that he is the Redeemer of the world, both from Adam's transgression and from our individual sins on condition of our repentance.

3—We must repent of all our sins, giving our hearts to God with the full intent of serving him.

4—We must be baptized in water for the remission of our sins, by one who is called of God and clothed with divine authority to administer in the ordinances of the gospel.

5—We must have the hands of those holding authority placed upon our heads, and through their ministrations receive the baptism of the Holy Ghost—the Spirit of truth and prophecy that guides us in all truth.

------
[5]Conf. Rep., Apr., 1943, p. 13.

6—We must be willing to serve the Lord with all our heart, mind, and strength, keeping his commandments even unto the end.

Upon these laws salvation is based, and the promised blessings are unto all men. These conditions are not severe, or grievous, and are within the power of the weakest of the weak, if they will only place their trust in their Redeemer.

All who repent and obey these laws, will be redeemed and saved from the sins of the world; but they who refuse and repent not will have to suffer for their own sins.[6]

INGRATITUDE FOR PLAN OF SALVATION. Ingratitude is, I think, the most prevalent of all sins, and one of the greatest, because every soul who refuses to abide in the truth, who will not walk in the light and understanding of the commandments which Jesus Christ has given, is ungrateful. He came and gave his life to redeem us from transgression. He was nailed to a cross and his blood was shed. What for? That we might live, that we might receive the remission of our sins, that we might, through obedience to the principles of the gospel, come back again into the presence of God the Father, and his Son Jesus Christ.[7]

IMMORTALITY AND ETERNAL LIFE

IMMORTALITY AND ETERNAL LIFE COMPARED. Immortality and eternal life are two separate things, one distinct from the other. Every man shall receive immortality, whether he be good, bad, or indifferent, for the resurrection from the dead shall come to all.

Eternal life is something in addition. None shall receive eternal life save it be those who keep the commandments of the Lord and are entitled thus to enter into his presence. When the Lord says, "Strait is the gate, and narrow is the way, which leadeth unto life, and few there

6*Salvation Universal,* p. 5; D. & C.   7Conf. Rep., Apr., 1944, pp. 49-50.
  19:4, 15-19; 20:18-28.

be that find it,"[8] he means that there will be very few of the children of men who will prove themselves worthy in this life, to go back and dwell in his presence. That is eternal life, to dwell in the presence of the Father and receive exaltation from him. He did not mean that those who passed through the gate which is strait, and the way which is narrow, were those who should be raised from the dead.

Very gladly would the Lord give to everyone eternal life, but since that blessing can come only on merit— through the faithful performance of duty—only those who are worthy shall receive it.

HIGHER KINGDOMS MINISTER TO LOWER. Yet, through his abundant mercy, the Lord will do for all the best that can be done, and therefore he will give to all a place somewhere—if not within the gates of the Holy City, then it must be on the outside—[9]where those who are not entitled to the fulness of blessings may be ministered to by those who have greater glory. For we read also here in this vision, where the glories are spoken of, that those who dwell in the celestial kingdom shall minister unto those of the terrestrial kingdom; those in the terrestrial kingdom shall minister to those of the telestial kingdom.

The Son may go to the terrestrial, but they who enter into that kingdom shall not receive the fulness of the Father; they will not see the greatness of his glory. He withholds that from them. They never come back again into the fulness of his presence. Those who enter into the telestial kingdom will not receive the fulness of the Father or of the Son. They will not visit there but will send messengers to visit the inhabitants of that glory and instruct them.

Those in the terrestrial kingdom shall visit those in the telestial kingdom, and those of the celestial shall visit those in the terrestrial kingdom. Where the Father is

---

[8]Matt. 7:14.   [9]Rev. 21:27; 22:14-15.

these cannot come, for the Lord has said: "Where God and Christ dwell they cannot come, worlds without end."[10] Yet in this very same section it is written that notwithstanding this fact, so great shall be the blessings that come to those who enter there that it is beyond our comprehension.[11] Such is the great mercy of the Lord. He will endeavor to save all his children and exalt as many as he possibly can.

COMPLETE OBEDIENCE BRINGS ETERNAL LIFE. But *to be exalted one must keep the whole law.* This is the great love he shows forth for his children: notwithstanding they sin and close their eyes against the truth, yet his arm is stretched out still, and he will feel after them and bring them back if they will keep his commandments; and if not, he will do for them just the best he can. He is going to bless them with all it is possible to give, and all shall be saved; all others will receive a place somewhere and it will be glorious unto them, but to receive the exaltation of the righteous, in other words eternal life, the commandments of the Lord must be kept in *all* things.

ETERNAL LIFE AND ETERNAL DAMNATION COM-PARED. There is another passage of scripture I want to read in connection with this. I want to read from section 29. The Lord here speaks of Adam and his punishment after he was cast out of the Lord's presence. "But, behold, I say unto you that I, the Lord God, gave unto Adam and unto his seed, that they should not die as to the temporal death"—they had already died the first death, the spir-itual death, and the Lord said he gave them power that they should not die the temporal death—"until I, the Lord God, should send forth angels to declare unto them repentance and redemption, through faith on the name of mine Only Begotton Son. And thus did I, the Lord God, appoint unto man the days of his probation,"—now

---

[10]*D. & C.* 76:112.   [11]*D. & C.* 76:86-89.

mark this—"that by his natural death he might be raised *in immortality unto eternal life."*

So you see the significance of it? Every man is raised *in immortality,* no more death, even *unto eternal life,* if he keeps the commandments of the Lord—not otherwise. Now I think that is a very significant reading here, "raised in immortality unto eternal life, even as many as would believe." Now mark this: *"And they that be-lieve not unto eternal damnation; for they cannot be redeemed from their spiritual fall, because they repent not."*[12]

The spiritual fall means banishment from the pres-ence of the Lord, and they cannot be redeemed from that because they do not repent. Now when they eventually do repent, if their deeds have been evil and they are not entitled to walk in the strait and narrow way and through the gate, they will have to take their place somewhere in some kingdom outside of his presence where they shall be taught, they shall be instructed by those who have gone beyond to exaltation.

ETERNAL LIFE IS GOD'S LIFE. One more thought. I want to read you a verse or two from the 17th chapter of John: "These words spake Jesus, and lifted up his eyes to heaven, and said, Father, the hour is come; glor-ify thy Son, that thy Son also may glorify thee: As thou hast given him power over all flesh, that he should give eternal life to as many as thou hast given him. And this is life eternal," now here you get it, "this is life eternal, that they might know thee the only true God, and Jesus Christ, whom thou hast sent."[13]

No man who does not receive the privilege of en-tering the celestial kingdom and coming face to face with the Father will be able to know what eternal life is, for he cannot know the Father unless he sees him and dwells with him, and partakes of the same life which the Father possesses for that is eternal life.

---

[12]D. & C. 29:42-44.   [13]John 17:1-3.

ETERNAL LIFE AND ETERNAL PUNISHMENT COM-
PARED. Now, again, my mind is called to another thought
I do not want to lose before I close. In the 19th section of
the *Doctrine and Covenants* we read of endless punishment. You know the idea of eternal punishment, endless
punishment, had troubled the world; and because the
scriptures speak of endless punishment and eternal punishment, men have stood before congregations of the
people and said unto them, "If you don't repent, if you
don't believe in the Lord Jesus Christ, you shall be
damned eternally; you shall go into a lake of fire and
brimstone where you will be ever burning but never consumed"; and thus they tortured the minds of the people
by teaching unto them such doctrine as that. The Lord
has revealed unto us what is meant by eternal punishment,
for he says: "For, behold, the mystery of godliness, how
great is it! For, behold, I am endless, and the punishment
which is given from my hand is endless punishment, for
Endless is my name. Wherefore—
  "*Eternal punishment is God's punishment.*
  "*Endless punishment is God's punishment.*"[14]
That is why it is called *endless.* Therefore, I say to
you, *eternal life is God's life; it is the life which he has,
that which he possesses.* Therefore, if he gives unto you
that life which he has, you have eternal life, and you will
not get it if you do not prove yourself worthy to enter into
his presence. Now, that is the gospel of Jesus Christ,
that is the great plan of salvation.[15]

ETERNAL LIFE IS EXALTATION. Now there is a difference between *immortality* and *eternal life. Immortality
is the gift to live forever.* It comes to every creature.
Eternal life is to have the kind of life that God has. All
those who become servants will have immortality, but
they who become sons and daughters of God will have
the *additional* gift of eternal life, which is the greatest
gift of God.[16]

---

[14]*D. & C.* 19:10-12.   [16]*Church News,* Apr. 22, 1939, p. 7;
[15]*Rel. Soc. Mag.,* vol. 7, pp. 10-13.   *D. & C.* 14:7.

Eternal life is life in the presence of the Father and the Son. Those who receive it become *members of the "Church of the Firstborn" and are heirs as sons and daughters of God. They receive the fulness of blessings. They become like the Father and the Son and are joint-heirs with Jesus Christ.*[17]

What is eternal life? It is to have "a continuation of the seeds forever and ever."[18] *No one receives eternal life except those who receive the exaltation.* Eternal life is the greatest gift of God; immortality is not. The Lord says: "Verily, verily, I say unto you, He that heareth my word, and believeth on him that sent me, hath everlasting life, and shall not come into condemnation; but is passed from death unto life." Everlasting life in this passage is the same as eternal life.[19]

KINDS OF SALVATION

SALVATION: CONDITIONAL AND UNCONDITIONAL. Christ's sacrifice and death did two things for us: it brought unto us *unconditional salvation* and *conditional salvation*. Sometimes we refer to these as *general salvation* and *individual salvation*. I am going to read what Orson Pratt said in relation to this. It is one of the clearest statements I know about. It is very concise and well thought out.

"The universal redemption of the posterity of Adam from the fall will be fully accomplished after the earth has been filled with its measure of inhabitants, and all men have been redeemed from the grave to immortality, and the earth itself has been changed and made entirely new."

Christ's mission is not finished until that time comes.

"But universal redemption from the effects of *original sin,* has nothing to do with redemption from our *personal sins;* for the original sin of Adam and the per-

[17]*Gen. & Hist. Mag.,* vol. 20, p. 40; Rom. 8:14-17; 1 John 3:1-3; Gal. 4:5-7; D. & C. 76:67, 94; 93:22.

[18]*Church News,* May 6, 1939, p. 8; D. & C. 132:19.

[19]Pers. Corresp.; Moses 1:39; John 5:24.

sonal sins of his children, are two different things. The
first was committed by man in his immortal state; the
second was committed by man in a mortal state; the former was committed in a state of ignorance of good and
evil; the latter was committed by man, having a knowledge of both good and evil. . . .

"The children of Adam had no agency in the transgression of their first parents, and therefore, they are
not required to exercise any agency in their redemption
from its penalty. They are redeemed from it without
faith, repentance, baptism, or any other act, either of
the mind or body."

REDEMPTION: CONDITIONAL AND UNCONDITIONAL.
"*Conditional redemption* is also universal in its nature;
it is offered to all but not received by all; it is a universal
gift, though not universally accepted; its benefits can be
obtained only through faith, repentance, baptism, the
laying on of hands, and obedience to all other requirements of the gospel.

"*Unconditional redemption* is a gift forced upon
mankind which they cannot reject, though they were dis-
posed. Not so with conditional redemption; it can be
received or rejected according to the will of the creature.

"Redemption from the original sin is without faith
or works; redemption from our own sins is given through
faith and works. *Both are the gifts of free grace;* but
while one is a gift *forced* upon us unconditionally, the
other is a gift merely *offered* to us conditionally. The
redemption of the one is *compulsory;* the reception of
the other is *voluntary.* Man cannot, by any possible act,
prevent his redemption from the fall; but he can utterly
refuse and prevent his redemption from the penalty of
his own sins."[20]

CHRIST REDEEMS ALL FORMS OF LIFE. We need
a little more explanation as to just what we mean by
unconditional redemption. That means to restore us

[20]*Millennial Star,* vol. 12, p. 69.

from this mortal state to the immortal state; in other words, to give unto us the resurrection. That comes to *every creature,* not only to men but also to the fish, the fowls of the air, and the beasts of the field, as the Lord tells us in section 29, of the *Doctrine and Covenants.*[21] All of them had spiritual existence before they were placed upon the earth; therefore they are to be redeemed.

Christ's blood not only redeems man but it also redeems every creature throughout this earth and the very earth itself. That comes as a free gift from Christ, without any asking on our part. We cannot prevent it. We have nothing to do with it, only to receive it, because we were not responsible for death. Therefore, as Paul says, "For as in Adam all die, even so in Christ shall all be made alive."[22]

But the conditional redemption is the redemption which will place us as sons and daughters of God in the kingdom of God.[23]

REDEMPTION AND SALVATION MEAN EXALTATION. *I want to discuss a little these three terms, redemption, salvation,* and *exaltation, used synonymously in the scriptures. Many places where you see the word redemption or where you see the word salvation it means exaltation, or in other words salvation in the kingdom of God; and yet sometimes there is a difference in meaning. While these three terms are used frequently in the scriptures synonymously,*[24] *in fact most of the time, yet they also do have different meanings describing three separate stages in the eternal progress of man.*[25]

SPECIAL MEANINGS OF REDEMPTION AND SALVATION. *Redemption* is the act of purchasing back, recovering from captivity, or restoring. So Christ becomes our Redeemer in bringing life back again where it was taken

---

[21]*D. & C.* 29:23-24; 77:2-3.
[22]1 Cor. 15:22.
[23]*Church News,* Mar. 9, 1935, p. 6.
[24]Redemption: *D. & C.* 29:42-46; 43:29; 35:25-26; 45:46; 133:52; 2 Ne. 2:6-7, 26; Mosiah 15:26-27;

Alma 9:27; Hela. 5:10; Ether 3:13-14; Morm. 7:7. Salvation: *D. & C.* 6:13.
[25]Redemption: *D. & C.* 88:14-17, 99; Alma 12:25; Morm. 9:12-13. Salvation: *D. & C.* 76:42-44.

away through the transgression. There will be some individuals who will be redeemed from death—I am
speaking now of the physical death—and that is all.
They will go out as sons of perdition to dwell with the
devil and his angels, as set forth in section 76 and other
scriptures. They are not redeemed from the spiritual
death, which is banishment from the presence of God.[26]

Salvation is preservation from impending evil; deliverance from sin and its penalty realized in a future
state; also, the means of deliverance from evil and ruin.
That is salvation. (I am giving you the dictionary
definition of these terms.)

Salvation will come to the great body of humanity.
The redemption of the soul is the resurrection. Salvation
is to find a place somewhere in that redeemed state, freed
from the realms "where their worm dieth not, and the fire
is not quenched"[27] in its fulness, or in other words redemption from that spiritual death which shall be pronounced upon the wicked when the Lord says unto them,
"Depart," and they go into the realms of Satan.[28]

Salvation will come to all who enter the terrestrial
kingdom. They will receive a higher grade of salvation
than will those in the telestial kingdom. Salvation will
come also to those who enter the celestial kingdom. That
will be a still higher grade of salvation.

SPECIAL MEANINGS OF REDEMPTION AND SALVA-
TION COMPARED. *Exaltation* is the act of being raised
or elevated, as in position or rank; it is to be magnified
or glorified. So in the celestial kingdom those who pass
by the gods who are set to guard the way to a fulness,
receive exaltation. The telestial kingdom is not a kingdom of exaltation; the terrestrial kingdom is not a
kingdom of exaltation, although it is higher than the
telestial kingdom; and there will be many who will enter
the celestial kingdom in their saved condition without

---

[26]*D. & C.* 76:30-49; 88:32-33; 2 Ne.   [27]*D. & C.* 76:44.
    9:15-16.   [28]*D. & C.* 29:41.

an exaltation in it, for there are different degrees even in the celestial kingdom.

Redemption, according to the gospel, is the gift of God to every creature born into the world, that he shall live again, being entitled to the resurrection. Christ is frequently spoken of in the scriptures as our Redeemer, and so refers to himself.

Salvation is the gift of God, according to the scriptures, to all men who do not sin against the light and become sons of perdition. Salvation is of varying stages or degrees. Every man is to be judged according to his works, and for this reason various degrees or kingdoms have been established.

Exaltation is to dwell in the presence of God and to be like him.[29]

WORKING OUT OUR SALVATION

GATE TO SALVATION IS STRAIT. "Enter ye in at the strait gate; for wide is the gate, and broad is the way, which leadeth to destruction, and many there be who go in thereat; Because strait is the gate, and narrow is the way, which leadeth unto life, and few there be that find it."[30]

Strange as it may appear, there are few people, very few in the world, who believe, if we are to judge them by their acts, in these words of our Redeemer. Mark you, this word *strait* is spelled *s-t-r-a-i-t* and not *s-t-r-a-i-g-h-t.* While no doubt, that path which leads into the presence of God is *straight,* it is also *strait,* which means that those who enter into it will find it restricted; it is narrow; they cannot take with them that which does not apply, or which does not belong to the kingdom of God. All such things must be left behind when we enter into this narrow way which leads into the presence of God, where we can receive life eternal. "Few there be that find it."[31]

[29]*Church News,* Apr. 22, 1939, p. 7.　[31]*Church News,* Feb. 12, 1938, p. 3.
[30]3 Ne. 14:13-14; Matt. 7:13-14; D. & C. 22:2; 132:22-25.

I have never been able in my teachings to make the gospel plan appear easy: that is, to hold out hopes to those who are indifferent, to those who are wayward, to those who wilfully break the commandments of the Lord and will not hearken unto these truths when every opportunity is given them to obey the truth.[32]

CHURCH MEMBERSHIP ALONE WILL NOT SAVE. *We are not going to be saved in the kingdom of God just because our names are on the records of the Church.* It will require more than that. We will have to have our names written in the *Lamb's Book of Life;* that is the evidence we have kept the commandments. Every soul who will not keep the commandments shall have his name blotted out of that book.[33] . . .

Oh, I wish we had the power, we who hold the priesthood, to reach every soul who is not faithful, who is not humbled in his heart—members of this Church— that we might bring them back to a full understanding of the gospel. Is it true that some among us have an idea that it matters not that we sin so long as it is not a grievous sin, a deadly sin, that we will yet be saved in the kingdom of God? Nephi saw our day. He said that people would be saying that. But I say unto you, we cannot turn away from the path of truth and righteousness and retain the guidance of the Spirit of the Lord.[34]

It is not possible, as some of us have supposed, for us to slip along easily through this life, keeping the commandments of the Lord indifferently—accepting some of the doctrines and not others, and indulging our appetites or desires, and, because we consider them little things, failing to understand and comprehend our duty to them—and then expect to receive a fulness of glory in the kingdom of God.[35]

[32]Conf. Rep., Apr., 1923, p. 138; 2 Ne. 9:27; Mosiah 15:26-27; Alma 34-31-35; 3 Ne. 12:20; 28:34-35.
[33] Ne. 27:16-21; 2 Ne. 31:16-21; Rev. 3:5; 13:8; 17:8; 20:12, 15; 21:27; 22:19.
[34]Conf. Rep., Sept., 1950, pp. 9-10, 12-13; 2 Ne. 28:7-9, 20-25.
[35]Rel. Soc. Mag., vol. 6, p. 464.

NOT HALF THE LATTER-DAY SAINTS TO BE SAVED.
Those who receive the *fulness* will be privileged to view
the face of our Father. *There will not be such an over-
whelming number of the Latter-day Saints who will get
there.* President Francis M. Lyman many times has declared, and he had reason to declare, I believe, that *if* we
save one-half of the Latter-day Saints, that is, with an
exaltation in the celestial kingdom of God, we will be
doing well. Not that the Lord is partial, not that he will
draw the line as some will say, to keep people out. He
would have every one of us go in if we would; but there
are laws and ordinances that we must keep; if we do
not observe the law we cannot enter.

Many come into the Church, like fish that are
gathered into the net, that have to be sorted and thrown
out again or put into piles where they belong. And so
it will be with us.[36]

The Savior compared the kingdom, in other words
the Church, to ten virgins, five of whom were wise and
five of whom were foolish;[37] and so we must not get the
understanding that because we are members of the
Church it is all well with us, and our salvation is secure,
that is, our exaltation is secure. It is not so.

We must continue to the end; we must obey the
commandments. We must keep the ordinances. We must
receive covenants, sealings, the sealing power, and privileges which are obtained in the temple of the Lord, and
then live in accordance with them. That we must do.[38]

NOT SAVED BY FAITH OF OUR FATHERS. We must
not lose sight of the fact that no man can lay claim to
salvation, or to the priesthood of God, simply because
he had a faithful father. . . .

If they are not faithful, then they will not receive
the fulfilment of the promise. The posterity of Joseph
Smith, like the posterity of any other elder of Israel, will
stand or fall on their own foundation which they have

---

[36]Matt. 13:47-50.   [38]*Rel. Soc. Mag.,* vol. 6, p. 469.
[37]Matt. 25:1-13.

builded. And *if the sons of Joseph Smith refuse to keep
the commandments, the blessings will pass them by;* but
God's work will continue until the consummation of all
things.[39]

SALVATION AND A CUP OF TEA. You cannot neglect
little things. "Oh, a cup of tea is such a little thing. It
is so little; surely it doesn't amount to much; surely the
Lord will forgive me if I drink a cup of tea."

Yes, he will forgive you, because he is going to
forgive every man who repents; but, my brethren, if you
drink coffee or tea, or take tobacco, are you letting a cup
of tea or a little tobacco stand in the road and bar you
from the celestial kingdom of God, where you might
otherwise have received a fulness of glory?

"Oh, it is such a little thing, and the Lord will forgive
us." Well, there is not anything that is little in the way
of sinning. There is not anything that is little in this
world in the aggregate. One cup of tea, then it is another
cup of tea and another cup of tea, and when you get them
all together, they are not so little. As we learned in the
Primary:

"Little drops of water, little grains of sand
Make the mighty ocean and the pleasant land."

What is a grain of sand? And yet the earth is composed of just such things as that.

Not long ago I was riding in an automobile. Something went wrong with it, and it refused to go. The
man was an expert who was driving, but I did not have
much time. I left matters till I hardly had time to get to
the train, which was 30 miles away. We went all over
his machine; every wire was in contact; everything was
just so; he could not find a thing in it that was wrong;
and yet he could not make it go.

"Well" I said to him, "here, you have done everything you know but one. There is just one thing now

[39]*Origin of the "Reorganized" Church,*
    p. 55; D. & C. 86:8-11.

that I want you to do: open up your carburetor, and let out a little gas, I believe it has water in it." He let it run off and closed the valve again, and the auto began to run immediately.

LITTLE SINS WILL KEEP US FROM SALVATION. But a little water in the carburetor was such a little thing, just a few drops, but they were in the road and they stopped the progress and nearly cost me reaching that train. Suppose we call that train salvation, could you afford to let a little thing like that stand between you and your salvation? . . .

God is not going to save every man and woman in the celestial kingdom. If you want to get there, and you have failings; if you are committing sins; if you are breaking the commandments of the Lord, and you know it; it is a good time right now to repent and reform, and not get the idea that it is such a little thing that the Lord will forgive you; just a few stripes, just a little punishment and we will be forgiven; for you may find yourselves cast out, if you insist and persist in such a course.[40]

CHURCH MEMBERS MUST ENDURE TO END. Unless it is a grievous sin we do not excommunicate people from the Church. We try to teach them their duty. We try to bring them to repentance. We try to make them understand the truth. But after they are in the Church, if they will not do these things and will not hearken to our counsels, you may be assured that they are going to be judged according to their works.

The fact that they are members of the Church will not save them. Every man and every woman will have to answer for the deeds done in the body. An ancient prophet said: "Wo unto him that has the law given, yea, that has all the commandments of God, like unto us, and that transgresseth them, and that wasteth the days of his probation, for awful is his state!"[41] . . .

---

[40]*Rel. Soc. Mag.*, vol. 6, pp. 472-473.   [41]2 Ne. 9:27.

"How shall we, that are dead to sin, live any longer therein?"[42]

Every baptized person who has fully repented, who comes into the Church with a broken heart and a contrite spirit, has made a covenant to continue with that broken heart, with that contrite spirit, which means a repentant spirit. He makes a covenant that he will do that.[43]

He is to endure to the end. It is essential that we endure to the end. In the revelation that was given at the time the Church was organized, the Lord said this:

"And we know that all men must repent and believe on the name of Jesus Christ, and worship the Father in his name, and endure in faith on his name to the end, or they cannot be saved in the kingdom of God."[44]

PROGRESS TOWARD SALVATION BEYOND THE GRAVE. Salvation does not come all at once; we are commanded to be perfect even as our Father in heaven is perfect. It will take us ages to accomplish this end, for there will be greater progress beyond the grave, and it will be there that the faithful will overcome all things, and receive all things, even the fulness of the Father's glory.[45]

I believe the Lord meant just what he said: that we should be perfect, as our Father in heaven is perfect. That will not come all at once, but line upon line, and precept upon precept, example upon example, and even then not as long as we live in this mortal life, for we will have to go even beyond the grave before we reach that perfection and shall be like God.

But here we lay the foundation. Here is where we are taught these simple truths of the gospel of Jesus Christ, in this probationary state, to prepare us for that perfection. It is our duty to be better today than we were yesterday, and better tomorrow than we are today. Why? Because we are on that road, if we are keeping

---

[42]Rom. 6:2.
[43]Mosiah 18:8-10; D. & C. 20:37.
[44]Conf. Rep., Oct., 1941, pp. 92-94; D. & C. 20:29.

[45]Salvation Universal, p. 17; Matt. 5:48; 3 Ne. 12:48; D. & C. 76:56; 84:38; 93:20-22, 27-28.

the commandments of the Lord, we are on that road to perfection, and that can only come through obedience and the desire in our hearts to overcome the world.[46]

THE UNCLEAN CANNOT BE SAVED. It is the duty of every man to try to be like his Eternal Father. This requires cleanliness of thought and action. We are instructed that *no unclean thing can inherit the kingdom of God.*[47] . . .

It is reasonable to think that every soul who desires to be a true follower of Jesus Christ would wish to be as nearly like him in all respects as it is possible.[48]

How SAINTS ARE MADE. Saints are not made by popes or any other creature. It is not within the jurisdiction of mortals to make saints, either when they are living or after they are dead. *Sainthood comes through obedience to the commandments of the Lord.*[49]

[46]Conf. Rep., Oct., 1941, p. 95.
[47]Alma 11:37; 3 Ne. 27:19; Moses
    6:57.
[48]*Church News*, Oct. 2, 1953, p. 4;
    3 Ne. 27:27.
[49]Pers. Corresp.

THE DEGREES OF GLORY

KINGDOMS OF GLORY

REASONABLE TO BELIEVE IN DEGREES OF GLORY. A place is prepared for every man where he shall be rewarded according to his works. For this reason Paul taught that there was a glory of the sun, a glory of the moon, and a glory of the stars, and as the stars differed in magnitude, so is it in the resurrection of the dead.[1] However, every man must repent, for every knee must bend and every tongue confess that Jesus is the Christ. None is exempt from this mandate which will finally be declared.[2]

Quite generally the idea has been taught that man is either to be saved in the kingdom of God or cast into hell. He is either in the presence of God, or else in the presence of the devil. No other place is provided where a man could go who is unworthy of the presence of the Lord and yet not worthy of the condemnation with Lucifer.

Is such a thought consistent? With serious reflection, can we believe that our Eternal Father, who is all-wise and just, has arranged salvation and damnation on any such foundation as this? Let us look at this question in the spirit of common sense. All of the principles of the gospel are reasonable. It was the Lord himself who declared that in his Father's house were many mansions.[3]

ALL SAVED EXCEPT SONS OF PERDITION. It is a very pleasing and consoling thing to know that the Lord will save *all* of his children, excepting the very few who wil-

---

[1] 1 Cor. 15:39-42; Rev. 20:12-15.
[2] Isa. 45:23; Rom. 14:10-11; Phil. 2:9-11; D. & C. 76:110; 88:104.
[3] *Millennial Star,* vol. 91, p. 675; John 14:2.

fully rebel against him. When his children have paid the penalty of their transgressions, they shall come forth from the clutches of the second death to receive a place somewhere in the great heavenly kingdoms, which are prepared for them with their several glories and degrees of salvation.[4]

It is the purpose of the Almighty to save all mankind, and all will enter into his kingdoms in some degree of glory, except sons of perdition who sin beyond the power of repentance and redemption, and therefore cannot receive forgiveness of sins. All the rest shall be saved, but not all with the same degree of glory or exaltation.[5] Every man will be judged according to his works, his opportunities for receiving the truth, and the intent of his heart.

CELESTIAL SALVATION. Those who keep the full law and obey all the commandments of God are heirs of *full salvation* in the celestial kingdom, the glory of which the sun is spoken of as being typical. These overcome all things and receive a fulness of the blessings, power, and glory of the Father.[6] All who have died without a knowledge of the gospel, or the opportunity to receive it, who would have accepted it had the opportunity been presented to them while living, are also heirs of this kingdom.[7]

TERRESTRIAL SALVATION. Into the next, or terrestrial, shall enter all those who die without law; "they who are the spirits of men kept in prison, whom the Son visited, and preached the gospel unto them, that they might be judged according to men in the flesh; Who received not the testimony of Jesus in the flesh, but afterwards received it"; "honorable men of the earth, who were blinded by the craftiness of men"; those who were

---

[4]*Era*, vol. 19, p. 428; *D. & C.* 63:17-18; 76:81-85.
[5]*D. & C.* 76:30-49; Heb. 6:4-8.

[6]*D. & C.* 76:50-70, 92-96; 84:38; 88:107.
[7]*Era*, vol. 20, pp. 360-361; Joseph Fielding Smith, *Teachings of the Prophet Joseph Smith*, p. 107.

not willing to receive a fulness of his glory; and those who were not valiant in the testimony of Jesus; "wherefore, they obtain not the crown over the kingdom of our God."[8]

TELESTIAL SALVATION. Those who enter into the telestial kingdom, where their glories differ as do the stars of heaven in their magnitude, and who are innumerable as the sands of the seashore, are the ungodly, the filthy who suffer the wrath of God on the earth, who are thrust down to hell where they will be required to pay the uttermost farthing *before* their redemption comes. These are they who receive not the gospel of Christ and consequently could not deny the Holy Spirit while living on the earth.

They have no part in the first resurrection and are not redeemed from the devil and his angels *until* the last resurrection, because of their wicked lives and their evil deeds. Nevertheless, even these are heirs of salvation, but before they are redeemed and enter into their kingdom, they must repent of their sins, and receive the gospel, and bow the knee, and acknowledge that Jesus is the Christ, the Redeemer of the world.[9]

In both the terrestrial and the telestial glories the inhabitants thereof will be limited in their powers, opportunities, and progression, because, like the sons of perdition, "they were not willing to enjoy that which they might have received."[10]

TELESTIAL DAMNATION. All who have been filthy and who would not receive the truth and have not had the testimony of Jesus Christ, must *suffer the torments of the damned until they are purged from their iniquity*, for the blood of Jesus Christ will not cleanse them from their sins without their own individual suffering.

Nevertheless they shall come out of the prison eventually. These are the rest of the dead, spoken of by John,

---

[8]*Era*, vol. 19, pp. 428-429; D. & C. 76:71-80.

[9]*Era*, vol. 20, pp. 360-361; D. & C. 76:81-90, 98-113.

[10]*Era*, vol. 19, p. 429; D. & C. 88:32.

who do not live during the millennial reign, but afterwards; and these are assigned to a kingdom known as
the telestial kingdom, and they are denied the privilege
of dwelling with the Father and the Son, "worlds without
end." The Lord will do for them the best he can under
the circumstances, but since they have denied his power
and have dwelt in iniquity, they cannot receive the
blessings of the kingdom of God.[11]

GOSPEL TRUTHS TAUGHT IN ALL KINGDOMS. Will
those in the other kingdoms besides the celestial, have
the gospel taught to them?

Yes, *all truth is gospel truth;* and every soul eventually must become acquainted with the plan of salvation, at least as far as it is possible for him to do. We
read that every knee must bow and every tongue confess
Jesus Christ as the Son of God. This being true, then
every soul must know something about him.

But matters which have been held in reserve for the
faithful and which have been kept hid from the world by
divine decree since before the foundation of the earth,
need not be known after the resurrection any more than
before, to those who are *not* entitled to receive them. For
instance, there will be covenants and obligations required
of these who enter into the exaltation which in no way
will apply to those who do not enter into the exaltation,
for they do not receive the fulness. In every kingdom
the inhabitants must know that they have been redeemed
from death, and have received such blessings as are
granted them, through the mercy of Jesus Christ.[12]

THE CELESTIAL KINGDOM

THE CELESTIAL IS THE KINGDOM OF GOD. *The
celestial kingdom is the kingdom spoken of in the scriptures as the kingdom of God,* which men are commanded
to seek first in preference to all else.[13] It is the place where

[11]*Church News,* Feb. 20, 1932, p. 8;   [12]Pers. Corresp.
   Rev. 20:5; D. & C. 19:4, 15-19;   [13]Matt. 6:33; D. & C. 6:7.
   29:17.

those who enter receive eternal life, in addition to immortality. Immortality is the gift to live forever given to all
men. Eternal life is life in the presence of the Father and
the Son and is the *kind* of life which they possess. It is
of the celestial kingdom the Lord was speaking when he
said: "Enter ye in at the strait gate: for wide is the gate,
and broad is the way, that leadeth to destruction, and
many there be which go in thereat: Because strait is the
gate, and narrow is the way, which leadeth unto life, and
few there be that find it."[14]

NATURE OF EXALTATION IN CELESTIAL KINGDOM.
Comparatively few of the children of men will find the
salvation which is found in the celestial kingdom, or in
other words the exaltation which will make of them heirs
of God and joint-heirs with Jesus Christ—even sons of
God. *Those who gain this exaltation receive the fulness
of the power, might, and dominion of that kingdom. They
overcome all things. They are crowned as priests and
kings and become like Jesus Christ.* While this doctrine
is taught in the *Bible,* the majority of mankind have lost
sight of it, and it has become one of the peculiar teachings
of the Church of Jesus Christ of Latter-day Saints.

Paul taught: "For as many as are led by the Spirit
of God, they are the sons of God. . . . The Spirit itself
beareth witness with our spirit, that we are the children
of God: And if children, then heirs; heirs of God, and
joint-heirs with Christ; if so be that we suffer with him,
that we may be also glorified together."[15]

John also taught that those who have kept the
commandments of the Lord in the full are sons of God,
and when Christ comes they shall be like him. "And,"
said John, "every man that hath this hope in him purifieth
himself, even as he is pure."[16]

This celestial kingdom is governed by immutable
law. It is only through obedience to the principles of the

[14]Matt. 7:13-14; 3 Ne. 14:13-14.   [16]1 John 3:1-3; Gal. 4:5-7.
[15]Rom. 8:14-17; D. & C. 76:50-70;
   84:38; 88:107; 93:20-28; 132:19-25.

gospel and the laws which pertain to this kingdom that its blessings are obtained. Since the majority of men refuse to take the course in righteousness, or enter the strait gate into the narrow way, which would make them heirs in the household of God, it will be a select few who receive these crowning blessings.[17]

SALVATION COMES TO THOSE WHO OVERCOME ALL THINGS. *We are preaching the gospel of salvation in the celestial kingdom.* I think it would be better if we would get into the habit of speaking more of exaltation than of salvation. According to the scriptures which are given to us, salvation means for a man to rise above his enemies, to conquer them. This does not mean enemies in the flesh, individuals, but it does mean sin, transgression of the law; and *as a man overcomes he is saved.*[18]

Through the atonement of Jesus Christ, *every soul* shall receive the resurrection; no matter when he lived or how, the resurrection will come to every individual. Even those who have lived upon the earth who shall be classed as sons of perdition shall receive their bodies, and the body and spirit shall be inseparably connected. This is a doctrine which seems to bother some. All others receiving the resurrection will find their places in one of these three great kingdoms.

But in order to enter into the celestial kingdom, which is the kingdom of exaltation, and the kingdom spoken of in the scriptures as the kingdom of God, one must accept and abide in the fulness of the gospel of Jesus Christ, adhering to the teachings, receiving the ordinances, and being true to the covenants which appertain to that salvation. . . .

The Prophet says a man may enter into the terrestrial or the telestial kingdom who has not been baptized with water and who has not in this life received these

[17]*Church News,* Feb. 27, 1932, p. 4.   [18]*D. & C.* 76:53, 60; Rev. 2:7, 11, 17, 26-28; 3:4-5, 12, 21; 21:7.

ordinances, but he can never enter into the celestial kingdom without complying with these eternal laws.[19]

Each kingdom, of course, is governed by laws. We have nothing to do with the laws of the telestial or terrestrial kingdoms, so far as the preaching of the gospel is concerned. *Our mission is to preach the salvation of the kingdom of God,* where he and Christ dwell, which is the celestial kingdom. And all of the principles of the gospel which have been given unto us pertain to the celestial kingdom.

Now, of course, if a man enters into one of the others because of disobedience, he will yet have to acknowledge Christ; he will have to believe in him as being the Son of God; he will have to bend the knee; for every knee must bow, and every tongue eventually must confess that Jesus is the Christ; that will be required of all, not merely those who are willing to keep the commandments and thereby receive exaltation.[20]

THIS EARTH TO BECOME CELESTIAL. This earth is going to become a celestial body and is going to be a fit abode for celestial beings *only;* the others will have to go somewhere else, where they belong. *This earth will be reserved for those who are entitled to exaltation,* and they are the *meek,* spoken of by our Savior, who shall inherit the earth. When the Lord said the meek shall inherit the earth, he had reference to those who are willing to keep the commandments of the Lord in righteousness and thus receive exaltation.[21]

MANY CELESTIAL EARTHS. This earth on which we dwell, like *many* that have gone before, is destined to become a *celestial sphere* and the righteous shall inherit it forever. "For, for this intent was it made and created," and after it has filled the measure of its mortal creation,

---

[19]Joseph Fielding Smith, *Teachings of the Prophet Joseph Smith,* p. 12.
[20]*Gen. & Hist. Mag.,* vol. 26, pp. 49-50; also: *Church News,* Jan. 5, 1935, pp. 2, 6.

[21]Conf. Rep., Apr., 1942, p. 28; Matt. 5:5; Ps. 37:11.

it shall be crowned with glory, even with the presence of God the Father. Like man, the earth also shall die, but it also shall be quickened again, and shall abide the power by which it is quickened, to continue throughout eternity as the celestial abode of man.[22]

THE TERRESTRIAL AND TELESTIAL KINGDOMS

JUDGMENT ACCORDING TO WORKS. Do you think that all are going to receive the gospel and come into the Church? No. There will be a great multitude, so great that you cannot count them, who will not receive the ordinances of the house of the Lord which would place them in the celestial kingdom and give them the blessings of exaltation. These will take their places in the terrestrial and telestial worlds, where they will be *denied many blessings and privileges* that are held in reserve for the faithful.[23]

Not all of the Lord's children are worthy of celestial glory, and many are forced to suffer his wrath because of their transgressions, and this causes the Father and the whole heavens to have sorrow and to weep.[24] The Lord works in accordance with natural law. Man must be redeemed according to law, and his reward must be based on the law of justice. Because of this, the Lord will not give unto men that which they do not merit, but shall reward all men according to their works.[25]

While all men shall be saved, except the few sons of perdition who wilfully reject the truth, yet our *place* and *station* will depend upon our integrity and willingness to obey the commandments of the Lord. Every man will be placed just where he belongs, according to his works. Justice will be meted out to all, and every man will find his level according to that which he was willing to receive.[26]

---

[22]*Era,* vol. 19, p. 431; *D. & C.* 88:17-26.
[23]*Gen. & Hist. Mag.,* vol. 17, pp. 149-150.
[24]Moses 7:28-31.

[25]Conf. Rep., Apr., 1923, p. 137.
[26]*Rel. Soc. Mag.,* vol. 5, pp. 680-681; Rev. 20:12; *D. & C.* 1:10; Alma 42:22-28.

CHURCH MEMBERS MAY GO TO ANY KINGDOM. We have our agency and many, very, very many members of this Church, when they come to the judgment and are judged according to their works, are going to be consigned to the telestial kingdom; others to the terrestrial kingdom; because that is the law that they have willed to obey; and *we are going to get our reward according to the law that we obey.*[27]

A man who has accepted the testimony of Jesus in the flesh may inherit *any* of the three kingdoms, according to the degree of faithfulness he has shown in keeping the commandments of the Lord. If he keeps the full law, he shall be entitled to enter the celestial kingdom.

If he is willing to abide by only a portion of the law, and rejects the covenants which govern in the celestial kingdom, notwithstanding he is honest, virtuous, and truthful, he shall be assigned to the terrestrial kingdom where other honorable men shall be found.

If he enters into the Church, but rejects the light, and lives a life of disobedience and corruption, he may be assigned to the telestial kingdom and obtain such blessings as he is willing to receive, because he was not willing to enjoy that which he might have received.[28]

THOSE WHO ARE NOT VALIANT. "These are they who are not valiant in the testimony of Jesus; wherefore, they obtain not the crown over the kingdom of our God."[29] These enter into the terrestrial glory.

Who are they? All who refuse to receive the fulness of the truth, or abide by the principles and ordinances of the everlasting gospel. They may have received a testimony; they may be able to testify that they *know* that Jesus is the Christ; but in their lives they have refused to accept ordinances which are essential to entrance into the celestial kingdom. They have refused to live the gospel, when they knew it to be true; or have been blinded

27*Church News,* Apr. 22, 1939, p. 8;   28*Era, vol.* 22, p. 623.
   D. & C. 88:21-33.   29*D. & C.* 76:79.

by tradition; or for other cause have not been willing to walk in the light.

In this class we could properly place those who refuse to take upon them the name of Christ,[30] *even though they belong to the Church;* and those who are not willing when called to go forth and preach to a perverse world "Jesus Christ, and him crucified."[31]

They may live clean lives; they may be honest, industrious, good citizens, and all that; but they are not willing to assume any portion of the labor which devolves upon members of the Church, in carrying on the great work of redemption of mankind.

We have known members of the Church who have gone out in the world and have mingled with those not of our faith, and these members were ashamed to have it known that they were Latter-day Saints. Such persons certainly are not valiant in the testimony of Jesus. The Lord has said: "Whosoever therefore shall be ashamed of me and of my words in this adulterous and sinful generation; of him also shall the Son of man be ashamed, when he cometh in the glory of his Father with the holy angels."[32]

SALVATION OF THOSE WITHOUT THE GOSPEL LAW. Through the mission of Jesus Christ a law has been given, the law of the gospel, and that law is binding upon all those who hear it, who come in contact with it; and provision has been made so that those who are without the law or who have not heard the name of Christ, who are ignorant of the plan of salvation, because the gospel has never reached them in any form, shall not be under the same restrictions and condemnation as will those who have received that law. And they who are without the law, Christ redeems through his blood, and does not require of them that which he requires of me and of you.[33]

---

[30]D. & C. 18:21-28; 20:37; Mosiah 5:7-14; Alma 5:38-39.
[31]1 Cor. 2:2.
[32]*Era,* vol. 22, pp. 623-624; Mark 8:38.
[33]*Church News,* Feb. 12, 1938, p. 3.

2 Ne. 9:25-27; Mosiah 3:11-12, 20-22; 15:24-27; Alma 9:15-16; 29:5; 42:21; Hela. 15:14-15; Moro. 8:22; *D. & C.* 45:54; 76:72; Acts 17:30; Rom. 2:12.

EVERY KNEE SHALL BOW; EVERY TONGUE CON-
FESS. I want to call attention to something that is stated
frequently in the scriptures, and I think very often misunderstood, and that is the statement that, "every knee
shall bow, and every tongue shall confess."[34] I wonder
how many of us have an idea that if a knee bows and a
tongue confesses, that is a sign of forgiveness of sin and
freedom from sin, and that the candidate is prepared for
exaltation? If you do, you make a mistake. It does not
mean that at all.

The time will come when "every knee shall bow,
and every tongue shall confess," and yet the vast majority
of mankind will go into the telestial kingdom eternally.
Let me read these verses: "The time shall come when
all shall see the salvation of the Lord; when every nation,
kindred, tongue, and people shall see eye to eye and shall
confess before God that his judgments are just."

It is a wonderful thing when men reach the stage
when they will be willing to confess that the judgments
against them are just, and they will bow the knee and
will understand "eye to eye." But see what this prophet
says further: "And then shall the wicked be cast out, and
they shall have cause to howl, and weep, and wail, and
gnash their teeth; and this because they would not
hearken unto the voice of the Lord; therefore the Lord
redeemeth them not." And yet they confess.

"For they are carnal and devilish, and the devil has
power over them; yea, even that old serpent that did be-
guile our first parents, which was the cause of their fall;
which was the cause of all mankind becoming carnal,
sensual, devilish, knowing evil from good, subjecting
themselves to the devil.

"Thus all mankind were lost; and behold, they
would have been endlessly lost were it not that God redeemed his people from their lost and fallen state."[35]

---

[34]Isa. 45:23; Rom. 14:10-11; Phil. 2:9-   [35]Mosiah 16:1-4.
11; D. & C. 76:110; 88:104.

So do not get an idea that because they bow the knee and confess with the tongue, or as it reads in the other scriptures, see eye to eye, that this is going to exalt them in the celestial kingdom of God, because they are going to be judged according to their works and receive their dominion according to the plan that has been appointed and prepared according to the justice, and tempered by the mercy, of the Lord.[36]

NO PROGRESSION FROM KINGDOM TO KINGDOM

No ADVANCEMENT FROM LOWER TO HIGHER. It has been asked if it is possible for one who inherits the telestial glory to advance in time to the celestial glory?

The answer to this question is, *No!*

The scriptures are clear on this point. Speaking of those who go to the telestial kingdom, the revelation says: "And they shall be servants of the Most High; *but where God and Christ dwell they cannot come, worlds without end.*"[37]

Notwithstanding this statement, those who do not comprehend the word of the Lord argue that while this is true, that they cannot go where God is "worlds without end," yet in time they will get where God *was,* but he will have gone on to other heights.

This is *false reasoning, illogical,* and creates mischief in making people think they may procrastinate their repentance, but in course of time they will reach exaltation in celestial glory.

KINGDOMS PROGRESS IN DIFFERENT DIRECTIONS. Now let us see how faulty this reasoning is. *If* in time those who enter the telestial glory may progress till they reach the stage in which the celestial is in *now*—then they are *in* celestial glory, are they not, even *if* the celestial has advanced? That being the case (I state this for the argument only, for it is not true), then they partake of all the blessings which are *now* celestial. That means

---

[36]*Church News,* Apr. 22, 1939, p. 7;   [37]*D. & C.* 76:112.
   D. & C. 76:108-112.

that they become gods, have exaltation, gain the fulness of the Father, and receive a continuation of the "seeds forever." The Lord, however, has said that these blessings, which are celestial blessings, they may *never have;* they are barred forever!

The celestial and terrestrial and telestial glories, I have heard compared to the wheels on a train. The second and third may, and will, reach the place where the first was, but the first will have moved on and will still be just the same distance in advance of them. *This illustration is not true! The wheels do not run on the same track, and do not go in the same direction. The terrestrial and the telestial are limited in their powers of advancement, worlds without end.*

LIMITATION ON CELESTIAL PROGRESSION. In section 131, the Lord has said, through the Prophet Joseph Smith: "In the celestial glory there are three heavens or degrees; And in order to obtain the highest, a man must enter into this order of the priesthood [meaning the new and everlasting covenant of marriage]; And if he does not, he cannot obtain it. He may enter into the other, but that is the *end of his kingdom;* he cannot have an increase."[38] So, we see, *even in the celestial, some are barred and cannot go on to exaltation.*

Further light is thrown on this in section 132: "For these angels did not abide my law; therefore, they *cannot* be enlarged, but *remain* separately and singly, *without exaltation,* in their saved condition, *to all eternity;* and from henceforth *are not gods,* but are angels of God *forever and ever.*"[39] These angels, spoken of here, include those who enter the celestial kingdom but do not gain the highest glory in that kingdom.

In this same section the Lord says: "Verily, verily, I say unto you, *except ye abide my law ye cannot attain to this glory.* For strait is the gate, and narrow the way that leadeth unto *the exaltation and continuation of the*

---

[38]D. & C. 131:1-4.   [39]D. & C. 132:17.

lives, and few there be that find it. because ye receive me not in the world neither do ye know me. But *if* ye receive me in the world, then shall ye know me, and shall receive your exaltation; that where I am ye shall be also.

"This is eternal lives—to know the only wise and true God, and Jesus Christ, whom he hath sent. I am he. Receive ye, therefore, my law. Broad is the gate, and wide the way that leadeth to *the deaths;* and *many there are that go in thereat, because they receive me not, neither do they abide in my law."*[40]

Now, if a man is deprived of the "continuation of the lives" for ever—and not to have these blessings is re- ferred to as leading to the deaths, or the lack of the con- tinuation of the lives, or increase—then he cannot "worlds without end" reach the celestial glory; *for the celestial glory is "the continuation of the lives" or increase eternally;* it is to be gods, even the sons of God.

DIFFERENCES IN KIND OF RESURRECTED BODIES. In section 88 of the *Doctrine and Covenants,* we are taught that there is a difference in the *kinds* of resurrection. Some will be raised with celestial bodies; some with terrestrial bodies, and some with telestial bodies; and yet others will be raised with bodies without any qualification or power of glory, and these will be sons of perdition. Read verses 17-33. Paul bears witness of this in the following words:

"But some man will say, How are the dead raised up? and with what body to they come? Thou fool, that which thou sowest is not quickened, except it die: And that which thou sowest, thou sowest not that body that shall be, but bare grain, it may chance ot wheat, or ot some other grain: But God giveth it a body as it hath pleased him, and to every seed his own body.

"All flesh is not the same flesh: but there is one kind of flesh of men, another flesh of beasts, another of fishes, and another of birds. There are also celestial bodies, and bodies terrestrial: but the glory of the celestial is one,

---

[40]*D. & C.* 132:21-25.

and the glory of the terrestrial is another. . . . So also is the resurrection of the dead."[41]

If a man will enter into life, then he must abide in the law of the gospel, keeping all of the commandments to the end of his mortal life. This is the doctrine of the Prophet Joseph Smith. "I . . . spoke to the people," he says, "showing them that *to get salvation we must not only do some things, but everything which God has commanded. Men may preach and practice everything except those things which God commands us to do, and will be damned at last.* We may tithe mint and rue, and all manner of herbs, and still not obey the commandments of God."[42]

---

[41]1 Cor. 15:35-41.

[42]Joseph Fielding Smith, *Teachings of the Prophet Joseph Smith,* p. 332.

CHAPTER 3

EXALTATION

JOINT-HEIRS WITH JESUS CHRIST

EXALTATION: TO BECOME LIKE GOD. Those who *receive exaltation in the celestial kingdom are promised the fulness thereof. "All things are theirs, whether life or death, or things present, or things to come."*[1] Our Father *in heaven is infinite; he is perfect; he possesses all knowledge and wisdom.* However, he is not jealous of his wisdom and perfection, but glories in the fact that it is possible for his children who obey him in all things and endure to the end to become like him.

Man has within him the power, which the Father has bestowed upon him, so to develop in truth, faith, wisdom, and all the virtues, that eventually he shall become *like the Father and the Son;* this virtue, wisdom, and knowledge on the part of the faithful does not rob the Father and the Son, but *adds* to their glory and dominion. Thus it is destined that *those who are worthy to become his sons and joint-heirs with our Redeemer, would be heirs of the Father's kingdom, possessing the same attributes in their perfection, as the Father and the Son now possess.*[2]

ALL THAT THE FATHER HATH. Those who are faithful in obtaining the priesthood and magnifying their calling become members of the Church of the Firstborn, receiving all that the Father hath; and this is according to an oath and covenant that cannot be broken. Now, *how are they to receive all that the Father hath, if something is withheld? And if something is not withheld, how*

---

[1] D. & C. 76:59.

[2] Pers. Corresp.; Joseph Fielding Smith, *Teachings of the Prophet Joseph Smith,* pp. 342-362, 369-376.

*can they receive all that he hath and not become as he is,
that is, be gods themselves? . . .*

*How can the saints receive of his fulness and be
equal with the Lord and not be as he is, that is, gods?*[3]

The Father has promised through the Son that all
that he has shall be given to those who are obedient to his
commandments. *They shall increase in knowledge, wisdom, and power, going from grace to grace, until the
fulness of the perfect day shall burst upon them.* They
shall, through the glory and blessing of the Almighty,
become *creators.* All power, and dominion, and might
shall be given to them, and they shall be the only ones
upon whom this great blessing shall be bestowed.

All others, no matter how much learning, wisdom,
and power, they may obtain, shall nevertheless be restricted in their several spheres, for they cannot attain
to the fulness which is held in reserve for those who are
permitted to pass by the angels and the gods who are set
to guard the way to this great exaltation.

GAINING A FULNESS OF LIGHT AND TRUTH. "If ye
continue in my word, then are ye my disciples indeed;
And ye shall know the truth, and the truth shall make
you free."[4] These are the words of our Master, and *it is
obedience to him and his word that unlocks the glories
and mysteries of the kingdom of heaven.* They cannot
be unlocked in any other way.

All light, all truth come from God. That which is
not from him does not edify but brings darkness. *If we
will continue in God; that is, keep his commandments,
worship him and love his truth; then the time will come
when we shall be bathed in the fulness of truth, which
shall grow brighter and brighter until the perfect day.*
Here then, we find power, wisdom, advancement, the
knowledge which is perfect and which can only be obtained through continuing in God by obedience unto him.[5]

[3]*Origin of the "Reorganized" Church,*
   pp. 89-90; *D. & C.* 84:33-40; 88:106-
   107; 93:16-20.
[4]John 8:31-32.
[5]*Church News,* June 19, 1937, pp. 4-5;
   D. & C. 50:23-28; 93:24-28.

FULL OBEDIENCE LEADS TO JOINT-HEIRSHIP. Now if we want to become heirs, joint-heirs with Jesus Christ, possessing the blessings of the kingdom, there is only one thing required of you and of me, and that is that we keep the *whole law,* not a part of it only. Do you think it would be fair, just, proper, for the Lord to say to us: "I will give unto you commandments; you may keep them if you will; you may be indifferent about the matter if you will; keep some, reject others; or, partially keep some; and I will punish you, but then I will make it up to you, and all will be well."[6]

SONS OF GOD

FAITHFUL BECOME SONS AND DAUGHTERS OF GOD. The destiny of the faithful man in this Church and the faithful woman is to become a son and daughter of God. That is the great gift that the Lord holds out to the members of the Church.[7]

John writes as follows: "Beloved, now are we the sons of God, and it doth not yet appear what we shall be: but we know that, when he shall appear, we shall be like him; for we shall see him as he is."[8]

Why? Because as sons of God we have lived to be like him; and John did not mean that we would see him in the form of a man. Every man is in that form, whether he repents of his sins or whether he does not. Every man was created in the image of God, in his likeness; but *when Christ comes, those who have kept the commandments and stand before him, will see themselves like they see him, a Son of God!* They will be entitled to the blessings of sons, heirs. The Lord has promised to them the fulness of his kingdom so they can go on through the eternities.[9]

PRIESTHOOD ESSENTIAL TO SONSHIP. John was speaking to the *men who held the priesthood. He calls them the sons of God.* We are the sons of God. That

6*Rel. Soc. Mag.,* vol. 6, p. 464.   8 1 John 3:1-3.
7*Church News,* Mar. 30, 1930, p 4.   9*Church News,* July 3, 1954.

same divine authority has been bestowed upon us. We, too, in this day should be just as grateful and just as willing to serve, and to keep the commandments of the Lord, and to magnify the callings which have been given unto us, as were these men in former days who were the sons of God.

I wonder if we realize the greatness of our callings — yes, all the elders in this Church — do they realize that they hold the Melchizedek Priesthood? Do they know that through their faithfulness and their obedience, according to the revelations of the Lord, they are entitled to receive all that the Father has — to become the sons of God, joint-heirs with our Elder Brother, Jesus Christ, entitled to the exaltations in the celestial kingdom? Do we realize that? We, too, if we do realize it, should be like those of former days, and every man that hath this hope in him, will purify himself even as Christ is pure.[10]

SONS OF GOD BECOME JOINT-HEIRS WITH CHRIST. I many times think of that passage of scripture, pertaining to those who keep the commandments of the Lord and are faithful and true to the end, that all that the Father hath shall be given unto them.[11] It is consoling and glorious to me. While we cannot comprehend the greatness of this blessing, yet a ray of light we do receive; an impression is made upon our minds to this effect, that if we will do the things the Lord requires of us, we shall become sons and daughters unto God. That is the meaning of this scripture.

As sons and daughters then, we are heirs of his kingdom and shall receive by right the fulness of the glory and be entitled to the great blessings and privileges which the Lord in his mercy has revealed to us in the dispensation of the fulness of times. "For as many as are led by the Spirit of God," Paul has written, "they are the sons of God. . . . The Spirit itself beareth witness with

---

[10]Conf. Rep., Oct., 1942, p. 18; Moses   [11]D. & C. 84:38.
  6:67-68; D. & C. 11:30; 35:2; 39:4;
  45:8; 76:24, 58; Mosiah 5:7.

EXALTATION   39

our spirit, that we are the children of God: And if children, then *heirs; heirs of God*, and *joint-heirs with Christ; if so be that we suffer with him, that we may be also glorified together.*"[12]

SONS OF GOD BECOME GODS. *If the faithful, who keep the commandments of the Father, are his sons, then they are heirs of the kingdom and shall receive of the fulness of the Father's glory, even until they become like the Father.* And how can they be perfect as their Father in heaven is perfect if they are not like him? ...

Now, if they overcome all things, then there are not some things which they do not overcome. If these are to receive "of his *fulness* and of his glory," and if into their "hands the Father has given *all things*," then the Father has not withheld some of the fulness of his glory, or some things. And if they receive his fulness and his glory, and if "all things are theirs, whether life or death, or things present, or things to come, all are theirs," *how can they receive these blessings and not become gods? They cannot.*[13]

FULL OBEDIENCE LEADS TO SONSHIP. Now how are we going to become the sons of God and, of course, daughters as well? How is it done? Can we become the sons and heirs of our Eternal Father simply by being baptized for the remission of our sins after we have repented and have had faith, and have had hands laid upon us for the gift of the Holy Ghost, and have come into the Church? No, it takes *more* than that.

Why, of course they are the children of our Father in heaven, those who do that, as are the people who are outside of the Church; but to become the sons and daughters of God, children, "heirs, heirs of God, and joint-heirs with Christ," we must suffer with him, that we may be glorified with him.[14] In other words, *we must receive in our hearts, accept in our hearts, every principle of the*

---

[12]*Rel. Soc. Mag.*, vol. 7, pp. 5-6; Rom. 8:14-19; Gal. 3:26, 29; 4:1-7.
[13]*Origin of the "Reorganized" Church,*
pp. 88-89; *D. & C.* 76:54-60; Rev. 3:21; 21:7; 3 Ne. 28:10; Matt. 5:48.
[14]Rom. 8:14-19.

gospel which has been revealed; and insofar as it is in our power to do so, we must live in accordance with these principles and keep the commandments of God in full.[15]

ENDOWMENT AND SEALING PRECEDE SONSHIP. The Lord has given unto us privileges, and blessings, and the opportunity of entering into covenants, of accepting ordinances that pertain to our salvation beyond what is preached in the world; beyond the principles of faith in the Lord Jesus Christ, repentance from sin, and baptism for the remission of sins, and the laying on of hands for the gift of the Holy Ghost; and these principles and covenants are received nowhere else but in the temple of God.

If you would become a son or a daughter of God and an heir of the kingdom, then you must go to the house of the Lord and receive blessings which there can be obtained and which cannot be obtained elsewhere; and you must keep those commandments and those covenants to the end. . . .

The ordinances of the temple, the endowment and sealings, pertain to exaltation in the celestial kingdom, where the sons and daughters are. The sons and daughters are not outside in some other kingdom. The sons and daughters go into the house, belong to the household, have access to the home. "In my Father's house are many mansions."[16] Sons and daughters have access to the home where he dwells, and you cannot receive that access until you go to the temple. Why? Because you must receive certain key words as well as make covenants by which you are able to enter. If you try to get into the house, and the door is locked, how are you going to enter, if you haven't your key? You get your key in the temple, which will admit you.

I picked up a key on the street one day, and took it home, and it opened every door in my house. You cannot find a key on the street, for that key is never lost that

---

[15]*Rel. Soc. Mag.*, vol. 6, pp. 463-464.   [16]John 14:2 .

will open the door that enters into our Father's mansions. You have got to go where the key is given. And each can obtain the key, if you will; but after receiving it, you may *lose* it, by having it taken away from you again, unless you abide by the agreement which you entered into when you went to the house of the Lord.[17]

ALL MEN TO BE EITHER SERVANTS OR SONS. You know what it says about servants in the scriptures. Those who become servants are those who are not willing to receive these blessings in the house of the Lord and abide in them. They are not sons; they are not daughters. They are children of God, it is true, for all men are his children. But they do not *inherit*, and therefore they *remain servants throughout eternity*, because they were not willing to receive that which they might have received, and the gift which was bestowed upon them or offered to them. They not only rejected the gift, but also the Giver of the gift. There will be a great many servants, but there will not be many heirs, "Because strait is the gate, and narrow is the way, which leadeth unto life, and few there be that find it."[18]

THE CHURCH OF THE FIRSTBORN

EXALTED BEINGS BELONG TO CHURCH OF FIRST-BORN. *Those who gain exaltation in the celestial kingdom are those who are members of the Church of the First-born; in other words, those who keep all the command-ments of the Lord.*[19] There will be many who are members of the Church of Jesus Christ of Latter-day Saints who shall *never become* members of the Church of the Firstborn.

The higher ordinances in the temple of God pertain to exaltation in the celestial kingdom. . . . In order to receive this blessing, one must keep the *full law*, must

[17]*Rel. Soc. Mag.*, vol. 6, pp. 465-469; D. & C. 130:10-11; 132:4-14
[18]*Gen. & Hist. Mag.*, vol. 21, p. 101; Matt. 7:14; D. & C. 76:112; 132:16-17, 24-25.
[19]*D. & C.* 76:54, 67, 71, 94-95, 102; 77:11; 78:21; 88:5; 93:22.

abide the law by which that kingdom is governed; for, "He who is not able to abide the law of a celestial kingdom cannot abide a celestial glory."[20]

So being ordained an elder, or a high priest, or an apostle, or even President of the Church, is not the thing that brings the exaltation, but obedience to the laws and the ordinances and the covenants required of those who desire to become members of the Church of the Firstborn, as these are administered in the house of the Lord. To become a member of the Church of the Firstborn, as I understand it, is to become one of the *inner circle*. We are all members of the Church of Jesus Christ of Latter-day Saints by being baptized and confirmed, and there are many who seem to be content to remain such without obtaining the privileges of exaltation.

How to Join Church of the Firstborn. *The Lord has made it possible for us to become members of the Church of the Firstborn, by receiving the blessings of the house of the Lord and overcoming all things.* Thus we become *heirs, "priests* and *kings,* who have received of his *fulness,* and of his glory," who shall "dwell in the presence of God and his Christ forever and ever," with full exaltation.[21] Are such blessings worth having?

I have said that only one man at a time on the earth holds the keys of this sealing power of the priesthood, but he may, and does, delegate power to others, and they officiate under his direction in the temples of the Lord. No man can officiate in these sealing ordinances *until* he receives the authority to do so by being set apart by the one who holds the keys, notwithstanding he may hold the priesthood. All the authority exercised in the temples is then, after all, the authority centered in *one man. He* has the power and calls upon others to officiate, and they seal upon us the keys and powers which, through our obedience, entitle us to become sons and daughters and members of the Church of the Firstborn, receiving all

---

[20]*Rel. Soc. Mag.,* vol. 5, p. 680;   [21]*D. & C.* 76:56, 62. *D. & C.* 88:22.

things in the kingdom. This is what we can get in the *temple, so that we become members of the family, sons and daughters of God, not servants.*[22]

THE PATH TO EXALTATION

EXALTATION OFFERED TO ALL. The Lord does not desire that the people should suffer. He is pained when a man does wrong and needs to be punished and fails to receive the crown or reward that is offered to those who are faithful and true. The Lord would have *every* man receive a *crown, every* man become *exalted, every* man become a *son*, and *every* woman become a *daughter* unto him. But this cannot be done, except on principles of righteousness and free agency.

Therefore, every soul has the right to choose for himself that which he will do. This is the gospel of merit. Every man shall receive that which he is entitled to receive. Every soul shall be blessed according to the diligence, willingness, and integrity put forth in the service of the Lord. The man who will not keep his commandments, the Lord will not exalt. The woman who rejects the light and refuses to abide by the doctrines of our Redeemer shall not be exalted. Those who will be exalted shall be crowned with glory, immortality, and eternal life in the presence of our Father.[23]

In order to obtain the exaltation we must accept the gospel and all its covenants; and take upon us the obligations which the Lord has offered; and walk in the light and the understanding of the truth; and "live by every word that proceedeth forth from the mouth of God."[24]

CELESTIAL MARRIAGE ESSENTIAL TO EXALTATION. Another thing that we must not forget in this great plan of redemption and exaltation, is that *a man must have a wife, and a woman a husband, to receive the fulness of exaltation.* They must be sealed for time and for all

---

[22]*Gen. & Hist. Mag.*, vol. 21, pp. 100-101; *D. & C.* 132:7.

[23]*Rel. Soc. Mag.*, vol. 7, p. 9.
[24]*D. & C.* 84:44.

eternity in a temple; then their union will last forever, and they cannot be separated because God has joined them together, as he taught the Pharisees.[25]

Parents will have eternal claim upon their posterity and will have the gift of eternal increase, if they obtain the exaltation. This is the crowning glory in the kingdom of God, and they will have no end. When the Lord says they will have no end, he means that all who attain to this glory will have the blessing of the continuation of the "seeds" forever. Those who fail to obtain this blessing come to the "deaths," which means that they will have no increase, forever. *All who obtain this exaltation will have the privilege of completing the full measure of their existence, and they will have a posterity that will be as innumerable as the stars of heaven.*[26]

If you want salvation in the fullest, that is exaltation in the kingdom of God, so that you may become his sons and his daughters, you have got to go into the temple of the Lord and receive these holy ordinances which belong to that house, which cannot be had elsewhere. *No man shall receive the fulness of eternity, of exaltation, alone; no woman shall receive that blessing alone; but man and wife, when they receive the sealing power in the temple of the Lord, if they thereafter keep all the commandments, shall pass on to exaltation, and shall continue and become like the Lord.* And that is the destiny of men; that is what the Lord desires for his children.[27]

ONLY EXALTED BEINGS GAIN FULNESS OF FATHER. No man can obtain that exaltation without receiving the covenants that belong to the priesthood. No woman can obtain this great honor and glory without receiving the blessings of faith, repentance and baptism, confirmation, and obedience to the covenants that are promised her and her husband in the temple of the Lord. Otherwise, there would be no progress, that is, to the fulness.

---

[25]Matt. 19:3-8.
[26]*Church News*, May 31, 1947, p. 8; D. & C. 132:16-25.

[27]*Elijah the Prophet and His Mission*, p. 31.

No man who is not willing to continue, even though he be a member of the Church, in receiving these cove-nants, and taking upon him these blessings and powers which the Lord has offered unto him by covenant, will ever reach the fulness. All such will be barred. There will come a certain place which they cannot pass. The fulness of knowledge, and understanding, and wisdom, by which men may become perfect even as God is perfect, can only be gained by a strict adherence to those eternal laws upon which this great blessing is based.

We fall short through lack of faithfulness if we re-fuse to receive covenants and take upon ourselves obligations that pertain to the exaltation. There will be a bar that will prevent us from continuing to that fulness.[28]

ENDOWMENTS AND SEALINGS PERTAIN TO EXALTA-TION. Baptism is the door into the celestial kingdom. All the ordinances of the gospel pertain to the celestial king-dom, and any person who is faithful to the covenant of baptism will be entitled to enter there, but no person can receive an exaltation in the celestial kingdom without the ordinances of the temple. The endowments are for ad-vancement in that kingdom, and the sealings for our perfection, *provided* we keep our covenants and obliga-tions.[29]

People baptized, and who are not endowed in the temple of the Lord, may enter the celestial kingdom. But that does not mean that a baptized person is going to get the exaltation in that kingdom. He is not going to pass on to the fulness just by being baptized. He will not pass on to the fulness even after he has been baptized and re-ceived an endowment in the temple. He has also to re-ceive the other ordinances so that he can become through his faithfulness and obedience a son of God. . . .

The first principles of the gospel are principles that

[28]*Church News,* July 3, 1954, p. 2; D. & C. 76:56, 71, 76-77, 86, 94; 93:4-28; 132:6, 19

[29]Pers. Corresp.; Smith, *Teachings of the Prophet Joseph Smith,* p. 12; D. & C. 124:28, 39.

save. By obedience to them we enter the celestial kingdom of God. Then, when we get into that kingdom, *if* we have received the other covenants, have been true and faithful to other obligations, we will advance until we shall become like God—his sons, his daughters, receiving a fulness of his kingdom. That is the promise.[30]

MAKING OUR CALLING AND ELECTION SURE. Those who press forward in righteousness, living by every word of revealed truth, have power to make their calling and election sure. They receive the more sure word of prophecy and know by revelation and the authority of the priesthood that they are sealed up unto eternal life. They are sealed up against all manner of sin and blasphemy except the blasphemy against the Holy Ghost and the shedding of innocent blood. But the mere fact of being married for time and eternity in the temple, *standing alone,* does not give them this guarantee. *Blessings pronounced upon couples in connection with celestial marriage are conditioned upon the subsequent faithfulness of the participating parties.*

Peter tells how the saints may make their calling and election sure in these words: "Grace and peace be multiplied unto you through the knowledge of God, and of Jesus our Lord, According as his divine power hath given unto us *all things that pertain unto life and godliness,* through the knowledge of him that hath called us to glory and virtue: Whereby are given unto us *exceeding great and precious promises:* that by these ye might be *partakers of the divine nature,* having escaped the corruption that is in the world through lust.

"And beside this, giving all diligence, add to your faith virtue; and to virtue knowledge; And to knowledge temperance; and to temperance patience; and to patience godliness; And to godliness brotherly kindness; and to brotherly kindness charity.

"For *if these things be in you, and abound,* they

---

[30]*Church News,* July 3, 1954, p. 2.

make you that ye shall neither be barren nor unfruitful in the knowledge of our Lord Jesus Christ. But he that lacketh these things is blind, and cannot see afar off, and hath forgotten that he was purged from his old sins.

"Wherefore the rather, brethren, *give diligence to make your calling and election sure: for if ye do these things, ye shall never fall:* For so an entrance shall be ministered unto you *abundantly* into the everlasting kingdom of our Lord and Saviour Jesus Christ. . . .

"We have also *a more sure word of prophecy;* whereunto ye do well that ye take heed, as unto a light that shineth in a dark place, until the day dawn, and the day star arise in your hearts."[31]

EXALTATION AND THE CREATION OF WORLDS. Now, according to the teachings of the Prophet Joseph Smith, we worship our Heavenly Father who governs in our universe, and we do all that we do in the name of the Son. We are informed that there are many earths or worlds which have been created, and were created by the Son for the Father. This was, of course, before he was born a Babe in Bethlehem.[32]

Evidently *his Father passed through a period of mortality even as he passed through mortality, and as we all are doing. Our Father in heaven, according to the Prophet, had a Father,* and since there has been a condition of this kind through all eternity, each Father had a Father, until we come to a stop where we cannot go further, because of our limited capacity to understand.[33]

We are sons and daughters of God in the spirit. Through the atonement of Jesus Christ, we receive the resurrection, the spirit and the body being united inseparably, never to be divided, so that we will never die again. We thus become immortal, and if we keep the

---

[31]Smith, *op. cit.,* pp. 149-151, 298, 305; 2 Pet. 1:2-19; Eph. 1:13-14; John 14:12-27; D. & C. 88:4; 124:124; 130:3; 131:5; 132:19-27, 49; 3 Ne. 28:10.

[32]Moses 1:29-40; 7:30; D. & C. 76:22-24; Heb. 1:1-4.

[33]Smith, *op. cit.,* pp. 345-346, 370, 373.

commandments which are given us, we will inherit
celestial glory. When we receive this great blessing, *we
will be sons of God, joint-heirs with Jesus Christ.*

The Father has promised us that through our faithfulness we shall be blessed with *the fulness of his kingdom.* In other words we will have the privilege of
becoming *like him. To become like him we must have
all the powers of godhood;* thus *a man and his wife when
glorified will have spirit children* who eventually will go
on an earth like this one we are on and pass through the
same kind of experiences, being subject to mortal conditions, and if faithful, then they also will receive the
fulness of exaltation and partake of the same blessings.
There is no end to this development; it will go on forever.
*We will become gods and have jurisdiction over worlds,
and these worlds will be peopled by our own offspring.*
We will have an endless eternity for this.[34]

EXALTATION IS WORTH REPENTANCE AND OBE-
DIENCE. What we need in the Church, as well as out of
it, is repentance. We need more faith and more determination to serve the Lord. . . . If the people of the world
walk in darkness and sin, and contrary to the will of the
Lord, there is the place for us to draw the line. Why
should we not uphold the standards of our faith? Why
should we not walk in strict accord with the regulations
of the Church notwithstanding what the world may
think?

The Lord has revealed the fulness of his gospel.
We have been fully informed regarding all of its principles pertaining to salvation. Is it worth while for us
to maintain our integrity and prove faithful to every
trust? *Is the pearl of great price—the fulness of the
glory, honor, and eternal life in the presence of the Father
and the Son—worth the sacrifice we may be called upon
to make? Are we, as the man spoken of in former times,
willing to sell all that we have in order that we may buy*

---

[34]Pers. Corresp.; Smith, *op. cit.,* pp.
    300-301; *D. & C.* 131:1-4; 132:18-32.

this field which will bring to us everlasting joy and exaltation as sons and daughters of God?[35]

SALVATION OF CHILDREN

FALSE DOCTRINE OF GUILT FOR ORIGINAL SIN. There are millions of people, professing to believe in Christ, who believe that little children are under condemnation and tainted with original sin—which is as *damnable a doctrine* as was ever taught among the children of men, for little children are not tainted with sin. They are not subject to sin until they reach the years of accountability, until they begin to know and to understand right from wrong, and become accountable before God according to the age which he himself has appointed, which is eight years. "Baptism availeth nothing," in the case of infants, because they cannot repent, and baptism is for the remission of sins.[36]

Christ paid the debt for Adam's transgression. "We believe that men will be punished for their own sins, and not for Adam's transgression,"[37] and the Lord has not placed *any* taint upon little children who come into this world. Through the blood of Christ they are redeemed from all that could be laid to their charge as descendants of Adam. Christ took that upon himself.

"The glory of God is intelligence, or, in other words, light and truth. Light and truth forsake that evil one. Every spirit of man was innocent in the beginning."[38]

CHILDREN INNOCENT IN BEGINNING. That means that in the beginning—before the foundation of the world was laid, and before Satan rebelled—when we were born, if you please, in that spirit world, we were innocent. There came a rebellion, and one-third of the hosts of heaven, we are told, rebelled against God, under the direction of Lucifer, and were cast out.

The two-thirds remaining were privileged to come

---

[35]*Gen. & Hist. Mag.,* vol. 21, p. 104;   [37]Second Article of Faith.
  Matt. 13:45-46.   [38]*D. & C.* 93:36-38.
[36]Moroni 8:5-24.

to this earth and receive tabernacles of flesh and bones.
Now the Lord says, in regard to men, at the time they
come into this world: "And God having redeemed man
from the fall, men became again, in their infant state,
innocent before God."[39]

Now, that is good, sound sense. To believe that the
Lord damns little children because parents, in a thought-
less mood, fail to have them sprinkled or otherwise baptized, and therefore, should they die, they are forever
damned, I repeat, is a *doctrine of the devil. There is no
truth in it. Baptism is for the remission of sins, and no
man can repent of a sin until he is accountable before
God.*[40]

BELIEF IN ORIGINAL SIN DENIES POWER OF ATONE-
MENT. Any man who believes that little children are born
in sin and are tainted by original sin, or the sin of somebody else, has failed to comprehend the nature of the
atonement of Jesus Christ. . . .

It is one doctrine, among all the doctrines that have
been corrupted, that seems to me to stand out as the *most
damnable,* denying the mercies of God to little children
who come into this world as innocent as they can be, and
then to put taint upon them. There may be a taint upon
the father, there may be a taint upon the mother, but that
little child is not responsible in any sense of the word for
either Adam's transgression, or your transgression, or
mine, or any other man's. I say again, *the man who believes that children are tainted by original sin cannot
understand and fails to comprehend the mission of Jesus
Christ.*

What was his mission? One part was to bring redemption to every soul from Adam's transgression; and
Christ paid the price. That is unconditional; it depends
neither upon repentance nor faith nor any other principle.
Every soul that comes into this world is cleansed—if
there is to be any cleansing—at least redeemed from the

[39]*D. & C.* 93:38.   [40]*Church News,* Feb. 12, 1938, p. 3.

consequences of Adam's transgression, because we were not in any sense responsible for it.

Why, of course we die; of course we suffer; of course we are subject to the vicissitudes of mortal life. We came here for that very purpose. Of course we inherit these from Adam; but to lay a sin on a child, because it was born into this world of mortal parents, I repeat, is a damnable doctrine. . . .

ALL CHILDREN ARE ALIVE IN CHRIST. *"Little children are redeemed from the foundation of the world."*[41] What does the Lord mean by that? He means that before the foundation of this earth was laid, this plan of redemption, the plan of salvation which we are supposed to follow in this mortal life, was all prepared; and God, knowing the end from the beginning, made provisions for the redemption of little children through the atonement of Jesus Christ. . . .

We teach that we are the offspring of God, we are his sons and daughters—that is a good *Bible* doctrine—and in the beginning of that spirit life every man was innocent. Likewise in the beginning of this mortal life—no matter how faithful, or how valiant, or otherwise, we were in that spirit world—when we come into this world, we come into it innocent as far as this world is concerned, just as we were innocent in the other world in the beginning. Every child—I don't care where it is born; I don't care what its color—that is born into this world comes into it innocent in its infant state.

Why, when you look into the face of a little babe and he looks up and smiles at you, can you believe that that little child is tainted with any kind of sin that will deprive it of the presence of God should it die? I have been reading to you about this Catholic doctrine of the "beatific vision," and these little children who are not sprinkled—or baptized if you want to call it that—in their infancy, being deprived of that glorious vision, and the

---

[41]*D. & C.* 29:46-50.

Lord softening their punishment or loss by dulling their comprehension so they do not understand and do not realize what they have lost. Can you think of anything that is more damnable than that?

FALSE TEACHING THAT UNBAPTIZED CHILDREN ARE LOST. I remember when I was in the mission field in England, there was an American family there. . . . One evening as we sat in their home, the man's wife turned to me and said: "Elder Smith, I want to ask you a question." Before she could ask her question, she began to cry. I did not know what the matter was. She sobbed, and when she had composed herself enough to ask the question, she told me this story:

When they went over to England, they had the misfortune of losing a little baby. They were attending the Church of England. They went to the minister and wanted to have that baby laid away with a Christian burial, as they had been attending the church. The minister said to her: "We can't give your child a Christian burial because it was not christened. Your baby is lost." That was a rather blunt way to put it, but that is the way she told the story; and that woman's heart had been aching and aching for two or three years. So she asked the question of me: *"Is my baby lost? Will I never see it again?"* I turned and read to her from the *Book of Mormon* the words of Mormon to his son Moroni.[42] I said: "Your baby is not lost. No baby is lost. Every baby is saved in the kingdom of God when it dies." . . .

ALL CHILDREN SAVED IN CELESTIAL KINGDOM. "And I also beheld that *all children who die before they arrive at the years of accountability, are saved in the celestial kingdom of heaven.*"[43] That is what the Lord said to the Prophet Joseph Smith by revelation in a vision that he had in the Kirtland Temple. Does not that sound good? Is it not just? Is it not right?

---

[42]Moroni 8:5-24 .   [43]Smith, *op. cit.,* p. 107.

It does not make any difference whether it is a Catholic baby, a Protestant baby, or a Mohammedan baby: no matter whose baby it is, it is not responsible for original sin; it is not responsible for any sin; and the mercy of God claims it; and it is redeemed.

But how is it with you and me? Here we are, capable of understanding, and the Lord says: "Whoso having knowledge, have I not commanded to repent?"[44] We are commanded to repent; we are commanded to be baptized; we are commanded to have our sins washed away in the waters of baptism, because we are capable of understanding, and we have all sinned. But I have not been baptized and you have not been baptized *for anything that Adam did.*

LITTLE CHILDREN NEED NO BAPTISM. I have been baptized that I might be cleansed from that which I have done myself (and so with you) and that I might come into the kingdom of God. Baptism is for two purposes. It is the door into the celestial kingdom of God; and so the Lord taught Nicodemus: "Except a man be born of water and of the Spirit, he cannot enter into the kingdom of God."[45]

That is true of men; it is true of women; but the Lord has made provisions for those who are without law, and little children are not subject to the law of repentance. How could you teach a little child to repent? It has not anything to repent of.

The Lord has placed—and that in his own judgment—the age of accountability at eight years. After we get to be eight years of age, we are supposed to have understanding sufficient that we should be baptized. The Lord takes care of those who are under that age. Now he has himself arbitrarily declared that. I did not set the age. I accept it because the Lord set the age, and that is the law.[46]

[44]*D. & C.* 29:49.
[45]John 3:5.
[46]*Church News,* Apr. 29, 1939, p. 7; *D. & C.* 68:27.

EXALTATION OF CHILDREN. Little children who die before they reach the years of accountability will automatically inherit the celestial kingdom, but not the exaltation in that kingdom *until* they have complied with all the requirements of exaltation. For instance:

The crowning glory is marriage and this ordinance would have to be performed in their behalf *before* they could inherit the fulness of that kingdom. The Lord is just with all his children, and little children who die will not be penalized as the Catholic Church penalizes them, simply because they happen to die. *The Lord will grant unto these children the privilege of all the sealing blessings which pertain to the exaltation.*

We were all mature spirits before we were born, and the bodies of little children will grow after the resurrection to the full stature of the spirit, and *all the blessings will be theirs through their obedience, the same as if they had lived to maturity and received them on the earth.*

NO BLESSING TO BE DENIED TO CHILDREN. The Lord is just and will not deprive any person of a blessing, simply because he dies before that blessing can be received. *It would be manifestly unfair to deprive a little child of the privilege of receiving all the blessings of exaltation in the world to come simply because it died in infancy.* The same thing is true of the young men who were deprived of these blessings and laid down their lives during the war. The Lord judges every soul by the intent of the heart.

All that we need do for children is to have them sealed to their parents. They need no baptism and never will, for our Lord has performed all the work necessary for them.

Children who die in childhood will not be deprived of any blessing. When they grow, after the resurrection, to the full maturity of the spirit, *they will be entitled to all the blessings which they would have been entitled to had they been privileged to tarry here and receive them.*

The Lord has arranged for that, so that justice will be given to every soul.

Boys and girls who die after baptism may have the endowment work done for them in the temple. Children who die in infancy do not have to be endowed. So far as the ordinance of sealing is concerned, this may wait until the millennium.

CHILDREN OF ALL RACES HEIRS OF SALVATION. The revelations of the Lord to the Prophet Joseph Smith declare that *all* little children who die are heirs of the celestial kingdom. This would mean the children of *every race. All the spirits that come to this world come from the presence of God and, therefore, must have been in his kingdom.*

Little children are redeemed by the Lord's decree from the foundation of the world through the ministry of Jesus Christ;[47] every spirit of man was innocent in the beginning;[48] and all who rebelled were cast out; therefore, *all who remained are entitled to the blessings of the gospel.*

The only souls coming to this world who are under restriction are the Negroes, and they cannot hold the priesthood; but Negroes may be baptized, and we have many Negroes in the Church. Therefore, by what right or reason are we going to deprive innocent children whether they are black, brown, or yellow who die in their infancy—innocent and without sin—from entering the celestial kingdom? If a Negro can receive the celestial kingdom by baptism, and the Chinese, Japanese and all other races, where would there be consistency in saying that any children, because they are born under adverse circumstances, should be deprived of entrance into that kingdom? It seems definitely clear that the Lord means exactly what he said to the Prophet Joseph Smith.

SALVATION OF MENTALLY DEFICIENT PERSONS. Mentally deficient persons, those who are incompetent

---

[47]*D. & C.* 29:46-47.   [48]*D. & C.* 93:38.

of understanding, are classed among those who are redeemed as little children through the atonement of our
Redeemer. *They need no baptism.*[49]

Mentally deficient children who are incompetent of
proper understanding, and hence are not to be baptized
themselves, should not be used for the ordinance of baptism for the dead. Any person acting vicariously must
be competent.

It would be proper, of course, for a mentally deficient person to be sealed to its parents. Babies are
sealed to their parents when they are too young to comprehend, but no one is to be baptized until he or she
reaches the age of accountability. We do not expect
mentally deficient children to remain so after the resurrection; the condition under which they suffer now is one
that pertains to the mortal condition, with all its defects
and restrictions.

CHILDREN IN THE RESURRECTION. When a baby
dies, it goes back into the spirit world, and the spirit as-
sumes its natural form as an adult, for we were all adults
before we were born.

When a child is raised in the resurrection, the spirit
will enter the body and the body will be the same size as
it was when the child died. It will then *grow after the
resurrection* to full maturity to conform to the size of the
spirit.

If parents are righteous, they will have their children
after the resurrection. Little children who die, whose
parents are not worthy of an exaltation, will be *adopted*
into the families of those who are worthy.

CHILDREN NEVER TO BE TEMPTED. Satan will be
loosed to gather his forces after the millennium. The
people who will be tempted, will be people living on this
earth, and they will have every opportunity to accept the
gospel or reject it. Satan will have nothing to do whatever with little children, or grown people who have

---

[49]Moroni 8:22.

received their resurrection and entered into the celestial
kingdom.

*Satan cannot tempt little children in this life, nor in
the spirit world, nor after their resurrection.* Little children who die before reaching the years of accountability
will not be tempted; those born during the millennium,
when Satan is bound and cannot tempt them, "shall grow
up without sin unto salvation."[50]

[50]Pers. Corresp.; *D. & C.* 45:58.

CHAPTER 4

CELESTIAL MARRIAGE

MARRIAGE AND EXALTATION

MARRIAGE: THE COVENANT OF EXALTATION. Marriage, as understood by Latter-day Saints, is a covenant ordained to be everlasting. *It is the foundation for eternal exaltation, for without it there could be no eternal progress in the kingdom of God.*[1]

The Lord taught Joseph Smith the doctrine of the eternity of the marriage covenant and the perpetuity of the family after death. This revelation has proved a wonderful, if not terrible shock to the believers in the doctrine that at death a man and his wife are forever separated and the family relationship comes to an eternal end. Yet there are very few, if they have natural feelings, who do not *hope* that the eternity of the family may prove to be a fact.[2]

There is no ordinance connected with the gospel of Jesus Christ of greater importance, of more solemn and sacred nature, and more necessary to the eternal joy of man, than marriage. Yet there is no principle which has been made the butt of coarser jokes, a greater jest by the vulgar and the unclean, and even by many who think themselves refined, than that of marriage.

MARRIAGE BRINGS CROWNING BLESSINGS OF GOSPEL. Marriage is a principle which, when entered, presents more serious problems than any other. It should be received in the spirit of patience and love, even that greater love which comes through the power of the Holy Spirit. *Nothing will prepare mankind for glory in the kingdom*

---

[1]*Era,* vol. 34, p. 704.　　　　　　[2]*Era,* vol. 23, p. 502; *D. & C.* 132.

*of God as readily as faithfulness to the marriage cove-
nant.* Through this covenant, perhaps more than any
other, we accomplish the perfect decree of the Divine
will, but this covenant is only *one of many* required of
man who seeks to do the will of the Father.

If properly received, this covenant becomes the
means of the greatest happiness. The greatest honor in
this life, and in the life to come—honor, dominion, and
power in perfect love—are the blessings which come out
of it. These blessings of eternal glory are held in reserve
for those who are willing to abide in this and all other
covenants of the gospel. Others shall not be so blessed.

Marriage is the grandest, most glorious, and most
exalting principle connected with the gospel. *It is that
which the Lord holds in reserve for those who become
his sons and daughters; all others are servants only,* even
if they gain salvation. They do not become members of
the household of our Father and our God, if they refuse
to receive the celestial covenant of marriage.[3]

MARRIAGE BY MAN'S AUTHORITY ENDS AT DEATH.
The Lord has informed us through his servants the
prophets, that *all things* are governed by law. His house
is a house of order, because all things within are obedient
to law. He will not accept at the hand of man, an offering,
vow, or contract, which is not entered into in accordance
with the laws which govern in his kingdom and which
he, the Lord, has established. *Man-made obligations and
agreements,* in which the Lord does not enter, and which
were not made by him, or by his word, which is his law,
shall come to an end when men are dead.

Therefore, all marriage contracts, as well as other
contracts and obligations made in this life by parties who
have not accepted the everlasting gospel, must come to
an end when the contracting parties have passed from
this existence. In order to make the marriage contract
valid and binding for eternity as well as for time, the

[3]*Era,* vol. 34, p. 643; *D. & C.* 76:50-
70; 131:1-4; 132:1-32.

contracting parties must enter into the marriage relationship in full obedience and accordance with the laws upon which such blessings are predicated.[4]

SAINTS COMMANDED TO MARRY FOR ETERNITY. The Lord has commanded us, as it is recorded in the revelations, that marriage among members of the Church should be performed in his holy house, and not for time only, but for time and all eternity. Therefore, those who are satisfied to receive a ceremony for time only, uniting them for this life, and are content with that, are *ignorant* of this fundamental principle of the gospel and its consequences, or they are in *rebellion* against the commandments of the Lord.

Now, what I want to say is intended very largely for the parents of the young people. I think the parents, perhaps, are more to be blamed, because, in many instances, very many instances, they have not taught their children the sacredness of the marriage covenant. . . .

It fills my heart with sadness when I see in the paper the name of a daughter or a son of members of this Church, and discover that she or he is going to have a ceremony and be married outside of the temple of the Lord, because I realize what it means, that *they are cutting themselves off from exaltation in the kingdom of God.*[5]

SORROW IN RESURRECTION IF NO ETERNAL MARRIAGE. These young people who seem to be so happy now, when they rise in the resurrection—and find themselves in the condition in which they will find themselves —*then* there will be *weeping,* and *wailing,* and *gnashing of teeth,* and *bitterness of soul;* and they have brought it upon themselves because of their lack of faith and understanding of the gospel, and from, I am sorry to say, the encouragement they have received many times from their own parents. . . .

[4]*Young Women's Journal,* vol. 31, p. 305; D. & C. 132:5-17.   [5]Conf. Rep., Apr., 1941, pp. 36-38; D. & C. 124:37-42; 132.

UNWORTHY NOT TO GO TO TEMPLE. Of course there are people who are not worthy to go to the temple, and therefore should not go to the temple. No one should go to the temple except those who are worthy, as the Lord has said, "who [have] overcome by faith," and are cleansed and are just and true.[6] Then they can go to the temple. *If they are unclean, if they lack the faith, they had better stay out until they get the faith and are clean.*[7]

CIVIL MARRIAGE MAKES SERVANTS IN ETERNITY. The Lord says in regard to marriage: "For whatsoever things remain are by me; and whatsoever things are not by me shall be shaken and destroyed. Therefore, if a man marry him a wife in the world, and he marry her not by me nor by my word, and he covenant with her so long as he is in the world and she with him, *their covenant and marriage are not of force when they are dead, and when they are out of the world;* therefore, they are not bound by any law when they are out of the world."[8]

That is, they are not bound by any law of the gospel. It has no claim upon them; when they are dead their contract, and obligations, and bonds come to an end; *they have no claim upon each other,* and *no claim upon their children. Their childern are left without parents,* only as they themselves through their own faithfulness may be adopted into some other man's family.

"Therefore, when *they* are out of the world *they neither marry nor are given in marriage;* but are appointed *angels* in heaven; which angels are *ministering servants, to minister for those who are worthy of a far more, and an exceeding, and an eternal weight of glory.*

"*For these angels did not abide my law; therefore, they cannot be enlarged, but remain separately and singly, without exaltation, in their saved condition, to all eternity; and from henceforth are not gods, but are angels of God forever and ever.*"[9]

---

[6]*D. & C.* 76:50-53.   [8]*D. & C.* 132:14-15.
[7]Conf. Rep., Oct., 1946, pp. 37-38.   [9]*D. & C.* 132:16-17.

The implication here is this, that they who are clean in their lives; who are virtuous; who are honorable; but who will not receive this covenant of eternal marriage in the house of God, shall come forth—and *they may even enter into the celestial kingdom,* but when they enter there they enter as servants—to wait upon those "who are worthy of a far more, and an exceeding, and an eternal weight of glory."

CHOICE BETWEEN WORLDLY THINGS AND EXALTATION. Do you want to go on in this brief span that is called mortality, loving the fashions—the temptations, the allurements, all that this world can offer—because they are pleasant, and then come up in the resurrection from the dead to be a *servant,* to wait upon those "who are worthy of a far more, and an exceeding, and eternal weight of glory"? That is what such persons are going to get. And it may be, if they are not honest and honorable, they may even go into the terrestrial or the telestial kingdoms and may miss the celestial kingdom altogether, because we are going to receive according to our works.

Now that is the *end,* as far as marriage is concerned, for those who are content to be married simply by the law of the land and not the law of God.

CELESTIAL MARRIAGE MAKES GODS IN ETERNITY. But if we are married for time and for all eternity and it is sealed upon our heads by those who have the authority so to seal, and *if we then keep our covenants and are faithful to the end,* we shall come forth in the resurrection from the dead and receive the following promised blessings:

"*Then shall they be gods,* because they have no end; therefore shall they be from everlasting to everlasting, because they continue; then shall they be *above all,* because all things are subject unto them. Then shall they be gods, because they have *all power,* and the angels are subject unto them."[10]

---

[10]*D. & C.* 132:20.

Who are the angels? Those who would not abide the law.

"Verily, verily, I say unto you, except ye abide my law ye cannot attain to this glory."[11]

Abide what law? The law of the new and everlasting covenant, which is all the covenants.

"For strait is the gate, and narrow the way that leadeth unto *the exaltation and continuation of the lives,* and few there be that find it, because ye receive me not in the world neither do ye know me.

"But if ye receive me in the world, then shall ye know me, and shall receive your *exaltation;* that where I am ye shall be also."[12]

What a wonderful promise! And it is open to us; it is a free gift; it doesn't cost us anything: *only righteousness, faith, obedience;* and surely we can pay that price. It means, of course, giving up the things of the world; but is that a sacrifice? Does anybody consider that giving up the things that pertain to this world is a sacrifice? Some people would look upon it that way, but it isn't. You cannot sacrifice anything for the gospel of Jesus Christ. It would be just as consistent if a man gave me a dollar and I gave him ten cents, and then I would go out and say that was a great sacrifice I made.

So if you want to enter into exaltation and become as God, that is a son of God or a daughter of God, and receive a *fulness* of the kingdom, then you have got to abide in his law—not merely the law of marriage but *all* that pertains to the new and everlasting covenant—and then you have the "continuation of the lives" forever, for the Lord says:

"This is *eternal lives*—to know the only wise and true God, and Jesus Christ, whom he hath sent. I am he. Receive ye, therefore, my law."[13]

---

[11]*D. & C.* 132:21.
[12]*D. & C.* 132:22-23.
[13]*D. & C.* 132:24.

UNMARRIED TO INHERIT THE DEATHS. Now what about the others? Let us see what the Lord says: "Broad is the gate, and wide the way that leadeth to *the deaths;* and many there are that go in thereat, because they receive me not, neither do they abide in my law."[14]

What does the Lord mean by "the deaths"? That does not mean annihilation; that does not mean they are not going to get immortality. Every man will get immortality, will live forever. That is a free gift of God. The resurrection will come to every soul. Then what does the Lord mean when he says those who enter into the broad way enter into "the deaths"?

He means they enter into the world-to-come "separately and singly," and they have no continuation of the "lives," no increase. That is death. They don't go on; *they come to an end as far as that progression is concerned.* The Lord calls it "the deaths," and I am sure, I am confident, that every soul who rejects this commandment of the Lord and enters into the broad way, will discover when he enters into the eternities that he surely has entered into "the deaths," he has reached the end—not the end of his life but *the end of increase.*[15]

MARRIAGE AND BECOMING SONS OF GOD. The gift promised to those who receive this covenant of marriage and *remain faithful to the end,* that they shall "have no end," means that they shall have the power of *eternal increase. Only those who have this power will truly "know the only wise and true God, and Jesus Christ, whom he hath sent."* Others may see the Lord and may be *instructed by him,* but they will not truly *know* him or his Father unless they become *like* them.

Who desires to enter the eternal world and be a *servant,* when the promise is held out that we may be sons and daughters of God? Yet there will be the vast majority who will enter into the eternal world as *servants,* and not as *sons,* and this simply because they think more

---

[14]*D. & C.* 132:25.   [15]*Church News,* May 6, 1939, pp. 7-8.

of the world and its covenants, than they do of God and his covenants; simply because in their blindness of heart, they refuse to keep these sacred and holy commandments. Oh, what bitterness there will be in the day of judgment, when every man receives his reward according to his works![16]

NO EXALTATION WITHOUT MARRIAGE. Since marriage is ordained of God, and the man is not without the woman, neither the woman without the man in the Lord, *there can be no exaltation to the fulness of the blessings of the celestial kingdom outside of the marriage relation.* A man cannot be exalted singly and alone; neither can a woman. Each must have a companion to share the honors and blessings of this great exaltation. Marriage for time and all eternity brings to pass the crowning glory of our Father's kingdom, by which *his children become his heirs, into whose hands he gives all things.*[17]

If a man and his wife are saved in separate kingdoms, for instance, the celestial and terrestrial, automatically the sealing is broken; it is broken because of the sins of one of the parties. *No one can be deprived of exaltation who remains faithful.* In other words, an undeserving husband cannot prevent a faithful wife from an exaltation and vice versa. In this case the faithful servant would be given to someone who is faithful.[18]

ETERNITY OF THE FAMILY

ETERNAL HAPPINESS BECAUSE FAMILY CONTINUES. Not only was marriage instituted by the Lord to endure eternally, but it also naturally follows that the same is true of the family. The plan given in the gospel for the government of man on this earth is typical of the laws governing in the kingdom of God. *Is it possible to imagine a greater source of sorrow than to be left in the eternal world without claim on father or mother or children?*

---

[16]*Era,* vol. 34, p. 706; Alma 41:12-15.   [18]Pers. Corresp.
[17]*Young Women's Journal,* vol. 31, p. 306, 1 Cor. 11:11.

The thought of a nation without the family unit as its fundamental foundation; where all the citizens are, comparatively, strangers to each other, and where natural affection is not found; where no family ties bind the groups together, is one of horror. Such a condition could lead to but one end—anarchy and dissolution. Is it not reasonable to believe the same thing true in relation to the kingdom of God? If in that kingdom, there were no family ties and all men and women were "angels" without the natural kinships, as many people believe, could it be a place of happiness—a heaven?

THE FAMILY OF GOD THE FATHER. The prevailing doctrines that there are no such ties and that sex disappears in the granting of salvation to the righteous, certainly are not in accord with the scriptures. The Lord said to John, "He that overcometh shall inherit *all things; and I will be his God, and he shall be my son.*"[19]

Moreover, Paul, writing to the Ephesian Saints said to them, "For this cause I bow my knees unto the Father of our Lord Jesus Christ, Of whom *the whole family in heaven* and earth is named."[20] Since all who obey the gospel in the fulness are to become *heirs, members of the household of God,* why should there not be such a thing as *the whole family of God in heaven?*

The scriptures inform us that we are the *offspring of God.*[21] He has called upon us to address him as *Father:* not in some mythical sense, but literally as our Father. It was in this manner that Jesus taught his disciples to pray,[22] and when he appeared to Mary after his resurrection, he said to her, "Touch me not; for I am not yet ascended to *my Father:* but go to *my brethren,* and say unto them, I ascend unto *my Father,* and *your Father;* and to my God, and your God."[23] Does not this indicate family organization?

---

[19]Rev. 21:7.   [22]Matt. 6:9.
[20]Eph. 3:14-15.   [23]John 20:17.
[21]Acts 17:29; Heb. 12:9.

Through the restoration of the priesthood held by Elijah, knowledge has been given to the Church that *each family unit,* where the parents have been married for time and for eternity, shall *remain intact through all eternity.* Moreover, each family unit is to be *linked to the generation which went before,* until all the faithful, who have proved their title to family membership through obedience to the gospel, shall be joined in *one grand family* from the beginning to the end of time, and shall find place in the celestial kingdom of God. *In this way all who receive the exaltation become heirs of God, and joint-heirs with Jesus Christ in the possession of eternal family relationships.*[24]

FAMILY UNIT CONTINUES ONLY IN CELESTIAL KINGDOM. There is no substitute for a righteous home. That may not be so considered in the world, but it is and ought to be in the Church of Jesus Christ of Latter-day Saints. The family is the unit in the kingdom of God. . . .

Outside of the celestial kingdom there is no family organization. That organization is reserved for those who are willing to abide in *every covenant* and *every obligation* which we are called upon to receive while we sojourn here in this mortal life.[25]

We believe that the family will go on. I get a great deal of comfort out of the thought that *if I am faithful and worthy of an exaltation, my father will be my father, and I will be subject to him as his son through all eternity;* that I will recognize and know my mother and she will be my mother in all eternity; and my brothers and sisters will be my brothers and sisters for all eternity; and that my children and my wives will be mine in eternity. I don't know how some other people feel, but that is a glorious thought to me. That helps to keep me sober.[26]

FAMILY CHAIN AMONG EXALTED BEINGS. *Every married man stands at the head of his household,* that is,

---

[24]*Church News,* Apr. 2, 1932, p. 6.   [26]*Church News,* May 6, 1939, p. 7.
[25]Conf. Rep., Oct., 1948, pp. 152-153.

his immediate family. Thus I, for instance, will stand at the head of my family group by virtue of the sealing for time and eternity, and my children will belong to me. I will belong to my parents in their family group. My father likewise, with his brothers and sisters, will belong to his father's unit in that family group, and his father to his father before him—all linked together generation to generation like a chain. So it will be of the righteous from the days of Adam down—Adam standing at the head as Michael, having authority and jurisdiction over his posterity in this large family group who have kept the commandments of God.

Now that is the order of the priesthood. Of course there will be chains that will be broken, links that will be missing, because we can not force people into the kingdom. Those who are unworthy to be joined in this grouping of families will have to stand aside, and those who are worthy will be brought together and the chain will go on just the same.[27]

Eventually, when this work is perfected, and Christ delivers up to his Father the keys and makes his report, and death is destroyed, then that great family from the days of Adam down, of all the righteous, those who have kept the commandments of God, will find that they are *one family, the family of God,* entitled to all the blessings that pertain to the exaltation.[28]

SPIRIT CHILDREN IN THE RESURRECTION. Those who attain to the exaltation in the celestial kingdom shall have the power of *eternal increase of posterity,* and they shall be "above all, because all things are subject unto them."[29] Children born to parents who have obtained, through their faithfulness, the fulness of these blessings, shall be *spirit children* not clothed upon with tabernacles of flesh and bones. *These children will be like we were*

---

[27]*Gen. & Hist. Mag.,* vol. 30, pp. 1-3;   [28]Conf. Rep., Oct., 1948, pp. 153-154.
  D. & C. 78:15-16; Dan. 7:9-14.   [29]*D. & C.* 132:20.
  21-27.

before we came into this world. We are taught in the scriptures that we are the offspring of God in the spirit, Jesus Christ being the Firstborn Son of our Eternal Father in that spirit world.[30]

ADAM AND CELESTIAL MARRIAGE

ADAM MARRIED BEFORE DEATH ENTERED WORLD. The Lord created man in his own image, *male* and *female,* and the woman was given as a companion to the man because the Lord said, "It is not good that the man should be alone."[31]

When Eve was given to Adam, the union was an eternal one. There was no death in the world, for the fall of man came later.[32] When the seeds of death were sown and man was banished from the presence of the Lord because of his transgression, the union previously formed was not severed.

The scriptures say that, "Adam began to till the earth, and to have dominion over all the beasts of the field, and to eat his bread by the sweat of his brow," and "Eve, also, his wife, did labor with him."[33] This holy companionship is destined to endure forever. Adam shall be known as the "prince of all, the ancient of days,"[34] and Eve shall be known as "the mother of all living."[35] Throughout eternity both shall be honored by their posterity.

It was not "good" for man to be alone in the beginning, and it never was and never will be "good" for man to be alone. That man or that woman who remains "separately and singly"[36] throughout eternity shall have *lost* the greatest blessing the Lord has prepared for them that love him. It is an inherent, or God-given desire, for a man when he becomes mature, to "leave his father and his mother" and "cleave unto his wife"[37] in a companionship

---

[30]Pers. Corresp.
[31]Gen. 2:18; Moses 3:18.
[32]2 Ne. 2:22-25.
[33]Moses 5:1.

[34]D. & C. 27:11.
[35]Gen. 3:20; Moses 4:26.
[36]D. & C. 132:17.
[37]Gen. 2:24; Moses 3:24.

and union that in all righteousness should endure
forever.[38]

ADAM'S MARRIAGE TO BE EVERLASTING. Paul declared that, "Neither is the man without the woman,
neither the woman without the man, in the Lord."[39] And
the Lord said he would give the man a companion who
would be a help *meet* for him:[40] that is, *a help who would
answer all the requirements, not only of companionship,
but also through whom the fulness of the purposes of the
Lord could be accomplished regarding the mission of man
through mortal life and into eternity.*

"Neither the man nor the woman were capable of
filling the measure of their creation alone. The union of
the two was required to complete man in the image of
God."[41] The Lord said, "Let us make man in our image,
after our likeness. . . . So God created man in his own
image, in the image of God created he him; male and
female created he them."[42]

Moreover when the woman was presented to the
man, Adam said: "This [woman] is now bone of my
bones, and flesh of my flesh."[43] From this we understand
that his union with Eve was to be everlasting. The Savior
confirmed this doctrine when he said to the Jews: "For
this cause shall a man leave father and mother, and shall
cleave to his wife: and *they twain shall be one flesh.*
Wherefore *they are no more twain, but one flesh.*"[44]
Then how can husband and wife be separated as we find
them so frequently among the people today and be justified in the sight of God? When a man and his wife
separate, the law of God has been broken.

The Prophet Joseph taught that "marriage was *an
institution of heaven,* instituted in the Garden of Eden;
[and] that it is necessary it should be solemnized by the
authority of the everlasting priesthood."[45]

---

[38]*Young Women's Journal.* vol. 31.
    p. 304.
[39]1 Cor. 11:11.
[40]Gen. 2:18; Moses 3:18.
[41]*Compendium*, p. 118.

[42]Gen. 1:26-27; Moses 2:26-27.
[43]Gen. 2:23; Moses 3:23.
[44]Matt. 19:5-6.
[45]*Era.* vol. 34, pp. 704-705.

GOD THE FATHER MARRIED ADAM AND EVE. Marriage as established in the beginning was an eternal covenant. The first man and the first woman were not married until death should part them, for at that time death had not come into the world. The ceremony on that occasion was performed by the Eternal Father himself whose work endures forever. It is the will of the Lord that all marriages should be of like character, and in becoming "one flesh" the man and the woman are to continue in the married status, according to the Lord's plan, throughout all eternity as well as in this mortal life.[46]

MARRIAGE IN HEAVEN

APOSTATE TEACHINGS DENY ETERNAL MARRIAGE. Righteous parents throughout the world long for the continuation of their union with each other and with their children beyond the grave. Poets have sung of such unions down through the ages. It is safe to say that no husband who dearly loves his wife, and who has been called upon to lay her away in death, ever did so without a yearning desire that he may meet her again and renew the companionship in eternity forever.

No parent ever laid away a child, if love dwelt in his heart, without having the same yearning desire. Yet the teachings of the world today deny to him this blessing.

It was not always so. This false doctrine, which has caused so many needless heartaches, is the outgrowth of apostasy and is based in large measure upon the misunderstanding of uninspired religious teachers, who misinterpret the words of the Lord to the unbelieving Sadducees.

These Sadducees, who denied the resurrection, endeavoring to catch the Lord in his words, set a trap for him.[47] In asking their question, they said that a certain woman had been married seven times, or at least had lived with seven men presumably as her husbands, in accordance with the law as designated by Moses. Since

---

[46]*Church News*, Mar. 26, 1932, p. 7.   [47]*Church News*, Mar. 13, 1948, p. 8.

these Sadducees did not believe in the resurrection, neither did they believe in marriage for eternity; and they thought there could be no suitable answer to their question.

The very fact that they asked the question indicates that the doctrine of marriage for eternity was taught and accepted by those who were not of their particular faith. Otherwise they never would have presented the question to the Savior. His answer was just such an answer as we would give today, and as we do give, and as the Lord has given it in the revelations to the Church.

No Marriage in Heaven for the Sadducees. This is the answer: *Marriage, like baptism, is an ordinance which has to be performed in this life; it cannot be performed after men are dead, except as in the case of baptism by proxy,* and so the Lord said that *they* neither marry nor are given in marriage in heaven. He might have answered those who questioned baptism, by saying, there is no baptism in heaven. All of the ordinances of the gospel given to us here pertain to this mortal probation and must be attended to here by the contracting parties or by some one in their behalf after they are dead . . . but they must be performed here.

The Savior, answering them according to their folly, said: "The children of *this world* [i.e. the world to which these Sadducees belonged] marry, and are given in marriage." I call your attention to the fact that the Lord said that he and his disciples did not belong to *this world;*[48] the Sadducees did.

Then he added: "But *they* [those of "this world" who do not keep the whole law] which shall be accounted worthy to obtain *that world* [i.e. even those who obtain the celestial kingdom but being unmarried do not obtain an exaltation in that kingdom], and the resurrection from the dead, neither marry, nor are given in marriage: Neither can they die any more: for they are equal unto

[48]John 17:9-16.

CELESTIAL MARRIAGE   73

the angels; and are the children of God, being the children of the resurrection."[49]

No Marriage in Heaven for Unrighteous. This is the *only* answer the Lord could have given to these *unbelievers*. It is in full accord with the revelation given to the Prophet Joseph Smith, wherein the Lord says that, "when *they* [those of "this world" who do not keep the whole law] are out of the world they neither marry nor are given in marriage; but are appointed angels in heaven; which angels are ministering servants, to minister for those who are worthy of a far more, and an exceeding, and an eternal weight of glory. For *these angels did not abide my law; therefore, they cannot be enlarged, but remain separately and singly, without exaltation, in their saved condition, to all eternity; and from henceforth are not gods, but are angels of God forever and ever.*"[50]

The answers are exactly the same and apply to those who may be worthy of *some salvation*, notwithstanding their rejection of the eternal marriage covenant.[51] *There will be no marrying, neither giving in marriage among those who reject the truth of the everlasting gospel. That privilege is confined to those who keep the commandments of the Lord in their fulness and who are obedient to the laws of God.*[52]

Restrictions will be placed upon those who enter the terrestrial and telestial kingdoms, and even those in the celestial kingdom who do not get the exaltation; *changes will be made in their bodies to suit their condition;* and there will be no marrying or giving in marriage, nor living together of men and women, because of these restrictions.[53]

LAWS GOVERNING ETERNAL MARRIAGE

Keys Required for Celestial Marriage. Now marriage for eternity can be performed only in the tem-

---

[49]Luke 20:27-37; Matt. 22:23-32.
[50]D. & C. 132:16-17.
[51]Pers. Corresp.

[52]*Young Women's Journal*, vol. 31, pp. 304-305.
[53]Pers. Corresp.

ples. It cannot be performed anywhere else. Authority by which such marriages are solemnized must be vested in the one who performs the ordinances, by virtue of appointment by the one who holds the keys.[54]

There is but one man living on the earth at a time who holds the keys of this binding or sealing power. No other man has the right to officiate in a marriage, or sealing ceremony, for time and all eternity, unless he has obtained the *direct appointment* from the one who holds the keys of this power.

That appointment may be cancelled at any time, when the one who holds those keys shall say the privilege is withdrawn. No man can officiate in these ceremonies unless he himself holds the holy priesthood. Any man who presumes to perform such marriages by virtue of his office in the priesthood, without having been appointed by the man who holds the keys of this power, is without authority and such acts are null and void.[55]

OBLIGATION OF MEN TO MARRY. Any young man who carelessly neglects this great commandment to marry, or who does not marry because of a selfish desire to avoid the responsibilities which married life will bring, is taking a course which is displeasing in the sight of God. Exaltation means responsibility. There can be no exaltation without it.

If a man refuses to take upon himself the responsibilities of married life, because he desires to avoid the cares and troubles which naturally will follow, he is taking a course which may bar him forever from the responsibilities which are held in reserve for those who are willing to keep in full the commandments of the Lord. His eternal progression will thus be limited. Like the Sadducees of old, he will be numbered among the angels who cannot be enlarged.[56] It will not be his privilege to be numbered among the sons of God, and thus be entitled

---

[54]*Church News,* May 6, 1939, p. 7.   [56]Luke 20:27-37; *D. & C.* 132:16-17.
[55]*D. & C.* 132:7.

as an heir to partake of the blessings reserved for those who receive an inheritance in the Father's kingdom.

DO NOT MARRY OUT OF CHURCH. For the reasons previously stated, it is a most serious error for a young man or a young woman to marry outside of the Church, for they cannot then be married with a promise of eternal union. No matter who should perform such a ceremony of marriage, it must be for time only, and then death will separate the contracting parties who will not have claim upon their children after they are dead.

This same condition will also prevail where both the contracting parties are members of the Church and refuse, or fail, to receive the ordinance in the proper way in the house of the Lord. However, there is a possibility that such may go to the house of the Lord later and have their blessings sealed upon them; but it is much better to have it done properly in the beginning, and then they will know they are on safe ground without danger of neglecting the opportunity until it may be too late.[57]

TEACH LAW OF ETERNAL MARRIAGE TO CHILDREN. May all Latter-day Saint fathers and mothers see to it that they teach their children the sacredness of the marriage covenant. Let them impress upon their children that in no other way than by honoring the covenants of God, among which the covenant of eternal marriage is one of the greatest and most mandatory, can they obtain the blessings of eternal lives.

If they refuse to receive this ordinance and other blessings of the house of God, then shall they be cut off from these higher blessings. *They shall wear no crown; they shall have no rule and sway no scepter; they shall be denied the fulness of knowledge and power,* and like the prodigal son, they *may* return again to their Father's house, but it will be *as servants,* not to inherit as *sons.*

---

[57] *Young Women's Journal,* vol. 31, pp. 305-307.

If they will be true to these commandments, their glory and exaltation shall have no bounds.[58]

MARRY RIGHT OR NOT AT ALL. I have heard President Joseph F. Smith say on several occasions that he would rather take his children one by one to the grave in their innocence and purity, knowing that they would come forth to inherit the fulness of celestial glory, than to have them marry outside of the Church, or even outside the temple of the Lord.

Why should he have been so emphatic? Because he had perfect knowledge of what marriage, according to the law of the Lord, means; and because he knew the consequences attending the rejection of this covenant in the house of the Lord. For those who refuse to receive this ordinance, as the Lord ordained, cannot enter into the fulness of celestial glory.[59]

EXALTATION FOR FAITHFUL UNMARRIED WOMEN. You good sisters, who are single and alone, do not fear, do not feel that blessings are going to be withheld from you. You are not under any obligation or necessity of accepting some proposal that comes to you which is distasteful for fear you will come under condemnation. If in your hearts you feel that the gospel is true, and would under proper conditions receive these ordinances and sealing blessings in the temple of the Lord; and that is your faith and your hope and your desire, and that does not come to you now; the Lord will make it up, and you shall be blessed—for *no blessing shall be withheld.*

The Lord will judge you according to the desires of your hearts when blessings are withheld in this life, and he is not going to condemn you for that which you cannot help.[60]

UNMARRIED WOMEN JUDGED BY DESIRES. According to modern custom, it is the place of the man to take

---

[58]*Era*, vol. 34, p. 706; Luke 15:11-32.   [60]*Elijah the Prophet and His Mission*,
[59]*Era*, vol. 34, p. 705.   p. 32.

the initiative in the matter of a marriage contract. Women are, by force of such custom, kept in reserve and whether it be right or wrong for a woman to take the lead and offer a proposal of marriage, she feels, and she knows that the public would also feel, that she was acting in a forward and unbecoming manner. This is all wrong, but nevertheless it is the fact. The responsibility therefore rests upon the man.

No woman will be condemned by the Lord for refusing to accept a proposal which she feels she could not properly accept. In my judgment it is far better for our good girls to refuse an offer of marriage when they think that the companionship of the man would be disagreeable, or if he is one they do not and believe they cannot learn to love.

If in her heart the young woman accepts fully the word of the Lord, and under proper conditions would abide by the law, but refuses an offer when she fully believes that the conditions would not justify her in entering a marriage contract, which would bind her forever to one she does not love, she shall not lose her reward. The Lord will judge her by the desires of the heart, and the day will come when the blessings withheld shall be given, though it be postponed until the life to come.

USE CARE IN CHOOSING MARRIAGE COMPANION. This life is short, and eternity is long. When we contemplate that the marriage covenant will endure forever, it is well that it should be given careful consideration. Hasty action in this most important step in life may fill the mortal lives of husband, wife, and children with endless sorrow. The results may and often do reach into eternity and cause irreparable regrets that will endure forever. Marriage, from the viewpoint of the Latter-day Saint, is the one thing in life where it might prove fatal to act in haste with the idea in mind that repentance could come at leisure.

The proper advice to our youth is to consider carefully with the view of choosing well a companion with an abiding faith in the gospel. Such a person is more likely to prove true to every vow and covenant. When the young man and the young woman are thoroughly grounded in the divine mission of our Lord and believe the gospel as revealed through Joseph Smith, the Prophet, the chances are all in favor of a happy union that will endure forever.

My advice is to our girls, if you cannot find a husband who would be true to his religion and have faith in the gospel of our Lord, it is better to abide in "single blessedness." It is better to suffer some denial in mortal life and receive life everlasting than to lose your salvation in the kingdom of God. Remember the Lord will make up to you in joy and eternal union more than you have temporarily lost if you will be true and faithful. "If in this life only we have hope in Christ, we are of all men [and women] most miserable."[61]

SECOND MARRIAGES OUT OF TEMPLE. When a person has been through the temple and has made solemn covenants, and then, after his companion has died, marries someone out of the Church, it shows a very grave lack of loyalty to covenants, of weakness in the faith, and of unbelief in the promises of the Lord.

A person who violates covenants and disregards commandments and proves himself unfaithful in the Church may lose not only his children but also his own salvation.

RAISING UP SEED UNTO ONE'S BROTHER. When a man and a woman are married in the temple for time and all eternity, and then the man dies and the woman marries another man, she can be married to him for time only.

When a man marries a woman who was married previously to her husband in the temple but who has now

---

[61]*Young Women's Journal*, vol. 31,
   pp. 307-308; 1 Cor. 15:19.

died, he does so, or should, with his eyes open. If the children are born to this woman and her "time" husband, he has no claim upon those children. They go with the mother. This is the law. Certainly a man cannot in reason expect to take another man's wife, after that man is dead, and rear a family by her and then claim the children.

If he wants a family of his own, then he should marry a wife that he can have in eternity. This is in full harmony with the patriarchal order. What was the law anciently? Was not the second husband supposed to raise up seed for his brother?[62]

---

[62]Pers. Corresp.; Deut. 25:5-10; Gen. 38:8; Ruth 3:13, 4:5, 10.

CHAPTER 5

SINS AGAINST THE MARRIAGE COVENANT

DIVORCE AND BROKEN HOMES

TRAGEDY OF BROKEN HOMES. Throughout our land we see the tragedy of broken homes, fathers and mothers separated, children denied the natural affections. Children have a right to the blessings coming from this sacred union. They are entitled to the love and care of faithful parents, and the happiness and devotion which true worship brings.

When these blessings are lost, the whole community suffers and the integrity of government is weakened. It is a shame and a disgrace that so much evil is coming out of broken homes, and this comes largely because we have forgotten God and our obligations to serve and honor him. Truly we have much room for repentance and a return to the simple worship of true Christianity.[1]

DIVORCE NOT PART OF GOSPEL PLAN. If all mankind would live in strict obedience to the gospel, and in that love which is begotten by the Spirit of the Lord, all marriages would be eternal, divorce would be unknown. Divorce is not part of the gospel plan and has been introduced because of the hardness of heart and unbelief of the people.

When the Pharisees tempted Christ saying: "Is it lawful for a man to put away his wife for every cause," he answered them: "Have ye not read, that he which made them at the beginning made them male and female, And said, For this cause shall a man leave father and mother, and shall cleave to his wife: and they twain shall

---

[1]Conf. Rep., Apr., 1943, p. 14.

be one flesh? Wherefore they are no more twain, but one flesh. What therefore God hath joined together, let not man put asunder."

Then when they asked why Moses permitted divorce, the answer of the Lord was: "Moses because of the hardness of your hearts suffered you to put away your wives: but from the beginning it was not so."[2] Moreover, *what God joins together is eternal.* Unfortunately most of the marriages performed are not by the will of God, but by the will of man. Marriages among Latter-day Saints are eternal marriages, if they are properly performed, because the Eternal Father gave the covenant of marriage which is received by couples who go to the temple to receive this blessing there.[3]

SALVATION LOST THROUGH DIVORCE. There never could be a divorce in this Church if the husband and wife were keeping the commandments of God.

Within the week, my attention was called to a case where a man and a woman, married in the temple for time and all eternity, have tired of each other. They have reared a family. Now he wants to go his way, and she wants to go her way. But they want to be friends! There are no hard feelings between them. They have just got tired. They want a change.

Do they have the spirit of the gospel in their hearts? I say to you, no, or they would not be tired of each other. That could not follow. They got tired of living the principles of eternal truth. *A man would not get tired of his wife, if he had the love of God in his heart.* A woman would not get tired of her husband, if she had in her heart the love of God, that first of all commandments. They could not do it!

And then think of the children. Here you have a broken home. These people get a divorce, and then they want to get a cancellation, perhaps, of their sealing. They want to marry somebody else. And there you have a

---

[2]Matt. 19:3-8.   [3]*Era*, vol. 34, p. 704.

broken home. What is going to become of the parents? What is going to become of the children? Haven't the children any rights?

The parents become separated. Each goes a different way, but they want to be friends! And then they expect to marry again for time and all eternity and enter into the celestial kingdom of God to receive all the blessings of exaltation! Are they entitled to do it? Not as I read the scriptures—they are not entitled to do it.

SOME DIVORCES JUSTIFIED. Of course, we have worse cases than that. We have cases, perhaps, where a woman is justified in seeking relief, to be separated from a brutal husband who lives after the flesh, whose incontinency is such that he makes her life miserable; and they are not keeping the commandments that were given to them when they were married in the temple for time and all eternity, where he is supposed to love and respect and care for his wife with all the humility, in all the faith, and the understanding of the gospel of Jesus Christ. And *the gospel of Jesus Christ is not carnal.*[4]

DISOBEDIENCE BRINGS DIVORCE. When divorce comes to those who are married in the temple, it has come because they have violated the covenants and the obligations they have taken upon themselves to be true to each other, true to God, true to the Church. If they will continue to live in that faithfulness, if they will have love in their hearts for each other, respect each other's rights and not one attempt to take an advantage unduly of the other but have the proper consideration, there will be no failures. . . .

CHILDREN HAVE RIGHT TO AN ENDURING FAMILY UNION. And when a man and a woman are married in the temple for time and all eternity and then seek through the courts a separation, and perhaps come to the President

---
[4]Conf. Rep., Apr., 1949, pp. 136-137.

of the Church to get a cancellation, what have they done? Children likely have been born, and *these children belong to God;* they are his children, sent to that home with all the *rights of protection* from father and mother, guidance from father and mother, to be built up and strengthened in the faith, and to go into the heavens, into the celestial kingdom with the father and mother to sit with them in exaltation and glory.

But frequently a man and a woman cannot live together, many times because of some trivial thing that arises, and they separate. *What have they done to those children? They have destroyed their God-given rights,* taken them away from them, destroyed a family. And how are they going to go into the eternities and face their Maker under those conditions?

Now I realize that there are some cases where a wife needs to have a separation, perhaps a husband should have a separation, but always because of a violation, a serious violation of the covenants that have been made.

But here you have the broken home, children left without one and maybe without both parents, to be taken perhaps through the mercy of the Almighty into some other faithful family, to be adopted in such a family to be theirs through all eternity. . . .

Those who violate this sacred and solemn covenant are going to have a sorry time of it if they are guilty when they come to the judgment seat of God, for they have broken the bands of an eternal union and lost their promise of exaltation in the kingdom of God.[5]

LORD'S PENALTY FOR DIVORCE. If you want to know how serious it is to seek a divorce, I want you to read what the Lord says in the Sermon on the Mount, which is repeated in the *Book of Mormon* in a similar sermon that was given to the Nephites. If we understood, if we

---

[5]Conf. Rep., Oct., 1951, pp. 121-122.

comprehended what the Lord says there, I want to tell you, people would be frightened rather than to seek a separation on some trivial matter—they would be frightened.[6]

Marriage according to the law of the Church is the most holy and sacred ordinance. It will bring to the husband and the wife, if they abide in their covenants, the fulness of exaltation in the kingdom of God. When that covenant is broken, it will bring *eternal misery to the guilty party,* for we will all have to answer for our deeds done while in the flesh. It is an ordinance that cannot be trifled with, and the covenants made in the temple cannot be broken without dire punishment to the one who is guilty.

PERFECTION COMES THROUGH MARRIAGE. When a couple are married in the temple, they should try to live in peace and harmony, and if both are faithful members of the Church, this should not be impossible. Young people should try to tolerate each other's weaknesses and overcome them. *If they live worthy of exaltation, they will enter the celestial kingdom without the frailties and weaknesses of mortality and will be perfect.*

POWER TO LOOSE IN HEAVEN. The Lord gives the President of the Church the keys of the kingdom; he has the right to bind on earth and in heaven; he has the right to loose on earth and in heaven. If circumstances warrant it, he may cancel the sealing and the Lord would sanction it. But in regard to trivial matters, there never should be a divorce.[7]

ABUSE OF MARRIAGE COVENANT DESTROYS NATIONS. The abuse of this ordinance has been the primary cause of the downfall of nations. When the sacredness of the marriage covenant is lost, and the vows are broken, destruction is inevitable. This principle cannot be re-

---

[6]*Church News,* May 6, 1939, p. 7;   [7]Pers. Corresp.; *D. & C.* 132:46.
    Matt. 5:31-32; 3 Ne. 12:31-32;
    Matt. 19:8.

ceived in the spirit of contempt and indifference. It is ordained to be more, far more, than a civil contract.

No nation can survive the abuse of this principle. Rome, Greece, Babylon, Egypt, and many other nations owe their downfall to the breaking of the sacred covenant of marriage. The anger of a just God was kindled against them for their immorality. The bones of dead civilizations on this American continent bear silent but convincing evidence that it was unchastity and the disregard of this sacred covenant which brought them to their final judgment.

BIRTH CONTROL

The Blessings of Birth into Mortality. Nothing should be held in greater sacredness and honor than the covenant by which the spirits of men—the offspring of God in the spirit—are privileged to come into this world in mortal tabernacles. It is through this principle that the blessing of immortal glory is made possible. *The greatest punishment ever given was proclaimed against Lucifer and his angels. To be denied the privilege of mortal bodies forever is the greatest curse of all. These spirits can have no progress, no hope of resurrection and eternal life! Doomed are they to eternal misery for their rebellion!*

And then to think that we are not only privileged, but also commanded to assist our Father in the great work of redemption by giving to his children, as we have obtained these blessings ourselves, the right to live and continue on even to perfection! *No innocent soul should be condemned to come into this world under a handicap of illegitimacy.* Every child has the *right* to be well born! *Every individual who denies them that right is guilty of a mortal sin.*

The importance of these mortal tabernacles is apparent from the knowledge we have of eternal life. Spirits cannot be made perfect without the body of flesh and bones. The body and its spirit are brought to immortality and the blessings of salvation through the resurrection. After the resurrection there can be no separation again, body and spirit become inseparably connected that man may receive a fulness of joy. In no other way, other than birth into this life and the resurrection, can spirits become like our Eternal Father.[8]

MAN COMMANDED TO BE FRUITFUL AND MULTIPLY. The obligations which married couples take upon themselves should conform in every particular to the commandments given by the Lord.

In the beginning, the Lord said when he gave Eve to Adam, "Be fruitful, and multiply, and replenish the earth, and subdue it."[9] This earth was created for the very purpose that the spirit children of our Father might have the *privilege of the temporal existence,* receiving bodies of flesh and bones as tabernacles for the spirits which occupy them, and then, through the atonement of Jesus Christ, receive the resurrection in which the spirit and the body become inseparably connected so that man may live again. . . .

Marriage is an eternal covenant, not to come to an end as taught so generally throughout the world when the covenanting parties are dead, but to endure forever. The real purpose of life is that the spirits of men thus clothed in bodies of flesh and bones may, through obedience to the gospel, come back into the presence of the Father and the Son, to receive the fulness of exaltation.

The Lord has revealed that when a man and a woman are married according to his law, children born to them will be theirs throughout all eternity.

The covenant given to Adam to multiply was renewed after the flood with Noah and his children after him. The Lord said to Noah: "And you, be ye fruitful, and multiply; bring forth abundantly in the earth, and multiply therein. And God spake unto Noah, and to his

[8]*Era,* vol. 34, p. 643.   [9]Gen. 1:28; Moses 2:28.

sons with him, saying, And I, behold, I establish my covenant with you, and with your seed after you."[10]

This covenant is still binding, although mankind has departed from the way of eternal life and has rejected the covenant of marriage which the Lord revealed.

BIRTH CONTROL IS WICKEDNESS. The abuse of this holy covenant has been the primary cause for the downfall of nations. When the sacred vows of marriage are broken and the real purpose of marriage abused, as we find it so prevalent in the world today, then destruction is inevitable.

No nation can endure for any length of time, if the marriage covenants are abused and treated with contempt. The anger of the Almighty was kindled against ancient nations for their immorality. There is nothing that should be held in greater sacredness than this covenant by which the spirits of men are clothed with mortal tabernacles.

When a man and a woman are married and they agree, or covenant, to limit their offspring to two or three, and practice devices to accomplish this purpose, they are guilty of iniquity which eventually must be punished. Unfortunately this evil doctrine is being taught as a virtue by many people who consider themselves cultured and highly educated. It has even crept in among members of the Church and has been advocated in some of the classes within the Church.

It should be understood definitely that this kind of doctrine is not only not advocated by the authorities of the Church, but also is condemned by them as wickedness in the sight of the Lord.

President Joseph F. Smith has said in relation to this question: "Those who have taken upon themselves the responsibility of wedded life should see to it that they do not abuse the course of nature; that they do not destroy the principle of life within them, nor violate any

---

[10]Gen. 9:7-9.

of the commandments of God. The command which he
gave in the beginning to multiply and replenish the earth
is still in force upon the children of men. *Possibly no
greater sin could be committed by the people who have
embraced this gospel than to prevent or to destroy life
in the manner indicated.* We are born into the world
that we may have life, and we live that we may have a
fulness of joy, and if we will obtain a fulness of joy, we
must obey the law of our creation and the law by which
we may obtain the consummation of our righteous hopes
and desires—eternal life."[11]

SPIRITS DESIRE BIRTH IN RIGHTEOUS FAMILIES.
President Brigham Young has this to say about birth
control, an abomination practiced by so-called civilized
nations, but nations who have forsaken the ways of life:

"There are multitudes of pure and holy spirits waiting to take tabernacles, now what is our duty? To prepare tabernacles for them; to take a course that will not
tend to drive those spirits into the families of the wicked,
where they will be trained in wickedness, debauchery,
and every species of crime. *It is the duty of every righteous man and woman to prepare tabernacles for all the
spirits they can.*"[12]

If these iniquitous practices find their place in our
hearts and we are guilty, then when we arrive on the
other side—and discover that we have deprived ourselves
of eternal blessings and are accused by those who were
assigned to come to us, because, as President Young has
said, they were forced to take bodies in the families of
the wicked—how will we feel? Moreover, *may we not lose
our own salvation if we violate this divine law?*[13]

BIRTH CONTROL LEADS TO DAMNATION. Instructing
the mothers of the Church, President Joseph F. Smith
said in June, 1917: "I regret, I think it is a crying evil,

---

[11]Joseph F. Smith, *Gospel Doctrine*,
4th ed., p. 347.
[12]Brigham Young, *Discourses of Brigham Young*, 2nd ed., p. 305.
[13]*Church News*, July 12, 1947, p. 5.

that there should exist a sentiment or a feeling among any members of the Church to curtail the birth of their children. I think that is a crime wherever it occurs, where husband and wife are in possession of health and vigor and are free from impurities that would be entailed upon their posterity. I believe that *where people undertake to curtail or prevent the birth of their children that they are going to reap disappointment by and by.* I have no hesitancy in saying that I believe that is *one of the greatest crimes of the world today, this evil practice.*"[14]

When young people marry and refuse to fulfill this commandment given in the beginning of the world—and just as much in force today—they rob themselves of the greatest eternal blessing. If the love of the world and the wicked practices of the world mean more to a man and a woman than to keep the commandment of the Lord in this respect, then they shut themselves off from the eternal blessing of increase. *Those who wilfully and maliciously design to break this important commandment shall be damned.* They cannot have the Spirit of the Lord.

Small families is the rule today. Husbands and wives refuse to take upon themselves the responsibilities of family life. Many of them do not care to be bothered with children. Yet this commandment given to Adam has never been abrogated or set aside. If we refuse to live by the covenants we make, especially in the house of the Lord, then we cannot receive the blessings of those covenants in eternity. *If the responsibilities of parenthood are wilfully avoided here, then how can the Lord bestow upon the guilty the blessings of eternal increase?* It cannot be, and they shall be denied such blessings.[15]

SINS BY HEIRS OF THE COVENANT

BLESSINGS OF BIRTH UNDER THE COVENANT. Death does not separate righteous parents who are joined by

---

[14]*Rel. Soc. Mag.,* vol. 4, p. 314.   [15]*Era,* vol. 34, p. 644.

decree and authority of the Father, neither does it take from these parents their righteous children, for they are born under the covenant, and therefore, their parents have claim upon them forever.

President Brigham Young has said: *"When a man and woman have received their endowments and sealings, and then had children born to them afterwards, these children are legal heirs to the kingdom and to all its blessings and promises, and they are the only ones that are on this earth."*[16] This is certainly true; how can children whose parents have not been married by divine authority be heirs of that kingdom?

It may be asked, what is the advantage coming to those born under the covenant? Being *heirs* they have claims upon the blessings of the gospel beyond what those not so born are entitled to receive. They may receive a greater guidance, a greater protection, a greater inspiration from the Spirit of the Lord; and then there is no power that can take them away from their parents. Children, on the other hand, who are born to parents who were married until death separates them, have no claim upon such parents, and such parents have no claim upon the children after the resurrection from the dead.

RECLAIMING CHILDREN BORN UNDER THE COVENANT. Those born under the covenant, throughout all eternity, are the children of their parents. Nothing except the unpardonable sin, or sin unto death, can break this tie. If children do not sin as John says, "unto death," the parents may still feel after them and eventually bring them back near to them again.[17]

On this point President Brigham Young has said: "Let the father and mother, who are members of this Church and kingdom, *take a righteous course, and strive with all their might never to do a wrong, but to do good all their lives;* if they have one child or one hundred children, *if they conduct themselves towards them as they*

---

[16]Young, *op. cit.,* p. 202.   [17]I John 5:16-17.

should, binding them to the Lord by their faith and prayers, I care not where those children go, they are bound up to their parents by an everlasting tie, and no power of earth or hell can separate them from their parents in eternity; they will return again to the fountain from whence they sprang."[18]

PARENTAL CLAIM ON CHILDREN BORN UNDER COVENANT. *All children born under the covenant belong to their parents in eternity, but that does not mean that they, because of that birthright, will inherit celestial glory. The faith and faithfulness of fathers and mothers will not save disobedient children.*

Salvation is an individual matter, and if a person who has been born under the covenant rebels and denies the Lord, he will lose the blessings of exaltation. Every soul will be judged according to *his works* and *the wicked cannot inherit eternal life. We cannot force salvation upon those who do not want it.* Even our Father's children had their agency before this life, and one-third of them rebelled.

It is the duty of parents to teach their children so that they will *walk uprightly* and *thus obtain the blessings of their birthright.*

But children born under the covenant, who drift away, are still the children of their parents; and the parents have a claim upon them; and *if* the children have not sinned away all their rights, the parents *may* be able to bring them *through repentance,* into the celestial kingdom, but *not* to receive the exaltation. Of course, if children sin too grievously, they will have to enter the *telestial* kingdom, or they may even become sons of perdition.

When a man and a woman are married in the temple for time and all eternity and then separate, the children will go with the parent who is justified and who has kept the covenants. If neither of them has kept his cove-

---

[18]*Church News,* Mar. 13, 1948, p. 8;
   Young, *op. cit.,* p. 322.

nants, the children may be taken away from both of them and given to somebody else, and that would be *by virtue of being born under the covenant.*

A child is not to be sealed the second time when born under the covenant, but by virtue of that birthright can be transferred.[19]

UNCHASTITY

ENORMITY OF SEX SIN. Every soul is entitled to the right to come into this world in a legitimate way— in the way the Father has willed that souls should come. Whosoever takes a course contrary to this is guilty of an almost irreparable crime.

Is there any wonder, then, that the Lord places the violation of this covenant of marriage and the loss of virtue as second only to the shedding of innocent blood?[20] Is there not, then, sufficient reason for the severity of the punishment which has been promised to those who violate this eternal law? Moreover, *have we not forgotten in large measure the enormity of the crime of unchastity and breaking of marriage vows?* Do those who are guilty think the enormity of the offense of maliciously or wickedly tampering with the laws of life will be overlooked by a just God? Do they think that only a few stripes, if any punishment at all, will amend this broken law?

The demand for personal purity is made by the Church upon both men and women equally. There is no double standard of judgment. *"If purity of life is neglected,"* President Joseph F. Smith once said, *"all other dangers set in upon us like the rivers of water when the flood gates are opened."*[21] Sexual impurity is a most deadly sin. Anciently it was considered so, and according to the law of God, those who were guilty were in danger of being put to death.[22] . . .

UNVIRTUOUS ARE DAMNED. President Brigham Young was also very emphatic in his denunciation of this

[19]Pers. Corresp.
[20]Alma 39:5-9.
[21]Smith, *op. cit.,* p. 392.
[22]Lev. 20:10.

evil, and I feel that we cannot be too emphatic in denouncing it. It is very prevalent and a universal evil. The world is fast coming to its destruction because of it. "Learn the will of God," said President Young, "keep his commandments and do his will, and you will be a virtuous person."

How wonderful is the peace and the joy which fills the soul of the virtuous person! *How terrible are the torments of the unvirtuous!* They shall have no place in the first resurrection. When the final judgment comes, they are they who remain filthy still. They cannot enter the Holy City, they are the "dogs, and sorcerers, and whoremongers, and murderers, and idolaters, and whosoever loveth and maketh a lie," who are cast out.[23]

ADULTERY AND REPENTANCE. How severe is the judgment on the man who has committed adultery, even though he apparently is repentant? In the *Doctrine and Covenants*, 42:24-26, the Lord has given us a key to this situation. If a person commits adultery and then repents with all his heart, he may be forgiven. If he repeats the offense, he is not to be forgiven, but is to be cast out. As I read it, the Lord has not provided that, under those circumstances, he can come back again.

Now this revelation was given *before the endowment* was made known. Since that time when a man is married in the temple, he takes a solemn covenant before God, angels, and witnesses that he will keep the law of chastity. Then if he violates that covenant it is not easy to receive forgiveness. I call your attention to this statement by the Prophet Joseph Smith: "If a man commit adultery, he cannot receive the celestial kingdom of God. Even if he is saved in any kingdom, it cannot be the celestial kingdom."[24]

Of course, a man may, according to the *Doctrine and Covenants*, 132:26, receive forgiveness, if he is willing to pay the penalty for such a crime: that is he "shall be

---

[23]*Era*, vol. 34, pp. 643-644; Rev. 22:15.   [24]*History of the Church*, vol. 6, p. 81.

destroyed in the flesh, and shall be delivered unto the buffetings of Satan unto the day of redemption," which is the time of the resurrection. We cannot destroy in the flesh, so what the Lord will require in lieu thereof, I do not know. Anciently when the Church was a theocratic power with authority in all things, this law was carried out. "And the man that committeth adultery with another man's wife, even he that committeth adultery with his neighbour's wife, *the adulterer and the adulteress shall surely be put to death.*"[25]

We have been taught that adultery is a crime second only to the shedding of innocent blood. We cannot treat it lightly. For a man to destroy another man's home is too serious an offense to be readily forgiven. Such a man should not be permitted to come back in the Church, under any circumstances, at least until years have elapsed. He should be placed on *probation* for that length of time to see if he can, or will, remain clean. Even then I confess I do not know what disposition the Lord will make of him. To permit him to come back within a short time has a very evil effect upon other members of the Church who begin to think that this enormous crime is not so serious after all.

SEALING BY THE HOLY SPIRIT OF PROMISE

Nature of the Sealing by the Spirit. I will make an explanation of the expression, "Sealed by the Holy Spirit of Promise." This does not have reference to marriage for time and all eternity only, but to *every ordinance and blessing of the gospel.* Baptism into the Church is sealed by this Spirit, likewise confirmation, ordination, and all ordinances as well as marriage for time and all eternity.

The meaning of this expression is this: *Every covenant, contract, bond, obligation, oath, vow, and performance, that man receives through the covenants and blessings of the gospel, is sealed by the Holy Spirit with*

---
[25]Lev. 20:10.

a promise. The promise is that the blessing will be obtained, if those who seek it are true and faithful to the end. If they are not faithful, then the Holy Spirit will withdraw the blessing, and the promise comes to an end.[26]

ISOLATED SCRIPTURES GIVE WRONG IMPRESSION. Verse 26, in section 132, is the most abused passage in any scripture. The Lord has never promised any soul that he may be taken into exaltation without the spirit of repentance. While repentance is not stated in this passage, yet it is, and must be, implied. It is strange to me that everyone knows about verse 26, but it seems that they have never read or heard of Matthew 12:31-32, where the Lord tells us the same thing in substance as we find in verse 26, section 132.

It is wrong to take one passage of scripture and isolate it from all other teachings dealing with the same subject. We should bring together all that has been said by authority on the question. If we were to make a photograph, it would be necessary for all of your rays of light to be focused properly on the subject. If this were not done then a blurred picture would be the result. This is the case when we try to obtain a mental picture, when we have only a portion of the facts dealing with the subject we are considering. Therefore we must find out what else has been said about salvation.

NONE EVER SAVED WITHOUT REPENTANCE. The Lord said by his own mouth: "And he that endureth not unto the end, the same is he that is also hewn down and cast into the fire, from whence they can no more return, because of the justice of the Father. And this is the word which he hath given unto the children of men. And for this cause he fulfilleth the words which he hath given, and he lieth not, but fulfilleth *all* his words. And *no unclean thing can enter into his kingdom; therefore nothing entereth into his rest save it be those who have washed*

---

[26]*D. & C.* 76:50-54; 88:3-5; 124-124;
   132:7; Moses 6:60.

their garments in my blood, because of their faith, and the repentance of all their sins, and their faithfulness unto the end."[27]

So we must conclude that those spoken of in verse 26 are those who, having sinned, have *fully repented* and are willing to pay the price of their sinning, else the blessings of exaltation will not follow. Repentance is absolutely necessary for the forgiveness, and the person having sinned must be cleansed.

John said: "There is a sin unto death." "If any man see his brother sin a sin which is not unto death, he shall ask, and he shall give him life for them that sin not unto death. There is a sin unto death: I do not say that he shall pray for it."[28]

The Lord, in verse 27, has pointed out some sins unto death for which there is no forgiveness. It will do no good for one to pray for his brother for forgiveness from such a sin. All other sins, including blasphemy against the Son of God, may be forgiven men, *on their true repentance.* If they do not repent, then no matter what the sin may be, or the covenant violated, the guilty party or parties will never enter into the kingdom of God!

DREADFUL PENALTY FOR CERTAIN SINS. Here is something which those who contend that the Lord has granted immunity from their sins to some, if they have received certain sealings by the Holy Spirit of promise, have overlooked in this passage. I call attention to these two things. If covenants are broken and enormous sins are committed, but not unto death, there are certain punishments to be inflicted. The mere confession is not enough; the sinners are: 1—to "be *destroyed in the flesh*"; and 2—to "be *delivered unto the buffetings of Satan unto the day of redemption.*"

Who in the world is so foolish as to wish to sin with the hope of forgiveness, if such a penalty is to be inflicted? No one but a fool! To be "destroyed in the flesh" means

---

[27] 3 Ne. 27:17-19.   [28] 1 John 5:16.

exactly that. We cannot destroy men in the flesh, because we do not control the lives of men and do not have power to pass sentences upon them which involve capital punishment. In the days when there was a theocracy on the earth, then this decree was enforced. What the Lord will do in lieu of this, because we cannot destroy in the flesh, I am unable to say, but it will have to be made up in some other way.

Then to be turned over to the buffetings of Satan unto the day of redemption, which is the resurrection, must be something horrible in its nature. Who wishes to endure such torment? No one but a fool! I have seen their anguish. I have heard their pleadings for relief and their pitiful cries that they cannot endure the torment. This was in *this* life. Add to that, the torment in the spirit world before the redemption comes—all of this, mark you, coming *after severe and humble repentance!*

FORGIVENESS SOMETIMES REQUIRES REPENTANCE AND PUNISHMENT. Some among us have the idea that to confess their sins with their lips and to turn away from them constitutes all that is required of the repentant. This is not *always* so. It is *our* duty to forgive, but the Lord *may* require a severe penalty *after* this humble repentance. David sorely repented; read some of his Psalms and realize how he cried in anguish for relief; yet we understand that he is paying the price to this day and will until the Son of God comes to relieve him.[29]

I said that when the Lord ruled in a theocracy that punishment by death was the edict for certain crimes. Here is an example: "And the man that committeth adultery with another man's wife, even he that committeth adultery with his neighbour's wife, the adulterer and the adulteress shall surely be put to death."[30] There were also other crimes for which this penalty was exacted.[31]

No, the Lord has not prepared for favoritism. He

[29]Ps. 16:10; 51:1-19; Acts 2:29, 34.　[31]Rom. 1:28-32; Ex. 35:2; Deut.
[30]Lev. 20:10.　　13:1-11; 17:1-7; 21:20-23.

has not placed exemption upon some because they have received marriage for time and for all eternity and had it sealed by the "Holy Spirit of promise." He has not given them the privilege of blaspheming his name, of committing any sin whatever, and then coming forth to receive an exaltation. We should all be grateful for the wonderful principle of repentance; we all need it. But we must not lose sight of the fact that *the celestial kingdom is reserved for those who are sanctified and none others.* Read Mormon 9:3-4.

Let it be remembered also that *those who sin must repent in this life; if they die in their sins, unrepentant, then no matter what blessings they have received, they are not re-instated.*[32]

HOLY SPIRIT BOTH SEALS AND UNSEALS. When a man and a woman, in all sincerity, enter into a covenant of marriage for time and all eternity (and after they have "overcome by faith," and are "just and true"),[33] *the Holy Ghost—who is the Spirit of promise—bears record of or ratifies that sealing.* In other words, *he seals the promises appertaining to the marriage covenant upon them.*

Now the Lord has said: "But *there is a possibility that man may fall from grace and depart from the living God;* Therefore let the church take heed and pray always, lest they fall into temptation; Yea, and *even let those who are sanctified take heed also.*"[34]

If one or both of these covenanting persons break that covenant by which they were sealed by the Holy Spirit of promise, then *the Spirit withdraws the seal* and the guilty party, or parties, stand as if there had been no sealing or promise given. *All covenants are sealed based upon faithfulness.*

Should a person endeavor to receive the sealing blessing by fraud, then the blessing is not sealed, not-

---

[32]Alma 34:31-35; 3 Ne. 12:20; 27:17-   [33]D. & C. 76:53.
   19.   [34]D. & C. 20:31-34.

withstanding the integrity and authority of the person officiating. Instead of a blessing they will receive a cursing, the heaviest of all.[35] Therefore, a person who may deceive the bishop or any other officer, will stand condemned before the Lord, for he cannot be deceived and justice will be meted out to all.

UNCLEAN SINNERS DAMNED. If a man thinks the Lord has placed upon him a seal by which he is exempt from his transgressions and is bound to inherit eternal life, no matter what he does, as long as he does not commit murder, or shed innocent blood, or deny the Holy Ghost, he is in the gall of bitterness, as a Nephite prophet would have said.[36]

No man is promised salvation who is not cleansed from all his sins, and if a man sins deliberately, thinking he is exempt, he will be damned!

"For behold, justice exerciseth all his demands, and also mercy claimeth all which is her own; and thus, none but the truly penitent are saved. What, do ye suppose that mercy can rob justice? I say unto you, Nay; not one whit. If so, God would cease to be God."[37]

---

[35]*D. & C.* 41:1.
[36]Alma 41:10-11.

[37]Pers. Corresp.; Alma 42:24-25.

CHAPTER 6

ELIJAH: THE MAN AND THE PROPHET

ELIJAH IN LEGEND

MANY NATIONS HAVE TRADITIONS ABOUT ELIJAH. Elijah occupies a place in the legends of many peoples. We are informed that among the Greeks he is the patron saint of the mountains, and many of the mountains in Greece are named for him. In the Roman Catholic Church, he is regarded as the founder of the order known as "the barefooted Carmelites."

The Mohammedans likewise have honored him in their traditions, and he is often confounded with the great and mysterious *El-Khudr,* the eternal wanderer, who having drunk the waters of life, remains in everlasting youth and appears from time to time to correct the wrongs of men. Of course this comes from the fact of Elijah's translation.

Among the Jews he finds a place of honor in their history second to none of the prophets. He is mentioned on many occasions in the New Testament, some of the time in reference to his labors and ministry in Israel when he dwelt among men, and at other times, in reference to his future mission.[1]

JEWISH BELIEF IN ELIJAH'S COMING. Edersheim in his work, *The Temple,* says: *"To this day, in every Jewish home, at a certain part of the Paschal service [i.e. when they drink the 'third cup']—the door is opened to admit Elijah the prophet as forerunner of the Messiah,* while appropriate passages are at the same time read which foretell the destruction of all heathen nations. It

---

[1]*Elijah the Prophet and His Mission,* p. 5; Matt. 16:14; 27:47; Mark 6:15; 15:35; Luke 4:25; 9:54; Rom. 11:2; James 5:17.

is a remarkable coincidence that, in instituting his own Supper, the Lord Jesus connected the symbol, not of judgment, but of his dying love, with his 'third cup.' "

It was, I am informed, on the third day of April, 1836, that the Jews, in their homes at the Paschal feast, opened their doors for Elijah to enter. On that very day Elijah did enter—not in the home of the Jews to partake of the Passover with them—but he appeared in the house of the Lord, erected to his name and received by the Lord in Kirtland, and there bestowed his keys to bring to pass the very things for which these Jews, assembled in their homes, were seeking.[2]

ELIJAH THE TISHBITE. I would like to spend just a little time dealing with the history, brief as it is, of Elijah's ministry.

He lived about 900 years B.C., in the reign of King Ahab of Israel—of whom it is recorded that he did more to cause Israel to sin than all the kings who were before him. Elijah appeared rather suddenly, so far as the history states. He is known as Elijah the Tishbite, of the inhabitants of Gilead; and that is about all we know of him so far as his place of birth and residence are concerned.

NOTION THAT ELIJAH HAD NO PARENTS. The fact that he appeared rather suddenly, and departed in a manner shrouded in mystery, and seemingly only mingled with the people on occasions when the Lord sent him with some instruction or command, has caused many people to look upon Elijah as being like Melchizedek— and in that, of course, they are wrong, for they misunderstand the scriptures. You know in the book of Hebrews, Melchizedek is spoken of in this wise, that he was "King of Salem, which is, King of peace; Without father, without mother, without descent, having neither beginning of days, nor end of life; but made like unto the Son of God; abideth a priest continually."[3]

---

[2]Conf. Rep., Apr., 1936, p. 75.   [3]Heb. 7:2-3.

Now, the world has commented upon that very greatly, and they have concluded because of this reading, that Melchizedek was not born in the world like other men, that he had no father or mother. But that is not the proper reading. And they have applied the same thing to Elijah, due to the fact that his was somewhat a mysterious nature. The proper reading of that passage of scripture should be as follows: "For this Melchizedek was ordained a priest after the order of the Son of God, which order was without father, without mother, without descent, having neither beginning of days nor end of life. And all those who are ordained unto this priesthood are made like unto the Son of God, abiding a priest continually."[4]

ELIJAH IN ANCIENT ISRAEL

ELIJAH SEALS THE HEAVENS. The first appearance of Elijah we read of is in the 17th chapter of 1st Kings, when he came before the king and said, "As the Lord God of Israel liveth, before whom I stand, there shall not be dew nor rain these years, but according to my word."[5]

There is something very significant in that edict. I want you to get it. Follow me again closely: "As the Lord God of Israel liveth, before whom I stand, there shall not be dew nor rain these years, *but according to my word.*" The reason I put emphasis upon this is to impress you with the sealing power by which Elijah was able to close the heavens, that there should be no rain or dew until he spoke.

After Elijah had made that prediction, he suddenly departed and made his abode upon the banks of the brook Cherith, where ravens fed him.

MIRACLES OF ELIJAH. After the brook dried up because of the drouth, the Lord directed him to go into a foreign land, so he departed and went to the city of

[4]*Inspired Version,* Heb. 7:3.   [5]1 Kings 17:1.

Zarephath of Zidon, as it reads, where a widow woman had been appointed by the Lord to feed him; and when he arrived he found her picking up sticks to make a fire. He asked for something to eat, and in her distress and anguish she said that she barely had enough meal and oil to make a cake; she was gathering sticks in order to make that cake for herself and her son and then they would die. But Elijah commanded her to go and prepare for him first. Do you think that selfish? No, not when you know the circumstances. The woman recognized him as a man of authority, so in faith she went and did as he had commanded her. The result was that during the time of the famine that woman's cruse of oil failed her not and her barrel of meal was not diminished.

It was while on this sojourn that Elijah raised her son from the dead and restored him to her again.

ELIJAH'S MEETING WITH OBADIAH. Three years passed, and then the word of the Lord came to him to return to the land of Israel to Ahab the king, with a message. So, Elijah returned, and on his way he met Obadiah, the king's chamberlain, or governor of his house. When Obadiah saw Elijah, he was startled and said to him, "Do you not know that my master has been searching for you everywhere, that he might put you to death?" But Elijah commanded him to go to the king with a message. I would like to read a little of this. Obadiah said:

"As the Lord thy God liveth, there is no nation or kingdom, whither my Lord hath not sent to seek thee: and when they said, He is not there; he took an oath of the kingdom and nation, that they found thee not. And now thou sayest, Go, tell thy lord, Behold, Elijah is here.

"And it shall come to pass, as soon as I am gone from thee" (I want you to mark this also carefully), "that the Spirit of the Lord shall carry thee whither I know not; and so when I come and tell Ahab, and he

cannot find thee, he shall slay me: but I thy servant fear
the Lord from my youth. Was it not told my lord what I
did when Jezebel slew the prophets of the Lord, how I
hid an hundred men of the Lord's prophets by fifty in a
cave, and fed them with bread and water? And now
thou sayest, Go, tell thy lord, Behold, Elijah is here:
and he shall slay me."[6] That is the way he felt about it.

ELIJAH WARNS WICKED KING AHAB. Let me pause
here to say a word about wicked Ahab. He had married
the daughter of Ethbaal, king of the Zidonians, and of
course she was idolatrous in her worship and led Ahab
to follow after her gods Baal and Asteroth. When Elijah
came with his message to the king and closed the heavens
that it should not rain, she became angry and searched
out the prophets of the Lord to put them to death, and
Obadiah, being a righteous man, took 100 of them and
hid them that they could not be found. And so he related
this to Elijah, I suppose to gain his sympathy, and have
him change his request that he should carry this message
to the king.

But Elijah answered him as follows: "As the Lord
of hosts liveth, *before whom I stand*, I will surely shew
myself unto him today."[7]

When Obadiah understood that he was going to
show himself to the king, he was ready to take the message, but Elijah went himself and confronted Ahab.
When they met, Ahab said to him, "Art thou he that
troubleth Israel?" And Elijah rebuked him, saying, he
(Ahab) was the man that troubled Israel. And then he
commanded Ahab to go and gather the priests and false
prophets of Baal and bring them to a certain place, that
he might meet them there. And the king hearkened to
him, and it was done.

ELIJAH CHALLENGES PRIESTS OF BAAL. When all
the people assembled, and the prophets of the false gods,

---

[6]1 Kings 18:10-14.   [7]1 Kings 18:15.

Elijah made a proposal to them. Said he: "We will take two bullocks, you take one and I will take one. You offer yours and sacrifice it unto Baal, and I will offer mine a sacrifice unto the God of Israel; and we will put no fire under them, but you pray to your gods and I will pray to the Lord; and if fire comes down and consumes your sacrifice, then we will worship Baal, but if fire comes down and consumes my sacrifice, then we will serve the Lord." It is not necessary for me to go into details.

The challenge Elijah gave to the priests was a challenge to the Phoenician god of fire—Baal the "sun-god." If he was the god of fire, then why should he not call down fire to consume the sacrifice offered in his name and thus prove in the eyes of Israel that he was in very deed all that his followers claimed for him? If he could not do such a thing and the God of Israel who had been forsaken could, was it not evidence that the children of Israel had broken the very first commandment given them by the Lord through Moses? "Thou shalt have no other gods before me. Thou shalt not make unto thee any graven image, or any likeness of anything that is in heaven above, or that is in the earth beneath, or that is in the water under the earth: Thou shalt not bow down thyself to them, nor serve them."[8]

ELIJAH CALLS DOWN FIRE FROM HEAVEN. The priests gathered and built their altar and prayed, beginning in the morning, and prayed until noon time, and then until the time of evening sacrifice. And Elijah mocked them when there was no answer, and called upon them to cry louder, for perhaps their god was asleep, perhaps he was on a journey, perhaps he was hunting—they were to call louder that they might get his attention. Then they began to cut themselves, according to their custom. When the day had passed and no answer came, then Elijah rebuilt an old, broken down altar. He took 12 stones, one for each tribe of Israel, placed his sacrifice

---

[8]Ex. 20:3-5.

upon it, built a trench around it, and had his servants pour water upon it until the trench was full; then he knelt down and prayed and fire came down and consumed his offering.

The result was that the priests of Baal were put to death, which angered Jezebel, and again Elijah was forced to flee. This time he went into the south country near to Beersheba—where he became discouraged and desired that the Lord would put an end to his life; but he was comforted by an angel, who brought him food and drink; he ate and was filled and went 40 days on the strength of it and departed from that place unto Mount Horeb. When he was there, the Lord called upon him and asked him what he was doing there; and in his sorrow, because of the hardness of the hearts of the people, he told the Lord the condition, that he alone remained, that they sought his life to take it away. But the Lord showed him that there were others who had remained true unto him, even 7,000.

ELIJAH CALLS ELISHA TO SUCCEED HIM. Then the Lord gave him a mission, that he was to return to Israel. He was to anoint Hazael to be king of Syria, Jehu to be king of Israel in the place of Ahab, and Elisha to be prophet in his stead. So, he returned on this mission and called Elisha to follow him.

In the meantime Ahab had murdered a man through covetousness. Naboth had a vineyard Ahab wanted, and so Ahab had him put to death. And Elijah met Ahab again suddenly and told him of his crime, predicting the wicked king's death, also the death of his wicked wife. And thus it came to pass, though after Elijah had spoken to the king he did repent, and the Lord turned away a portion of his wrath. However the judgments of the Lord followed Ahab's sons, who walked in the unrighteous course set them by their father.

Elijah called Elisha to follow him, and finally, when

Elijah was taken into heaven in a chariot of fire, Elisha became the prophet in Israel in the stead of Elijah.[9]

Now, there was a *reason* for the translation of Elijah. *Men are not preserved in that manner unless there is a reason for it.* Moses was likewise taken up, though the scriptures say that the Lord buried him upon the mountain. Of course, the writer of that wrote according to his understanding; but *Moses, like Elijah, was taken up without tasting death, because he had a mission to perform.* We will refer to that as we pass along.

APOCRYPHA RECITES ELIJAH'S DEEDS. I made the statement, in the beginning, that the Jews in later generations had great respect for Elijah. They had some understanding regarding his mission. I have here a statement that I have copied from Ecclesiasticus, the writings of the son of Sirach. He was not one of the inspired writers, and this book is one of the books of the Apocrypha, but he gives us an idea of the feeling that existed among the Jews in his day in regard to Elijah. I will read it:

"Then stood up Elias the prophet as fire, and his word burned like a lamp."

Now, let me say this interpretation *Elias* ought not to be Elias; it should be *Elijah.* The references to Elijah in the New Testament, where it is interpreted Elias, should be Elijah. In the modern version, it is so. There is a big difference between Elias and Elijah, but I shall not refer to that right now.

"Then stood up Elias the prophet as fire, and *his word burned like a lamp.* He brought a *sore famine* upon them, and by his zeal he diminished their number. By the word of the Lord he *shut up the heaven,* and also *three times brought down fire.*

"O Elias, how wast thou honoured in thy wonderous deeds! and who may glory like unto thee! Who didst

---

[9]1 Kings 17; 18; 19; 21:17-29; 2 Kings
1; 2; 3:11; 9:36; 10:10, 17; 2 Chron.
21:12-15.

raise up a dead man from death, and his soul from the
place of the dead, by the word of the Most High: who
broughtest kings to destruction and honorouble men from
their bed: who heardest the rebuke of the Lord in Sinai,
and in Horeb the judgment of vengeance: who anointedst
kings to take revenge, and prophets to succeed after him:
who wast *taken up in a whirlwind of fire,* and in a chariot
of fiery horses: who was ordained for reproofs in their
times, to pacify the wrath of the Lord's judgment, before
it break forth into fury, and *to turn the heart of the father
unto the son,* and to restore the tribes of Jacob.

"Blessed are they that saw thee, and slept in love;
for we shall surely live."[10]

NEW TESTAMENT DOCTRINE OF ELIJAH AND ELIAS

ELIJAH, ELIAS, AND JOHN THE BAPTIST. When John
the Baptist came out of the wilderness preaching—and
he was a character that had more or less mystery about
him—the Jews wondered, and the Pharisees sent messengers unto John to question him as follows:

"And this is the record of John, when the Jews sent
priests and Levites from Jerusalem to ask him, Who art
thou? And he confessed, and denied not; but confessed,
I am not the Christ. And they asked him, What then?
Art thou Elias? And he saith, I am not. Art thou that
prophet? And he answered, No. Then said they unto
him, Who art thou? that we may give an answer to them
that sent us. What sayest thou of thyself? He said, I
am the voice of one crying in the wilderness, Make
straight the way of the Lord, as said the prophet Esaias.

"And they which were sent were of the Pharisees.
And they asked him, and said unto him, Why baptizest
thou then, if thou be not that Christ, nor Elias, neither
that prophet? John answered them, saying, I baptize
with water: but there standeth one among you, whom
ye know not; He it is, who coming after me is preferred

10*The Apocrypha,* Ecclesiasticus 48:1-
11.

before me, whose shoe's latchet I am not worthy to unloose. These things were done in Bethabara beyond Jordan, where John was baptizing."[11]

They wondered who John was. He came as one with authority, and they knew that the prophets of old had testified that Elijah was to come again. And so they wondered if John were Elijah. It is written *Elias* here, but in the modern version, I say, it is written Elijah, as it should be. And so they asked him, "Are you the Christ," because *they knew the Christ would have that power.* He said, "I am not."

"Are you Elias?" "No, I am not."

"Well then, why do you do these things—don't you know that these things were reserved for Elias, who was to be the forerunner of the Christ?—and then, if you are not that prophet, why do you do these things?" That was their query regarding John.

MOSES AND ELIJAH APPEAR ON MOUNT OF TRANS-FIGURATION. Again, after the Savior came down off the Mount, his disciples began to question him:

"And as they came down from the mountain, Jesus charged them, saying, Tell the vision to no man, until the Son of man be risen again from the dead. And his disciples asked him, saying, Why then say the scribes that Elias must *first* come?"

You see, these three, Peter, James, and John, who had been on the Mount, where Moses and Elijah had appeared to them, began to inquire of the Savior the meaning of it all. So they asked: "Why then say the scribes that Elias must *first* come?"

"And Jesus answered and said unto them, *Elias truly shall first come, and restore all things.* But I say unto you, That Elias is come already, and they knew him not, but have done unto him whatsoever they listed. Likewise shall also the Son of man suffer of them. Then the

[11]John 1:19-28; Luke 1:17; Matt. 11:14.

disciples understood that he spake unto them of John the Baptist."[12]

Now, this passage of scripture has caused a great deal of confusion in the minds of many people; and because the Lord said Elias had already come, the world has interpreted that to mean that John the baptist was the Elias, or the fulfillment of the predicted coming of Elijah, and they refer to his passage as their evidence. The Lord had *two* thoughts in mind: *Elijah must first come and restore all things, but Elias has already come.*

ELIJAH AND MOSES: TRANSLATED BEINGS

MOSES AND ELIJAH GAVE KEYS TO PETER, JAMES, AND JOHN. When Moses and Elijah came *to* the Savior and to Peter, James, and John upon the Mount, what was their coming for? Was it just some spiritual manifestation to strengthen these three apostles? Or did they come merely to give comfort unto the Son of God in his ministry and to prepare him for his crucifixion? No! That was not the purpose. I will read it to you. The Prophet Joseph Smith has explained it as follows:

"The priesthood is everlasting. *The Savior, Moses, and Elias [Elijah, in other words] gave the keys to Peter, James, and John, on the Mount when they were transfigured before him.* The priesthood is everlasting—without beginning of days or end of years; without father, mother, etc. If there is no change of ordinances, there is no change of priesthood. Wherever the ordinances of the gospel are administered, there is the priesthood. . . . Christ is the Great High Priest; Adam next."[13]

WHY MOSES AND ELIJAH WERE TRANSLATED. From that we understand why Elijah and Moses were preserved from death: because *they had a mission to perform,* and it had to be performed *before* the crucifixion of the Son of God, and *it could not be done in the spirit.*

---

[12]Matt. 17:1-13; Mark 9:2-13; Luke 9:28-36.   [13]Joseph Fielding Smith, *Teachings of the Prophet Joseph Smith,* p. 158.

They had to have tangible bodies. Christ is the first fruits of the resurrection; therefore if any former prophets had a work to perform preparatory to the mission of the Son of God, or to the dispensation of the meridian of times, it was essential that they be preserved to fulfill that mission *in the flesh.* For that reason *Moses disappeared* from among the people and was taken up into the mountain, and the people *thought* he was buried by the Lord. The Lord preserved him, so that he could come at the proper time and *restore his keys,* on the heads of Peter, James, and John, who stood at the head of the dispensation of the meridian of time.[14] He reserved Elijah from death that he might also come and bestow his keys upon the heads of Peter, James, and John and prepare them for their ministry.

But, one says, the Lord could have waited until after his resurrection, and then they could have done it. It is quite evident, due to the fact that it did so occur, that it had to be done before; and there was a reason. There may have been other reasons, but that is one reason why *Moses and Elijah did not suffer death in the flesh, like other men do.*

WHAT ELIJAH RESTORED. After the resurrection of Christ, of course, they passed through death and the resurrection, and then *as resurrected beings* came to fulfill a mission of like import in the dispensation of the fulness of time.[15]

Why was Elijah reserved? What keys did he hold? What keys did he bestow on Peter, James, and John? Exactly the same keys that he bestowed upon the head of Joseph Smith and Oliver Cowdery. And what were they? Some of you may be saying the keys of baptism for the dead. No, it was not just that. Some of you may be thinking it was the keys of the salvation of the dead. No, it was not just that, that was only a *portion* of it. *The keys that Elijah held were the keys of the everlasting*

---

[14]Deut. 34:5-6; Alma 45:18-19.   [15]D. & C. 110:11-16; 133:54-55.

*priesthood, the keys of the sealing power, which the Lord
gave unto him.* And that is what he came and bestowed
upon the heads of Peter, James, and John; and that is what
he gave to the Prophet Joseph Smith; and that included
*a ministry of sealing for the living as well as the dead—
and it is not confined to the living and it is not confined
to the dead, but includes them both.*[16]

THE COMING OF ELIJAH

ELIJAH'S RETURN PRESAGES SECOND COMING OF
CHRIST. One of the most important events connected
with the restoration and consummation of the purposes
of the Lord in the last days is the coming of the Prophet
Elijah with his message and authority, turning the hearts
of the fathers to the children, and the hearts of the children to the fathers, lest the Lord come and smite the
earth with a curse.

Just what is meant by Malachi, and how it is to be
accomplished, has been one of the outstanding mysteries
of *Bible* prophecy.[17] Some commentators have thought
that this prophecy was fulfilled in the coming of John
the Baptist in the meridian of time, but a careful reading
will soon dispel such a thought. The days of John, and
those which followed during the ministry of Jesus Christ
and his apostles, were *not* the days of vengeance and
burning in which the wicked would be as stubble and
the earth would be cleansed from all its iniquity.

This day of preparation by turning the hearts of
the fathers to the children and of the children to the
fathers, it is very evident from the context, is reserved
until the *last days,* or *the day of restitution of all things.*
It is an event to take place, according to the plain prediction, *shortly preceding the great and dreadful day of
the Lord.* The great and dreadful day of the Lord, this
prophecy proclaims, is *the day of the coming of our Lord
in the clouds of heaven in great glory and when he shall*

[16]*Elijah the Prophet and His Mission,*   [17]Malachi 4:5-6; *D. & C.* 2:1-3; 27:9;
pp. 6-18.   110:13-16.

take vengeance upon the ungodly. It is to be a day dreadful to all who are unrepentant and full of sin, but to the just it shall be a day of peace and salvation. However, *before* it comes there is to be some mighty work performed by the restoration of Elijah's authority, which is so potent that it will save the earth from destruction, or from being smitten with a curse.

ONLY THE SAINTS UNDERSTAND PROPHECIES ABOUT ELIJAH. One of the doctrines peculiar to the Latter-day Saints, and to them alone, is the doctrine that Elijah has already come, and that he has restored his keys and has turned the hearts of the fathers to the children and the hearts of the children to their fathers, in preparation for the coming of our Redeemer in power and glory to reign on the earth.

Moreover the Latter-day Saints are the only people on the earth who have a clear understanding of the meaning of this prophecy and can knowingly apply it. This comes to them by revelation. It was on the third day of April, 1836, that Elijah came to fulfill this prediction, and on that date he bestowed upon Joseph Smith and Oliver Cowdery the keys of his priesthood and said unto them: "Therefore, the keys of this dispensation are committed into your hands; and by this ye may know that the great and dreadful day of the Lord is near, even at the doors."[18]

WHY ELIJAH WAS CHOSEN TO RESTORE SEALING POWER. It has been a mystery to many members of the Church why this important mission was reserved for Elijah and why these authorities could not have been bestowed by some other prophet, or prophets, presumably Peter, James, and John, who held the keys of authority in the days of the dispensation of the meridian of time. Without question Peter, James, and John could have bestowed this authority, if they had been commissioned;

---

[18]*Church News,* Jan. 9, 1932, p. 8;
   D. & C. 110:16.

so could Adam, for he held the keys of all the dispensations. The reason why Elijah was reserved for this mission, according to the Prophet Joseph Smith, was
that:

"Elijah was the *last prophet* that held the keys of the
priesthood, and who will, before the last dispensation,
restore the authority and deliver the keys of the priesthood, in order that all the ordinances may be attended to
in righteousness. It is true the Savior had authority and
power to bestow this blessing; but the sons of Levi were
too prejudiced. . . . Why send Elijah? Because *he holds
the keys of the authority to administer in all the ordinances of the priesthood; and without the authority
is given, the ordinances could not be administered in
righteousness.*"[19]

No BAPTISM FOR DEAD IN DAYS OF ELIJAH. Since
Elijah was the last of the ancient prophets to hold this
authority, he was the prophet chosen to come in the last
days and restore that fulness. But what was the particular nature of the keys held by Elijah? Some have
thought it was the keys of baptism for the dead; but it
was not just that. *There was no baptism for the dead in
the days of Elijah, or before Christ bridged the gulf which
separated the righteous in paradise from the wicked in
the spirit world.* Christ was the first to declare the gospel
to the dead, and it was not until after his resurrection
that the privilege of baptism for the dead was granted.

The keys held by Elijah were the keys of the sealing
power of the priesthood.[20]

---

[19]Smith, *op. cit.,* p. 172.   [20]*Gen. & Hist. Mag.,* vol. 27, p. 50.

CHAPTER 7

ELIJAH: HIS MISSION AND SEALING POWER

MISSION OF ELIJAH

ELIJAH'S LATTER-DAY MISSION FORETOLD. "Behold, I will send you Elijah the prophet before the coming of the great and dreadful day of the Lord: And he shall turn the heart of the fathers to the children, and the heart of the children to their fathers, lest I come and smite the earth with a curse."[1]

I suppose there is no passage of scripture that has caused more controversy, that has been called in question more, that has been less understood than this passage in the last chapter of Malachi. It took a revelation from God in this age in which we live to make known what it means. This passage of scripture has reference to the salvation of *both* the living and the dead.

ELIJAH PROVES JUSTICE AND MERCY OF GOD. Now in justice, and we know the Lord is just; and in mercy, and we know the Lord is merciful; there must be provision made by which men who die in various parts of the earth and in various ages—without having heard the gospel of Jesus Christ, and without knowing the plan of salvation—might also have the opportunity of repentance and of accepting the principles of eternal truth and thus have opened up to them the gates of eternal life. Otherwise there would be no justice. *If provision had not been made for this, then men could say that God is unjust and that he is a respecter of persons.*

MISSION OF ELIJAH KNOWN ONLY BY REVELATION. Yet this doctrine was lost after the apostles fell asleep

---
[1]Mal. 4:5-6.

and was not understood. It has come down in perverted
form in one of the churches, and in others it has been
discarded entirely. And it took a revelation from the
Lord to make it known. It was not understood in the
beginning of this Church. Elijah came and fulfilled his
mission on the third day of April, 1836.[2]

The first inkling, I suppose, that the Prophet got
of this new doctrine—new to the world, but old because
it comes down from the beginning—was in the teachings
he received from the Angel Moroni. But in his youth
and inexperience he was unable to understand the significance of it, and it was not until January of 1836, just
a short time before the coming of Elijah, that the vision
of salvation for the dead was made known to Joseph
Smith.[3]

ELIJAH'S MISSION IN ANCIENT ISRAEL. A great
many people have the idea that Elijah held the keys,
somehow, of baptism for the dead. Elijah's mission in
ancient Israel was not to hold the keys of baptism for
the dead. *There was no baptism for the dead before the
days of the Son of God and until after he had risen from
the dead,* because he was the first who declared the gospel unto the dead. No one else preached unto the dead
until Christ went to them and opened the doors, and
from that time forth the elders of Israel, who have passed
away, have had the privilege of going to the spirit world
and declaring the message of salvation.[4]

Elijah's earthly mission was not baptism for the
dead; his mission among men was not a mission to the
dead, but a mission to the *living.* It was by virtue of the
coming of Elijah to the Prophet Joseph Smith that the
Prophet received the *sealing power,* in connection with

[2]*D. & C.* 110:13-16.
[3]*Church News,* Jan. 5, 1935, p. 6;
Joseph Fielding Smith, *Teachings
of the Prophet Joseph Smith,* pp.
106-107.

[4]Moses 7:36-40; Luke 16:19-31; 1 Pet.
3:18-21; Isa. 42:7; 61:1; *D. & C.*
76:73; 88:99; Pres. Joseph F. Smith,
"Vision of the Redemption of the
Dead," *Gospel Doctrine,* 4th ed.,
pp. 596-602.

the priesthood, which made valuable that which he did for the salvation of the human family.

Elijah's mission was the sealing power. He held the keys by which the parents could be sealed together and children sealed to parents. He bestowed these keys upon the Prophet Joseph Smith. And that *applies to the dead as well as the living since the coming of the Lord Jesus Christ.*[5]

ELIJAH'S MISSION IN MODERN ISRAEL. But what was the nature of his mission to the earth in these latter days? It was to restore power and authority which once was given to men on the earth and which is essential to the complete salvation and exaltation of man in the kingdom of God. In other words, Elijah came to *restore* to the earth, by conferring on mortal prophets duly commissioned of the Lord, *the fulness of the power of priesthood. This priesthood holds the keys of binding and sealing on earth and in heaven of all the ordinances and principles pertaining to the salvation of man,* that they may thus become valid in the celestial kingdom of God.

During the days of his ministry Elijah held this authority, and the Lord gave him power over *all things* on earth and that through his ministry whatever was done should be ratified, or sealed, in the heavens and recognized of full force by the Eternal Father. This power effects and vitalizes *every ordinance* performed by duly commissioned officers holding divine power on the earth.

It is by virtue of this authority that ordinances are performed in the temples for *both* the living and the dead. It is the power which unites for eternity husbands and wives, when they enter into marriage according to the eternal plan. It is the authority by which parents obtain the claim of parenthood, concerning their children, through all eternity and not only for time, which makes eternal the family in the kingdom of God.[6]

---

[5]*Gen. & Hist. Mag.,* vol. 13, pp. 57-58.   [6]*Church News,* Jan. 16, 1932, p. 8.

RESTORATION OF SEALING POWER

MORONI FORETELLS ELIJAH'S RETURN. On the night of September 21st, 1823, Moroni, an angel from the presence of the Lord, appeared to Joseph Smith and instructed him. He quoted the last verses of the prophecy of Malachi, but with some difference from the *Bible* version, as follows:

"Behold, *I will reveal unto you the Priesthood*, by the hand of Elijah the prophet, before the coming of the great and dreadful day of the Lord. And he shall *plant* in the hearts of the children the promises made to the fathers, and the hearts of the children shall turn to their fathers. If it were not so, the whole earth would be *utterly wasted* at his coming."[7]

Elijah came on April 3rd, 1836, to Joseph Smith and Oliver Cowdery, in fulfilment of this promise, and gave them the keys of his priesthood, and said to them that by this event they should know that the great and dreadful day of the Lord was near, even at the door.[8]

SEALING POWER OF PRIESTHOOD RESTORED. What was the nature of this restoration? It was the conferring upon men in this dispensation of *the sealing power of the priesthood*, by which *all things are bound in heaven as well as on earth*. It gave the authority to Joseph Smith to perform in the temple of God *all the ordinances essential to salvation for both the living and the dead.*

Through the power of this priesthood which Elijah bestowed, husband and wife may be sealed, or married for eternity; children may be sealed to their parents for eternity; thus the family is made eternal, and death does not separate the members. *This is the great principle that will save the world from utter destruction.*

Vicariously the dead may obtain the blessings of the gospel—baptism, confirmation, ordination, and the higher blessings, which are sealed upon them in the temples of the Lord, by virtue of the authority restored

[7]Joseph Smith 2:38-39; D. & C. 2:1-3.   [8]D. & C. 110:13-16.

by Elijah. Through the restoration of these keys, the work of the Lord is fully inaugurated before the coming of Jesus Christ in glory.[9]

NATURE OF KEYS OF SEALING. These keys of the binding, or sealing power, which were given to Peter, James, and John in their dispensation, are keys which make valid *all* the ordinances of the gospel. They pertain more especially to the work in the temples, both for the living and for the dead. *They are the authorities which prepare men to enter the celestial kingdom and to be crowned as sons and heirs of God.*

These keys hold the power to *seal husbands and wives for eternity* as well as for time. They hold the power to seal children to parents, the key of adoption, by which the family organization is made intact forever. This is the power which will save the obedient from the curse in the coming of the great and dreadful day of the Lord. Through these keys the hearts of the children have turned to their fathers.[10]

ELIJAH NOW RESURRECTED. When Elijah came to the Prophet Joseph Smith, he was not a translated being. He was a resurrected being. He had received his resurrection, and he came to Joseph Smith just as did Peter, James, and John, and gave to Joseph Smith and Oliver Cowdery—as he did to Peter, James, and John at the transfiguration—the keys of sealing power, so that the work *now*, not only for the living but also for the dead, may be done. Since the same ordinances are required for the dead as for the living, these keys also pertain to the salvation of the dead.[11]

SPIRIT BEINGS PARTICIPATE IN WORK OF ELIJAH. We go into the temples and are sealed for time and for eternity and also perform like ordinances vicariously for

[9]*Millennial Star,* vol. 89:774-775; Joseph Fielding Smith, *op. cit.,* pp. 323, 330, 335-338.

[10]*Church News,* Sept. 16, 1933, p. 4. [11]*Church News,* Jan. 5, 1935, p. 6; D. & C. 133:55.

our dead. Generation will be joined to generation, as far as it is in our power to perform the labor. The obligation rests heavily upon us, and when we have exhausted all the information which we are able to obtain through our research, and have obtained all the names of the dead within our power, we may be content.

President Brigham Young has said that during the millennium those on the other side will work hand in hand with those in mortality and will furnish the names of the dead which we are unable to obtain through our research, and thus every soul that is entitled to these blessings shall be ferreted out and his work done for him. I fully believe that *many among the dead,* those who are worthy, are even now engaged in *compiling records* and *arranging information,* if it has not already been done, for this very purpose. Why should they not be so engaged?[12]

EARTH CURSED EXCEPT FOR ELIJAH

WHY EARTH WOULD BE CURSED. The question naturally arises in the inquiring mind, "Why would the whole earth be smitten with a curse had not Elijah come with the keys of sealing which he held?"[13]

The family organization must be intact. First husbands and wives must be sealed for time and for all eternity. When this is done, children born to them belong to them for time and all eternity and the family units are preserved.

Parents who have been married out of the new and everlasting covenant must be sealed for time and all eternity and then have their children sealed to them. When this is done, the ordinance is just as valid as it is in the case of those who were originally married according to the law of the Lord. In like manner, the children who are living may have the same ordinances performed for their ancestors who are dead.

---

[12]*Rel. Soc. Mag.,* vol. 5, p. 678; *Discourses of Brigham Young,* 2nd ed., pp. 626-628.

[13]Mal. 4:5-6.

Then each generation must be joined to the one which went on before. In this way eventually all the families which are entitled to celestial exaltation are joined together, from generation to generation, back to the time of our first parents, Adam and Eve. This will not all be done before the coming of our Lord, but the great work of the millennium will be the temple ordinances for the dead who are worthy to receive it.

The sealing power of Elijah makes it possible for this joining of the families, generation to generation, back to the beginning. Now, if these units of authority were not here, then the work of sealing, by which the family units are preserved, could not be performed; then the binding power by which all blessings are sealed in heaven, as well as on earth, would be lacking. *If this were so, the earth would be smitten with a curse, for all work which had been done, without these binding or sealing ordinances, would fall to the ground unfulfilled.*[14]

EARTH WASTED EXCEPT FOR ELIJAH'S COMING. If Elijah had not come, we are led to believe that all the work of past ages would have been of little avail, for the Lord said the whole earth, under such conditions, would be *utterly wasted* at his coming.[15] Therefore his mission was of vast importance to the world. It is not the question of baptism for the dead alone, but also the sealing of parents and children to parents, so that there should be a "whole and complete and perfect union, and welding together of dispensations, and keys, and powers, and glories," from the beginning down to the end of time.[16]

If this sealing power were not on the earth, then confusion would reign and disorder would take the place of order in that day when the Lord shall come, and, of course, this could not be, for all things are governed and controlled by perfect law in the kingdom of God.[17]

---

[14]*Gen. & Hist. Mag.*, vol. 27, pp. 52-53.   [16]*D. & C.* 128:18.
[15]*D. & C.* 2:1-3.   [17]*Rel. Soc. Mag.*, vol. 5, pp. 677-678.

Why would the earth be wasted? Simply because if there is not a welding link between the fathers and the children—which is the work for the dead—then we will all stand rejected; the whole work of God will fail and be utterly wasted. Such a condition, of course, shall not be.[18]

SALVATION AND THE SEALING POWER OF ELIJAH. "He shall turn the heart of the fathers to the children, and the heart of the children to their fathers." The Prophet says that this is not the correct translation—the word *turn* should be translated *seal* or *bind*.[19] Now you get a glimpse of what is meant in this scripture which says that the whole earth would be smitten with a curse if Elijah did not first come.

Why would it be smitten? Because there could be no sealing up against the day of destruction, no sealing of parents to each other, no sealing of children to parents, no contracts, bonds, obligations entered into that would be valid on the other side—because the clinching power was not there; and it was necessary that Elijah should come and bestow those things spoken of as *all things* in the scriptures.[20] . . .

There is power in the Church for salvation and exaltation, and the Lord, when he comes, will not find it necessary to smite this earth with a curse, because that sealing power is here, and the leaven is at work, so that all men who will may receive salvation and exaltation and the sealing powers. Thanks be unto God that he sent Elijah into the world to bestow these blessings.[21]

PROOF THAT ELIJAH CAME

TO WHOM DID ELIJAH COME? The world does not believe that Elijah came to Joseph Smith and Oliver Cowdery, but they have no record in the world that he has come to anyone else. There has been no appearance

---

[18]*Origin of the "Reorganized" Church,*
   pp. 43-44.
[19]Mal. 4:5-6; Smith, *op. cit.,* p. 330.

[20]Matt. 17:11; Acts 3:21.
[21]*Elijah the Prophet and His Mission,*
   pp. 23, 32.

and no claim of an appearance and a restoration of his priesthood to anyone else.

May we not, then, with perfect consistency, put forth the claim that he did come on that occasion and that he did restore his keys of authority to these two humble men, which turned the hearts of the fathers to their children and the hearts of the children to their fathers?

No one else has ever disputed this claim by the giving of another claim. *And why could he not come to Joseph Smith and Oliver Cowdery as well as to anybody else?* I testify to you that he did come, and if the world wants to know it also, it can. We have an abundance of evidence that this story is true.

If Joseph Smith and Oliver Cowdery had lied, it would have been impossible for them to have turned the hearts of the fathers to their children and the hearts of the children to their fathers. Surely, they would not have any power to do that. It is true that following the declaration by them that Elijah had come, the hearts of the children commenced to turn to their dead fathers.[22]

WORLD GIVES PROOF OF ELIJAH'S COMING. One of the outstanding evidences bearing witness that Joseph Smith and Oliver Cowdery spoke the truth, when they declared that Elijah had come to them and conferred upon them his priesthood, is the fact that *since* that time the hearts of the children have in a miraculous way turned towards their fathers.

It might be contended with some semblance of logic that Joseph Smith and his successors could yield an influence over the members of the Church and have them go to the temples to do ordinance work for their dead, in order that the saying could go abroad that this prophecy by Malachi had been fulfilled, and the hearts of the children have turned to their fathers.

It would be unreasonable to say, however, that Joseph Smith, or the entire body of the Church, could

22Conf. Rep., Apr., 1948, pp. 132-133.

wield the power to persuade millions who are not members of the Church, also, to turn their attention towards their dead fathers; yet it is a fact that the hearts of millions have so turned, *since* the proclamation of the coming of Elijah in 1836.[23]

JOSEPH SMITH'S TESTIMONY ABOUT ELIJAH. Joseph Smith and Oliver Cowdery declare in words of soberness to all the world that Elijah, in fulfillment of the prediction that was made, came to them in the Kirtland Temple in the year 1836 and committed unto them the priesthood which the Prophet Malachi said was to be bestowed, before the coming of the great and dreadful day of the Lord.

Now, we have the testimony of Joseph Smith; we have the testimony of Oliver Cowdery, and *their testimony will stand through all time as a witness against all these who refuse to hearken unto it.*

But is that all? Are we dependent solely upon the testimony of these two men for evidence that Elijah came and restored his priesthood? No other men, so far as we know, beheld this vision; no one else was present when the angel came in fulfillment of this remarkable prophecy; but is there no evidence that can be pointed to which will corroborate their testimony and prove that they spoke the truth?

GENEALOGICAL RESEARCH PROVES ELIJAH CAME. I believe that I can point to evidence, circumstantial it may be, yet evidence that ought to be convincing in any court in the land, that would prove beyond the possibility of doubt that Joseph Smith and Oliver Cowdery spoke the truth.

How will I do it? Simply this way. *Before* the year 1836 there was very little, if any, research being made anywhere in this world in behalf of the dead. It is true that here and there some man may have been searching

---

[23]*Church News,* Jan. 30, 1932, p. 4.

out a genealogical record, but what was his object? To prove title to some estate.

There were no genealogical societies; there were no genealogical organizations; there were no genealogical researches of any systematic character anywhere in the world. That is significant, is it not?

What do we discover now? One year *after* this revelation was given and these keys were bestowed, we find in Great Britain the government passing laws compelling the preservation of duplicate records of the dead on the part of those who kept them. This is a significant fact, one link that points in the direction of the truth of the statement of the Prophet Joseph Smith. It did not occur the year *before* this vision.

In the year 1844, the year of the martyrdom, the first organization for the purpose of gathering together the records of the dead, and compiling genealogical records, was formed in the city of Boston. It was the New England Historical and Genealogical Society. In 1869, in the city of New York, another society, the New York Genealogical and Biographical Society, was organized.

Since that day societies have sprung up all over the land. There are hundreds of them along the Atlantic border. The state of Massachusetts is full of them. We find the same thing in Virginia, in the Carolinas, and along the Atlantic Coast from Maine to Georgia, where the first settlements in this country were made. The hearts of the children have *since* that day turned to their fathers, and they are searching out the records of their dead.

Fascinating Nature of Genealogical Research. It was my privilege in the year 1902 to go back to Massachusetts, for the purpose of hunting out the records of my own dead, and while there I had conversations with men who are engaged in this research work. I asked them, "Why are you doing this?" The answer was, "We are interested in the work." One man made the statement that when he took hold of it, he could not let go. There was something about it that was fascinating, and when he started on this work of genealogical research, he had to continue. He was neglecting his profession and was spending his time in the research of the dead.

GROWTH OF RESEARCH SINCE ELIJAH CAME. In the year 1902 the Legislature of the State of Massachusetts passed a measure providing for the compiling of the vital records of all the towns of the state, from their settlement down to the year 1850, and the genealogical organizations have the privilege of making these compilations. Robert Henry Eddy left a portion of his estate for the purpose of gathering out the vital records of Massachusetts, and that was the incentive for the Legislature, which caused them to take that action.

Following this the people in Rhode Island, and I understand also Connecticut and other states, have followed the lead of Massachusetts and are providing for the publication of the vital records of all towns in those states, from the beginning to the year 1850. All these things are significant.[24]

In Great Britain, genealogical societies have been organized in practically every county in that land and in Scotland. These records have been kept and filed also in other countries in Europe, the countries from which the Latter-day Saints have come. The spirit has taken hold of the people, not only in the Church, but also of many who are not of the Church, and they too are searching the records, and compiling them, of the dead. . . .

FAMILY HISTORIES PUBLISHED SINCE ELIJAH CAME. Now here is something which I think is interesting. In 1935 Mr. T. B. Thompson published *A Catalogue of British Family Histories*. It included the titles and years

---

[24]*Gen. & Hist. Mag.*, vol. 9, pp. 19-21.

of publication of some 2,071 families and was supposed to be a complete list of all such published records up to that date. Here are his figures from the date of the invention of printing:

From 1450 to 1600, were published 2 family histories.

From 1600 to 1700, were published 18 family histories.

From 1700 to 1800, were published 72 family histories.

From 1800 to 1836, when Elijah came, were published 100 family histories.

From 1837 to 1935, were published 1,879 family histories.

These were records *in Europe,* and since the year 1836, there have been published in Great Britain and the United States *thousands* of records of the dead.[25]

Here, then, is this *vast array of witnesses,* who are engaged in genealogical research, scattered throughout our own land and all over the civilized world, bearing record to the fact that Joseph Smith spoke that which was true, when he said Elijah came to him and bestowed upon him the keys of his priesthood, which turned the hearts of the children to their fathers.[26]

TURNING OF HEARTS OF CHILDREN AND FATHERS. Who are the fathers spoken of by Malachi, and who are the children? *The fathers* are our dead ancestors who died without the privilege of receiving the gospel, but who received the promise that the time would come when that privilege would be granted them. *The children* are those now living who are preparing genealogical data and who are performing the vicarious ordinances in the temples.[27]

The turning of the hearts of the children to the fathers is placing or planting in the hearts of the children that

---

[25]Conf. Rep., Apr., 1948, pp. 132-133, 135.
[26]*Gen. & Hist. Mag.,* vol. 9, p. 21.

[27]*Millennial Star,* vol. 89, p. 775; Moses 7:36-40; Isa. 42:7; 61:1; Abra. 2:8-11; Zech. 11:9.

*feeling and desire which will inspire them to search out
the records of the dead.* Moreover the planting of the
desire and inspiration in their hearts is necessary. This
they must have in order that they might go into the house
of the Lord and perform the necessary labor for their
fathers, who died without a knowledge of the gospel, or
without the privilege of receiving the fulness of the
gospel.[28]

DUTY TO SEEK KNOWLEDGE OF OUR FATHERS. The
Lord has called upon us to look after our dead, to seek
out their genealogy. This spirit has gone forth, the keys
that were bestowed by Elijah are here, and the hearts
of the children have turned to their fathers. One of the
greatest evidences of the truth of the story told by the
Prophet Joseph Smith that Elijah came to him and Oliver
Cowdery is the fact that people who are not connected
with this Church, who have no sympathy, perhaps, with
the Church, are gathering the records of the dead. Their
hearts have turned to the fathers.

Our duty, of course, is to seek after our dead. We
have a department in the Church, the Genealogical Society, where we are gathering in these records for the
benefit of the members of the Church, where we can
receive information, and are able to give help and encouragement in relation to these matters that pertain to
the salvation of our families.[29]

---

[28]*Gen. & Hist. Mag.*, vol. 9, pp. 15-16.   [29]Conf. Rep., Apr., 1934, pp. 19-20.

CHAPTER 8

SALVATION UNIVERSAL

SALVATION OFFERED TO ALL

JUSTICE OF GOD VS. CREEDS OF MEN. Where can you look in all the world for a faith which teaches the justice of God in granting to *all men* the same or an *equal* right to receive salvation? I mean by this, where the chance is given to every soul, whether living or dead, to obtain the remission of sins and find the way into the kingdom of God, through obedience to the gospel?

Are not the creeds of men narrowed in this respect to include only those who have believed in Christ in this mortal life? Is such a narrowing warranted by scripture? Is such a doctrine consistent with reason, with justice, with eternal love?

LIVING AND DEAD JUDGED BY SAME LAW. It is a fact that the kingdom of God is governed by law, and *all* who enter it must accept the conditions and obey the ordinances which the Father has prepared for such a blessing. No man can come unto God except by his law, and that law must be by his own appointing, not by man's appointing.

It is not man's privilege to say which regulation will have to be observed and which will not have to be. *It is not man's privilege to set up churches and to establish rules of conduct insuring salvation in the kingdom of God.* The Lord alone has that right. We mortals have the privilege of obeying or rejecting divine law, for we have our agency; but we cannot change, annul, or circumscribe the laws of God.[1]

---

[1] *D. & C.* 1:38; 88:34-42; 130:20-21; 132:5, 8-12.

What then of the dead who knew not Christ? They, too, must subscribe to the law the same as the living, for the same principles and ordinances apply to both. For hundreds of years the declaration has thundered into the ears of the inhabitants of the earth that all who died without confessing Christ are damned, no matter if it were no fault of their own. It was taught that no provision was made in the gospel plan for the redemption of the dead. What a gloomy outlook! . . .

FALSE LIMITATIONS ON HOPE OF SALVATION. Let us reflect for a moment on this teaching that only those who confess the name of Christ or who are baptized in this life shall be saved; that all who have died without confessing Christ, or without having had the privilege of hearing him, are forever lost and are cast into hell; that there is no salvation for them, although it is no fault of their own that they did not hear. Think of the countless multitudes who have died without the privilege of hearing of Jesus Christ! Are all these to be eternally consigned to torment with the damned? And this, because they were unfortunate as to *time* and *place* of birth!

GOSPEL TRUTHS REFUTE FALSE CREEDS. We are taught that God is no respecter of persons;[2] he is a God of mercy and love.[3] Then, surely, he does not wish to see his children suffer. Through modern revelation, or speaking properly, in revelation given anciently and now restored, we are taught that his great work and glory is to bring to pass the immortality and eternal life of man.[4] Also, that man is created that he may have joy.[5]

Nothing that our Eternal Father has created has been created to be destroyed.[6] No man was ever born into this world predestined to suffer eternally without any chance for relief from pain, anguish, or remorse. True it is, those who fight against him and sin against

[2]Acts 10:34-35; Rom. 2:5-12.   [5]2 Ne. 2:25.
[3]Ex. 34:6-7; 1 John 4:7-11   [6]D. & C. 93:33; 132:14; Eccles. 3:14.
[4]Moses 1:39.

the Holy Ghost, *after* they have received his power, shall be cast off without redemption, but not so with any others.[7]

Is it not stated in the scriptures that sins may be forgiven beyond the grave?[8] There are punishments to be endured in the spirit world; but is not the promise made that the prisoner may come forth from the prison, when the uttermost farthing is paid?[9] Sin may be forgiven, if not a sin unto the second death. The second death is not destruction of spirit and body, but banishment from the presence of the Lord.[10]

WORTHY DEAD SAVED IN KINGDOM OF GOD. *The Lord is not narrow*, for he has granted the privilege to all those who have died or who may yet die without knowing the principles of the gospel, and without repenting of their sins and receiving a remission, to receive these privileges in the spirit world, and through their acceptance of the principles of the gospel and their belief in the Lord Jesus Christ to be redeemed from their sins and have *a place in his kingdom*. That is what he intends, and he never did intend to reject and cast down to hell forever all those who died without receiving a remission of their sins or who failed to have the opportunity of hearing the name of the Son of God.

REBELLIOUS DEAD SAVED IN LOWER KINGDOMS. There are many religious teachers in the world who stand before their people and declare that those who die without confessing the Lord Jesus Christ are subject to the torments of hell, without any means of redemption. The Lord never has said it. Truly he has declared that *those who reject his truth shall be damned*, but he has *not* said that when they have paid the penalty of their transgression they shall not come forth from the prison house.

[7]*D. & C.* 76:30-49.
[8]Matt. 12:31-32.
[9]Isa. 42:7; 61:1; *D. & C.* 128:22; Matt. 5:25-26.

[10]*Millennial Star*, vol. 91, pp. 674-676; 1 John 5:16-17; *D. & C.* 29:41.

But on the other hand, he has said that *after* they have paid the penalty of their transgression, they shall come forth, and they shall receive their reward. Their reward will not be as great as it would have been had they embraced the truth and lived faithfully all the principles of the gospel, but nevertheless those who have not sinned unto death shall be redeemed, in the due time of the Lord, and shall come forth from the dead and receive *a place in one of his kingdoms.*[11]

ALL MEN TO HEAR THE GOSPEL

GOSPEL PREACHED TO LIVING AND DEAD. *In the justice of the Father, he is going to give to every man the privilege of hearing the gospel.*[12] Not one soul shall be overlooked or forgotten. This being true, what about the countless thousands who have died and never heard of Christ, never had an opportunity of repentance and remission of their sins, never met an elder of the Church holding the authority? Some of our good Christian neighbors will tell you they are lost forever, that they cannot believe in the grave, for there is no hope beyond.

Would that be fair? Would it be just? No! *The Lord is going to give to every man the opportunity to hear and to receive eternal life, or a place in his kingdom.* We are very fortunate because we have had that privilege here and have passed from death unto life.

The Lord has so arranged his plan of redemption that all who have died without this opportunity shall be given it in the spirit world. There the elders of the Church who have died are proclaiming the gospel to the dead. All those who did not have an opportunity here to receive it, who there repent and receive the gospel, shall be heirs of the celestial kingdom of God. The Savior *inaugurated* this great work when he went and preached to the spirits held in prison, that they might be *judged according to men in the flesh* (or in other words, accord-

---

[11]*Gen. & Hist. Mag.,* vol. 9, p. 17;   [12]*D. & C.* 1:1-3.
    D. & C. 76:71-112.

ing to the principles of the gospel) and then live according to God in the spirit, through their repentance and acceptance of the mission of Jesus Christ who died for them.[13]

ISRAEL ACCEPTS GOSPEL IN SPIRIT WORLD. It is our opportunity, in this dispensation, and our privilege and duty to spend our time in searching out our dead. We are of the house of Israel. We learn that through revelation; and that being true, then we reach the conclusion, unless we have been adopted through the gospel and were gentiles, that our ancestors were also of the house of Israel. In other words, the promise made to Abraham, that through the scattering of his seed all nations would be blessed, has been fulfilled, and our lineage has come down generation after generation through the loins of Abraham and the loins of Israel.

Therefore *our fathers are more likely to receive the gospel* (if they did not hear it in this life, to receive it *in the spirit world*), *than are those whose descendants are not in the Church* and who refused to receive the gospel here.[14]

ACCEPTING GOSPEL SAVES LIVING AND DEAD. The Lord has made it known that his mercy extends to the uttermost bounds and that every soul is entitled to hear the gospel plan, either in this life or in the spirit world. *All who hear and believe, repenting and receiving the gospel in its fulness, whether living or dead, are heirs of salvation in the celestial kingdom of God.*

Those who reject the gospel, but who live honorable lives, shall also be heirs of salvation, but not in the celestial kingdom. The Lord has prepared a place for them in the terrestrial kingdom.

Those who live lives of wickedness may also be heirs of salvation, that is, they too shall be redeemed from death and from hell *eventually.* These, however, must suffer in hell the torments of the damned *until* they pay

---

[13]*Gen. & Hist. Mag.,* vol. 17, pp. 148-149; John 5:24-27; 1 John 3:14; 1 Pet. 3:18-21; 4:6.   [14]Conf. Rep., Apr.; 1942, p. 26; Abra. 2:8-11; Gen. 12:1-3.

the price of their sinning, for the blood of Christ will not cleanse them. This vast host will find their place in the telestial kingdom where their glories differ as the stars of the heavens in magnitude.

Sons of perdition are those who have rejected the light and the truth after having received the testimony of Jesus, and they are the only ones who are not redeemed from the dominion of the devil and his angels.[15]

MILLIONS NEVER HEAR GOSPEL IN MORTALITY. Knowing of the love the Father has for his children, we may rightfully conclude that the Father has arranged the plan of salvation so that all his children may have the *fullest* opportunity of salvation. How is this opportunity coming to them? We know that millions of people have died without a knowledge of the gospel, or of the name of Christ our Redeemer. Millions are now living who have never heard. Notwithstanding all the efforts that we can put forth to preach the truth, millions will die without hearing, much less receiving it.

It would be foolish on our part to think that the Lord would condemn all these to eternal damnation without the privilege of a hearing. Such a thing would not be just; it would not be merciful; it would not be godlike. Yet, has not the Lord said that no man may enter his kingdom except he be born again, and that only those may enter who accept his laws and endure to the end?[16]

SALVATION AND LAW OF GOSPEL ACCEPTANCE. *No person has been overlooked, no one will be forgotten.* He who can number the stars of heaven and who knows them all, he who takes notice when a sparrow falls will also take notice of *all* his children. *All* who have not had the privilege of repentance and acceptance of the plan of salvation in this life will have that opportunity in the world of spirits.

Those who repent there and believe when the mes-

---

[15]*Gen. & Hist. Mag.*, vol. 21, p. 145-146; D. & C. 19:3-20; 29:17; 76:30-112.

[16]John 3:3-5; Mark 16:15-16; 2 Ne. 9:23-24; 3 Ne. 27:19-20; *D. & C.* 84:74.

sage is declared to them are heirs of salvation and exaltation. The ordinances which pertain to the mortal life will be performed for them in the temples. *It is the duty of all men who hear the gospel to repent. If they reject the gospel when it is declared to them here, then they are damned.* The Savior has said it. If they receive and endure to the end, they shall receive the blessings. Every man has his agency. "I know," said Alma, "that he allotteth unto men according to their wills, whether they be unto salvation or unto destruction."[17]

TRUE CHURCH OFFERS SALVATION TO ALL

SAINTS OPEN PRISON DOORS FOR DEAD. We are doing the work in these temples for *those who have died without a knowledge of the gospel.* We have the privilege of acting vicariously for the dead, in performing the ordinances which pertain to this life. They who go into the spirit world, who hold the priesthood of God, teach the dead the everlasting gospel in that spirit world; and when the dead are willing to repent and receive those teachings, and the work is done for them here vicariously, they shall have the privilege of coming out of the prison house to find their place in the kingdom of God; and thus the Lord, in his justice and mercy, meets the demands, the requirements which the gospel has placed upon us.[18]

ONLY ONE CHURCH TEACHES SALVATION FOR DEAD. The principles of the gospel having general application and being required of all generations, naturally brings before us the question: What becomes of those who die without the opportunity of hearing and accepting the gospel? The justice and mercy of the Lord is admitted by all who profess faith in God; yet the Church of Jesus Christ of Latter-day Saints is the *only church* that holds out hope for those who have died without the opportunity of embracing the gospel in this mortal life. *No other church teaches the doctrine of salvation for the dead,*

[17]*Gen. & Hist. Mag.,* vol. 20, pp. 40-41; [18]*Church News,* Feb. 12, 1938, p. 7, Alma 29:4.

based on obedience to the principles of the gospel as that obedience may be given in the spirit world.

Could we justly make the claim that the Lord is no respecter of persons, and deals out equitably justice and mercy to all, if the dead who had no opportunity to embrace his everlasting truth, who never heard of Jesus Christ, were barred from the privilege of participating in the blessings of salvation on *equal terms* with those who received the message in mortality, and that such condition prevailed simply because the dead were unfortunate in living at a *time* and *place* where the message could not reach them?

FALSE CATHOLIC ORDINANCES FOR DEAD. Obedience to the gospel being essential and demanded of all who enter the kingdom, and the mercy and justice of the Lord being perfect, we must conclude, as a matter of *common sense*, that the Lord has provided means whereby this message of salvation will reach all, no matter in what age they lived. The plan of salvation would be imperfect if this were not the case.

It is an astonishing fact that in all the Christian churches, except the Church of Jesus Christ of Latter-day Saints, there is no teaching of the doctrine of salvation for those who died without the opportunity of hearing the gospel. *Prayers for the dead and the burning of candles do not meet the requirements of the gospel law.* There must be obedience to the principles and ordinances of the gospel by those who are dead as well as by the living, and the vicarious work must be performed for the dead by the living.

APOSTATE CHURCHES OFFER NO SALVATION FOR DEAD. In this connection I recall the story told by Motley in his *Rise of the Dutch Republic.* When Christianity was taken to the tribes of Europe, Radbod, a Frisian chief, was apparently converted and ready for baptism. Just before the ceremony was to be performed a singular thought crossed his mind, and he asked, "Where are my dead forefathers at present?" Wolfran, the Catholic bishop, very unwisely and ignorantly replied, "In hell, with all other unbelievers." "Mighty well," said the heathen chieftain, "then will I rather feast with my ancestors in the halls of Woden, than with your little starveling band of Christians in heaven."[19]

What else had the church of that day to offer for the dead? *What have those who profess Christianity to offer today?* Ask yourselves the question, and *let it come home to you.* Which was right, the bishop with nothing better to give, or the heathen chieftain? Who would think the kingdom of God to be a very desirable place if those whom they loved were barred forever from salvation because they in this mortal life had never heard the gospel?

Thousands upon thousands have died without repentance and remission of sins simply because they never heard the plan of salvation, and yet they were in all respects just as worthy as you and I. The justice of God will not bar them from his kingdom just because they never heard the gospel message; but the same conformance to the principles and obedience to law will be required of them as the Lord requires of the living. This is both just and reasonable; it is also scriptural.[20]

SALVATION FOR DEAD PROVES DIVINITY OF CHURCH. This wonderful knowledge made known in our dispensation was like the piercing of the rays of the sun into the abyss of darkness. Before this knowledge was revealed, it was taught that all who died without confessing Christ or believing on his name, were eter-

---

[19]J. L. Motley, *The Rise of the Dutch Republic,* vol. 1, pp. 20-21. Though the Frisian *converts* to Catholicism were being made Lucifer-like, without agency, at the point of a sword, yet Radbod maintained his personal integrity to the end. "Entreaties and threats" Motley says, "were unavailing. The Frisian declined positively a rite which was to cause an eternal separation from his buried kindred, and he died as he had lived, a heathen." Radbod was conquered in 692 A.D.

[20]*Millennial Star,* vol. 89, pp. 770-771.

nally and irredeemably lost. There was no ray of hope for them no matter how circumspect their lives had been.

Now the mercy of a just Redeemer, banishing the darkness and ignorance of this benighted religious world of unbelief, has shone forth with resplendent glory. Thousands have been made to rejoice among the living and hundreds of thousands among the dead. It is not very strange that this doctrine of salvation through obedience to the principles and ordinances of the gospel for the dead is taught *solely* by the Church of Jesus Christ of Latter-day Saints, for it is *one of the vital signs of the true Church of Jesus Christ,* and all men may be perfectly assured—for it is a divine truth—*where this doctrine is not taught and practiced, there the true Church is not to be found.*[21]

"FAITH ALONE" VS. SALVATION FOR DEAD

FALSE "FAITH ALONE" DOCTRINE. Latter-day Saints have been severely criticized by many professing Christians for believing it necessary to comply with these first principles of the gospel. We are told that such views make us narrow and illiberal, for we reject and damn all who do not accept Mormonism and the ministration of our elders, while they on the other hand, give a broader interpretation of the scriptures, holding it but necessary to believe in Christ—to confess him with the mouth and to believe in the heart that Christ was raised from the dead.

Or, as it is expressed,

> Nothing, either great or small,
> Remains for me to do;
> Nothing—Jesus paid it all,
> All the debt I owe.

SALVATION COMES BY FAITH PLUS OBEDIENCE. Nevertheless, there is but *one* plan of salvation and *one* door into the sheepfold. "He that entereth not by the

[21]*Gen. & Hist. Mag.,* vol. 26, p. 5.

door into the sheepfold, but climbeth up some other way, the same is a thief and a robber."[22]

We have not made the way *narrow* nor the gate *strait*, that few there be that find it! Nor was ours the edict, "Not every one that saith unto me, Lord, Lord, shall enter into the kingdom of heaven; but he that doeth the will of my Father which is in heaven."[23]

The fact that certain laws must be observed and ordinances complied with is not the ruling of the Latter-day Saints, but the divine mandate of the Author of our salvation, who has said he will judge all men according to their works and opportunities. We are merely complying with the teachings of the Master which we have received and which are requisite to salvation.

If belief alone were sufficient, then even the devils, who fear and tremble, would be saved. They recognized the Savior and declared on several occasions that he was the Son of God. And the devils in the days of the sons of Sceva declared that they knew Jesus and Paul, yet they were far from the road to salvation.[24]

MANKIND DAMNED BY "FAITH ALONE" DOCTRINE. Notwithstanding the apparently narrow construction of the Latter-day Saints pertaining to the scriptures—and we most emphatically declare that all men must obey these laws if they would be saved, excepting those who die without law,[25] and therefore are not judged by law— we are broader and more liberal in our teachings than the believers in the faith-only theory of salvation.

They would save all who profess a belief in the name of the Redeemer, but reject all others, consigning them to everlasting destruction without one ray of hope, simply because they did not confess that Jesus was the Christ. This view condemns all who lived at a *time* or *place* that the knowledge of the Redeemer of the world could not reach them. *They would reject this vast major-*

---

[22]John 10:1.
[23]Matt. 7:13-23.
[24]Mark 5:2-9; Luke 40:33-34; Acts 19:13-16.
[25]Moro. 8:22.

*ity of the human family, men, women, and children, to
eternal damnation, without the fault being their own!*

With the Latter-day Saints, this is not so. While it
is true we teach that a man must comply with these principles of the gospel in order to receive salvation and
exaltation in the kingdom of heaven—which is proved
by many passages of scripture—nevertheless, we hold
out the hope that *all may be saved,* excepting the sons
of perdition, a class that wilfully rejects the atonement
of the Savior, for the Lord intends to save all the workmanship of his hands, save these few who will not receive
salvation. Our doctrine consigns none others to perdition,
but holds forth the hope that all will eventually be saved
in some degree of glory.[26]

"FAITH ALONE" DOCTRINE DENIES JUSTICE OF GOD.
For hundreds of years the idea has prevailed among a
large portion of the so-called Christian world that all
that is necessary to insure salvation for each soul is for
each to believe in Jesus Christ. . . .

*The weakness of this "faith alone" doctrine is made
manifest in that it precludes and denies salvation to all
who have been so unfortunate as to die without the
privilege of hearing the name of Christ or of believing
on his name.*

In the revelations given by the Lord to the Latter-
day Saints through their Prophet, Joseph Smith, the
knowledge is imparted that *all* men will have the privilege
of hearing the name of Christ—not only that, but also of
receiving or rejecting his gospel truth, the plan of salvation. This promise of necessity means that the dead as
well as the living shall have the gospel preached unto
them. . . .

This broader view, while it makes the requirement
of all who receive a place in the kingdom of God of repentance and obedience to the laws and ordinances of the
gospel, nevertheless is just and in full accord with the

---

[26]*Salvation Universal,* pp. 7-8.

mercy of our Eternal Father. It gives to each individual the chance to escape, whether living or dead, from the power of sin and the chains of hell, and it does not consign to everlasting torment those who were unfortunate in not having heard the gospel in this mortal life and therefore had no privilege of repentance.[27]

LAW OF VICARIOUS SALVATION

VICARIOUS ORDINANCES PART OF GOSPEL. Since it is necessary for all who enter the kingdom of God to comply with the ordinances of the gospel, it must be necessary for the dead to conform to this plan. If a man cannot enter the kingdom of God without baptism, then the dead must be baptized. But how can they be baptized in water for the remission of their sins?

It is easy to understand how they in person could believe in Christ and even obtain the spirit of repentance; but water is an element of this world, and how could spirits be baptized in it, or receive the laying on of hands for the gift of the Holy Ghost? The only way it can be done is vicariously, someone who is living acting as a substitute for the dead.

SALVATION BASED ON VICARIOUS WORK. But, says one, this cannot be; it is impossible for one man to stand for another. The answer to this is: *The whole system of Christianity is based on vicarious work, One without blemish and without sin standing for all as the Redeemer.* You answer, "This is granted in the case of Jesus Christ, for he is God, but it cannot be granted in the case of man for man."

What of the commandments given by the Lord to Moses in the case of the sin offerings and of the scapegoat for Israel? On the head of the goat Aaron placed his hands and confessed over it all the iniquity of the children of Israel, all their transgressions, and all their

[27]*Church News,* Feb. 13, 1932, p. 4.

sins, putting them upon the head of the goat, and then sent it away "by the hand of a fit man into the wilderness." And the goat bore upon him all their iniquities into the wilderness "unto a land not inhabited." If this was done then, is it beyond the power of the Lord to permit a man now to act as proxy for the man who is dead and unable to help himself in person?[28]

That one man cannot stand or answer for another's sins, but that every man must stand for himself, is true so far as it is possible to be done. But occasions have arisen where the man guilty of transgressing the law was unable to redeem himself. And punishment for sin is for the propitiation of sin, and in such cases there is nothing in the scriptures forbidding one to stand vicariously for another when circumstances render it impossible for the first to comply with the law.[29]

TEMPLE PROXIES REPRESENT THE DEAD. When we go into the temple to do work for the dead, we go representing the dead, acting vicariously and as proxies for the dead. We are not treating those dead individuals as if they were dead. What are we doing? We are treating them as beings living in the flesh, and we are representing them. What are we doing? Giving unto them in person by proxy that which they must receive and which should have been received here and would have been received by them here had the privilege come.

So we are only presenting to the dead such ordinances and privileges as pertain to those who are living here and now. So far as faith is concerned, they exercise that where they are. So far as repentance is concerned, they repent where they are. We are baptized for them because they cannot be baptized there. We are confirmed and ordained for them. Why? Because they cannot receive those ordinances there. Why? Because these ordinances pertain to mortal life, and *all we are doing for the*

---

[28]*Millennial Star*, vol. 89, pp. 773-774;   [29]*Salvation Universal*, pp. 9-10.
   Lev. 4; 5; 16:20-22.

dead is to give them that which pertains to this mortal existence in which we find ourselves.[30]

IMPORTANCE OF SALVATION FOR DEAD

PURPOSE OF ORDINANCE WORK FOR DEAD. Temple work is for the purpose of giving to every man and to every woman the blessings of the higher ordinances of the gospel that are essential to salvation in the kingdom of God. There is not an ordinance performed in the temple that does not pertain to this mortal life.

When we go into the temple and act for somebody else, we are treating that person as though we were that person living here, doing for him just what he would have to do if he were in mortal life. Thus *we bring to pass his salvation,* and we learn through these keys the knowledge of God which is made manifest through these ordinances, these blessings, these signs, all that is given to us in the temple of the Lord.[31]

GRANDEUR OF DOCTRINE OF SALVATION FOR DEAD. This doctrine of giving an *equal* chance to the dead to hear and receive the truth, wherein they were denied that privilege while living, is *one of the grandest, most reasonable, and soul satisfying doctrines ever revealed to man.* I would that all men might ponder over it and then, obtaining the spirit, seek to bless their dead by making it possible for the ordinances of the gospel to be performed for them in the temples of the Lord. By this means we may help to save those who have gone before and in our limited way become *saviors to many people.* How great shall be the satisfaction of the man and the woman who have performed those ordinances for their dead, when they stand in the presence of their dead, and see their joy and hear expressions of gratitude.[32]

---

[30]*Church News,* Jan. 5, 1935, p. 7.
[31]*Gen. & Hist. Mag.,* vol. 30, ;'. 3; D. & C. 84:19-20; 124:28-41.

[32]*Millennial Star,* vol. 89, pp. 782-783; Obad. 21.

UNSELFISH NATURE OF SALVATION FOR DEAD. There is no work connected with the gospel that is of a more unselfish nature than the work in the house of the Lord for our dead. Those who work for the dead do not expect to receive any earthly remuneration or reward. It is, above all, a work of love, which is begotten in the heart of man through faithful and constant labor in these saving ordinances. There are no financial returns, but there shall be great joy in heaven with those souls whom we have helped to their salvation.

It is a work that enlarges the soul of man, broadens his views regarding the welfare of his fellowman, and plants in his heart a love for all the children of our Heavenly Father. *There is no work equal to that in the temple for the dead in teaching a man to love his neighbor as himself.* Jesus so loved the world that he was willing to offer himself as a sacrifice for sin that the world might be saved. We also have the privilege, in a small degree, of showing our great love for him and our fellow beings by helping them to the blessings of the gospel which now they cannot receive without our assistance.[33]

BLOOD OF OUR DEAD RESTS ON US. In an editorial in the *Times and Seasons,* written by the Prophet, he speaks of the remarks made by the Savior to the Jews, that upon them should come all the righteous blood shed upon the earth from the blood of righteous Abel, unto the blood of Zacharias, son of Barachias, who was slain between the temple and the altar.[34]

Then the Prophet declares, in most emphatic terms, that the reason why this blood was to come upon these Jews was that since, *"They possessed greater privileges than any other generation, not only as pertaining to themselves, but to their dead, their sin was greater, as they not only neglected their own salvation but that of their*

---

[33]*Era,* vol. 20, p. 362.   [34]Matt. 23:35-36.

progenitors, and hence their blood was required at their hands."[35]

Now, if these Jews were to answer for the blood of their progenitors because they neglected the salvation of their dead, then, may we not ask: *Will not we have to answer for the blood of our dead, if we neglect these ordinances in their behalf?* It matters not even if we have been baptized and have had hands laid on our heads for the reception of the Holy Ghost, if we wilfully neglect the salvation of our dead, then also we shall stand rejected of the Lord, because we have rejected our dead; and just so sure their blood will be required at our hands.[36]

OUR MOST IMPORTANT RESPONSIBILITIES

OUR OWN SALVATION COMES FIRST. We have these two great responsibilities—every man holding the priesthood—first, to *seek our own salvation;* and, second, our duty to our fellow men. Now I take it that my first duty is, so far as I am individually concerned, to seek my own salvation. That is your individual duty first, and so with every member of this Church.[37]

Our duty to our fellow men in the world is a responsibility resting especially on the shoulders of the men holding the priesthood. *Our duty is to preach the gospel,* to teach the nations of the earth, to go out and bring people into the Church. *That duty is upon the Church.* The Lord has arranged it so that certain men are called to certain offices in the Church with that peculiar duty on their shoulders. The Twelve, the seventies, are the missionaries of the Church, but every man in the Church has this responsibility as a man holding the priesthood.

PRIESTHOOD RESPONSIBILITY FOR TEMPLE WORK. Now, of course, the Lord says that our greatest *individual responsibility* is to seek after our dead; but as men hold-

[35]Joseph Fielding Smith, *Teachings of the Prophet Joseph Smith*, pp. 222-223.
[36]*Origin of the "Reorganized" Church,* pp. 45-46.
[37]Matt. 16:26; Mark 8:36-37; Luke 9:25.

ing the priesthood our responsibility is—so far as temple work is concerned—to teach, to instruct, to persuade, to prevail upon men and women who are not inclined to take advantage of their opportunities and receive these blessings for themselves, to go into the temple where they can do this work. That is our responsibility as men holding the priesthood.

It does not make any difference whether we are high priests, seventies, or elders. *We are trying to place this burden especially upon the high priests of the Church.* The seventies preach the gospel—that is where they belong—the elders are ministers at home. The high priests, also, are ministers at home, and we are also trying to train them to take upon themselves this responsibility of teaching their fellow men in all that pertains to exaltation and to help prepare them to go to the temple to do these labors in behalf of their dead. That is our responsibility, and it is a great responsibility.[38]

RESPONSIBILITIES OF THE CHURCH AND THE INDIVIDUAL. The Lord has given to the Church the responsibility of preaching the gospel to the nations of the earth. *This is the greatest responsibility of the Church.*[39] Men are to be taught the gospel and called to repentance and warned. When they refuse to heed the warning, they must be left without excuse.

The Lord has also placed upon the individual members of the Church a responsibility. *It is our duty as individuals to seek after our immediate dead*—those of our own line. This is the greatest *individual responsibility* that we have, and we should carry it through in behalf of our fathers who have gone before.[40]

OUR GREATEST INDIVIDUAL RESPONSIBILITY. The Prophet Joseph Smith declared, *"The greatest responsibility in this world that God has laid upon us is to seek after our dead."*[41] The reason for this is that all the dead

---

[38]*Gen. & Hist. Mag.,* vol. 30, pp. 3-4. [40]*Gen. & Hist. Mag.,* vol. 20, pp. 42-43.
[39]Smith, *op. cit.,* p. 113. [41]Smith, *op. cit.,* p. 356.

must be redeemed from their sins through obedience to the gospel just as the living are. It is required of us to perform this labor in their behalf.

Moreover, we cannot be made perfect without our faithful dead who are also heirs of celestial exaltation. There must be a welding, or joining together of generations, from Adam down. Parents must be sealed to each other and children to parents, in order to receive the blessings of the celestial kingdom. Therefore *our salvation and progression depends upon the salvation of our worthy dead with whom we must be joined in family ties.* This can only be accomplished in our temples.

The Prophet further declared that the doctrine of salvation for the dead is the "most glorious of all subjects belonging to the everlasting gospel."[42] The reasons for this are the great magnitude of the labor, and the fact that we have the privilege of officiating for the dead and assisting in giving to them the privileges that we also enjoy, through our obedience to the gospel.[43]

SAINTS SEEK TO SAVE THEIR DEAD

MIGHTY WORK OF THIS DISPENSATION. While many honorable men and women in the world are accomplishing a great work in searching out and compiling genealogical data, their labors serve only as the means to the end. The greatest work, after all, devolves on the members of the Church who have the priesthood, power, and privilege to go into the temples, taking the names from these compiled records, and from all other authentic sources, and performing the ordinances in behalf of their dead.

We live in the greatest dispensation of the world's history, that of the fulness of times, when all things are to be gathered and restored to their proper order, ushering in the millennial reign of the Redeemer and the righteous. *Do we Latter-day Saints fully realize the impor-*

---

[42]*D. & C.* 128:17.   [43]*Era*, vol. 20, p. 361; *D. & C.* 128:18.

tance of the mighty responsibility placed upon us in
relation to the salvation of the world?

CHURCH PROGRESS IN MANY FIELDS. We are doing
a great deal in the attempt to convert and save a perverse
and wicked generation; we are sending hundreds of
missionaries into all parts of the earth, and are spending
hundreds of thousands of dollars annually in this very
necessary labor, with results that are not so very startling.
We are spending hundreds of thousands of dollars in
the building of meetinghouses, church schools and other
buildings, and in the education of the youth of Israel, in
developing and improving our lands, building cities and
increasing our communities, publishing periodicals and
magazines, and in every way diligently striving to
improve our own people and disseminate knowledge that
will convert the world to the gospel.

But what are we doing for the salvation of our dead?
Many there are, it is true, who comprehend this greater
work, and are faithfully discharging their duties in the
temples of the Lord, but of others this cannot be said.
The temple in Salt Lake City is frequently so crowded
with anxious, earnest workers, that it is necessary many
times to turn large numbers away because there is not
sufficient room. This is a good sign, showing the willingness and activity of the saints.

NONE EXEMPT FROM WORK FOR DEAD. But this
condition does not relieve from responsibility the inactive,
dilatory members, who are doing nothing for their dead.
These persons cannot expect to receive credit for what
others may be doing. The responsibility rests with equal
force on all, according to our individual ability and opportunities.

It matters not what else we have been called to do,
or what position we may occupy, or how faithfully in
other ways we have labored in the Church, none is exempt
from this great obligation. It is required of the apostle
as well as the humblest elder. Place, or distinction, or

long service in the Church, in the mission field, the stakes of Zion, or where or how else it may have been, will not entitle one to disregard the salvation of one's dead.

Some may feel that if they pay their tithing, attend their regular meetings and other duties, give of their substance to the poor, perchance spend one, two, or more years preaching in the world, that they are absolved from further duty. But *the greatest and grandest duty of all is to labor for the dead.*

WORK FOR DEAD OBLIGATORY UPON US. We may and should do all these other things, for which reward will be given, but if we neglect the weightier privilege and commandment, notwithstanding all other good works, we shall find ourselves under severe condemnation.

And why such condemnation? Because "the greatest responsibility in this world that God has laid upon us, is to seek after our dead," because we cannot be saved without them. "It is necessary that those who are going before and those who come after us should have salvation in common with us; and *thus hath God made it obligatory upon man,"* says the Prophet Joseph Smith.[44] From this, then, we see that while it is necessary to preach the gospel in the nations of the earth, and to do all other good works in the Church, yet the greatest commandment given us, and made obligatory, is the temple work in our own behalf and in behalf of our dead.[45]

RESURRECTED BEINGS TO FURNISH GENEALOGICAL DATA. The Lord expects of us all that we do what we can for ourselves and for our dead. He wants us to make the search for our ancestry because he does not do for us what we can do for ourselves. And after we have done all we can, then means will be furnished, or the way will be opened for the furnishing of the information which we are unable to discover.

---

[44]Smith, *op. cit.,* p. 356.   [45]*Salvation Universal,* pp. 24-26.

The time will come when the dead, or at least those who have passed through the resurrection unto life, will work hand in hand with those who are still in mortality, and they will furnish the information. There will be no mistakes about it then, and we will have the privilege of going into the temple of the Lord and doing the work, until every soul for whom this work is intended shall be ferreted out, and not one soul shall be overlooked.[46]

DO WORK FOR ALL ANCESTORS. We must not slacken in our labors. The Lord will hold us accountable for our own actions regarding our own selves. We should take diligent heed concerning our dead, that none shall be overlooked. It is our privilege and our duty to perform the labor in the temple for all our ancestors whose names we can obtain, unless for good and sufficient reason they should be barred, according to the rules, from having that work done in the temple, and then we leave the matter in the hands of the Lord. If some of them for whom we labor are unworthy, the Lord will do the eliminating. That is not for us to do. Our work is to go to the temples and perform the labor.[47]

YOUNG AND OLD SHOULD DO TEMPLE WORK. A man does not have to be old, nor does a woman, to understand temple work. We do not have to get along in years before we get the spirit of salvation for the dead. True, it is largely the older people who go to the temples and devote their time. I can see reason in this, because younger people are occupied and their time is required in other pursuits while the aged people have laid aside the cares of the world, more or less, and have more time to go to the temple and devote their time to the salvation of the dead. And therefore, necessarily and logically, we find more aged people in the temple than we do younger people.

But, the younger people must not get the idea that this is only an old person's work. It is for *all* the Latter-

---

[46]*Gen. & Hist. Mag.*, vol. 13, p. 58.   [47]*Gen. & Hist. Mag.*, vol. 14, pp. 17-18.

day Saints, and *young people can attend to these matters* and get the spirit of this work just as much as those who are advanced in years.[48]

SUGGESTED MINIMUM TEMPLE SCHEDULE. If we spent one day each month in the temples saving our dead, just 12 days out of the 365 of the year, brethren and sisters, would any of us be doing more than our share? Could we even feel that we were doing our full duty, when the responsibility given us is so great, and, *"The saints have not too much time to save and redeem their dead, and gather together their living relatives, that they may be saved also, before the earth will be smitten, and the consummation decreed falls upon the world"?*[49]

Again, suppose each one of us should fill out one baptismal blank of 20 names and send it to the temple every month, . . . is this more than we ought to do? Is it more than we are capable of doing? It certainly is a great deal more than we are doing; and, too, there are many individuals who are baptizing more than 20 every month.

If a few can do it, why can not more? The fact is, this question has not appealed to many of us; we have been so busy in other pursuits, principally in the accumulation of worldly goods that we cannot carry with us, that we have had no time or inclination to do the work for our dead. If one hundredth part of the energy expended by the members of the Church in other ways were directed in the channels of temple work where it properly belongs, we could accomplish a great deal more work than we are now doing for the salvation of the dead.

ASSIST OTHERS IN TEMPLE WORK. But one will say: "I have done the work for all my ancestors of whom I have any knowledge. My genealogy can only be traced to my great-grandfather, beyond that all is dark. How can I be baptized each year for 20, 40, 60, or more of my dead when we have not their records?"

[48]*Gen. & Hist. Mag.,* vol. 13, p. 67.   [49]Smith, *op. cit.,* p. 330.

To such a person I reply: "If you have done the work for all your known dead, and your record cannot be traced but one or two generations, you still have the privilege of assisting your neighbor who lacks sufficient help and therefore cannot do the work for all his dead. Assist him and assist the temples with your financial as well as your moral support, and the way may be opened before you that you can obtain more knowledge of your own dead."[50]

CONVERSION TO TEMPLE WORK NEEDED. We may, without any suffering so far as we are concerned, act as *saviors on Mount Zion by going into the temple and doing for our dead the things they cannot do for themselves.* But there are thousands of Latter-day Saints who seem to be uncertain about this.

They are willing to go to meeting, willing to pay their tithing and attend to the regular duties of the Church, but they do not seem to feel or understand the importance of receiving the blessings in the temple of the Lord which will bring them into exaltation. It is a strange thing. People seem to be content just to slide along without taking advantage of the opportunities presented to them and without receiving these necessary covenants that will bring them back into the presence of God as sons and daughters.

RESPONSIBILITY OF GENEALOGICAL WORKERS. Now this is our duty as men holding the priesthood: To teach them and make them understand the importance of this. We will go to them as missionaries, we will labor with them, we will try to show them, we will try to convince them, we will try to persuade them to go to the temple for their own salvation and for the salvation of their dead; and when we have done that, we have done our duty.

So I want to say that to all those who are engaged in the genealogical work in the stakes of Zion, that work

---

[50]*Salvation Universal,* pp. 30-31.

of persuasion is assigned to you. We want you as men holding the priesthood, and the sisters laboring with you, to persuade, to teach, to do everything in your power by persuasion and by teaching the members of the Church to get them to the temple to do the thing that will bring them the fulness of the glory of God.[51]

[51]*Gen. & Hist. Mag.,* vol. 30, p. 4.

CHAPTER 9

SALVATION FOR THE DEAD

THE PROMISES MADE TO THE FATHERS

NATURE OF PROMISES MADE TO FATHERS. What was the promise made to the fathers that was to be fulfilled in the latter-days by the turning of the hearts of the children to their fathers? It was the promise of the Lord made through Enoch, Isaiah, and the prophets, to the nations of the earth, that *the time should come when the dead should be redeemed*. And the turning of the hearts of the children is fulfilled in the performing of the vicarious temple work and in the preparation of their genealogies.[1]

At various times during the history of the world the opportunity for mankind to receive the blessings of the gospel has been denied them. For instance, during the time of the apostasy, following the ministry of our Savior and his apostles down to the time of the restoration, the opportunity for men to receive the remission of their sins by baptism and partake of the other ordinances essential to exaltation was impossible. The Church with its authorized ministers was not on the earth. It is true that similar conditions have existed at other and more remote periods of time.

CERTAIN ORDINANCES RESERVED FOR LATTER-DAYS. Even when the priesthood has been on the earth and every opportunity given to men generally to repent and embrace the gospel, many individuals have died without that opportunity who, perhaps, would have done so had the privilege been presented to them.

---

[1] *Salvation Universal*, p. 20; *D. & C.* 2:1-3.

Moreover, is it not probable that in the present dispensation we are privileged to perform ordinances for the dead which were denied them when living, notwithstanding their faithfulness and obedience to the gospel in their day? The Lord said to Joseph Smith: *"For I deign to reveal unto my church things which have been kept hid from before the foundation of the world, things that pertain to the dispensation of the fulness of times."*[2]

. . .

ISAIAH'S PROMISES OF SALVATION FOR DEAD. Some of these promises made to the fathers are found in the scriptures. For instance, Isaiah said in reference to our Savior: "I the Lord have called thee in righteousness, and will hold thine hand, and will keep thee, and give thee for a covenant of the people, for a light of the Gentiles; To open the blind eyes, *to bring out the prisoners from the prison,* and them that sit in darkness *out of the prison house."*[3]

Isaiah also says: "And it shall come to pass in that day, that the Lord shall punish the host of the high ones that are on high, and the kings of the earth upon the earth. And they shall be gathered together, *as prisoners are gathered in the pit,* and shall be *shut up in the prison,* and after many days shall they be visited."[4] This is spoken of those who keep not the law who live in latter-days.

Again, he says: "The Spirit of the Lord God is upon me; because the Lord hath anointed me to preach good tidings unto the meek; he hath sent me to bind up the brokenhearted, to *proclaim liberty to the captives, and the opening of the prison to them that are bound."*[5] This was spoken of as the mission of the Redeemer, *both* his work for the living and the dead, who were prisoners that were bound.

---

[2] D. & C. 124:41; 128:18.   [4] Isa. 24:21-22.
[3] Era, vol. 25, pp. 829-831; Isa. 42:6-7.   [5] Isa. 61:1.

CHRIST FULFILS ISAIAH'S PROMISES. When the Savior commenced his ministry, he entered into the synagogue in the city of Nazareth, his home town, on the Sabbath day. The book of Isaiah was handed him; he turned to this passage and read, closed the book, handed it back to the minister, and while the eyes of all the congregation were riveted upon him, he said, "This day is this scripture fulfilled in your ears."[6]

But the Jews rejected him, and his testimony, and with violence drove him from the city. Nevertheless, he continued to proclaim liberty to the captives, declaring that he came not alone to save the living but also to save the dead.

ENOCH'S KNOWLEDGE OF SALVATION FOR DEAD. This vicarious salvation for the dead is not a new doctrine. It is new and strange for this generation it is true, but only because of a lack of comprehension of the revelations of the Lord. The Prophet Joseph Smith said *it is the burden of the scriptures.*[7] It has been taught among the Lord's people from the earliest times.

Enoch saw in vision the kingdoms of the world and all their inhabitants down even to the end of time. The Lord told him of Noah and the flood and how he would destroy the people of the earth for their iniquity. Of these rebellious ones who rejected the truth and paid no heed to the preachings of Noah and the ancient prophets, the Lord said: "I can stretch forth mine hands and hold all the creations which I have made; and mine eyes can pierce them also, and among all the workmanship of mine hands there has not been so great wickedness as among thy brethren.

"But behold, their sins shall be upon the heads of their fathers; Satan shall be their father, and misery shall be their doom; and the whole heavens shall weep over them, even all the workmanship of mine hands; wherefore

---

[6]Luke 4:16-21.   [7]Joseph Fielding Smith, *Teachings of the Prophet Joseph Smith,* p. 193.

should not the heavens weep, seeing these shall suffer? But behold, these which thine eyes are upon shall perish in the floods; and behold, *I will shut them up; a prison have I prepared for them.* And That which I have chosen hath plead before my face. Wherefore, he suffereth for their sins; inasmuch as they will repent *in the day that my Chosen shall return unto me, and until that day they shall be in torment."*[8]

From this we learn that the Lord has prepared a prison for the souls of all those who rejected the testimony of the antediluvian prophets, where they were to remain in torment *until* the time when Jesus should atone for their sins and return to the Father.[9]

PROMISES OF MALACHI AND OBADIAH. Perhaps the most direct promise recorded in the scriptures is that by Malachi: "Behold, I will send you Elijah the prophet before the coming of the great and dreadful day of the Lord: And he shall turn the heart of the fathers to the children, and the heart of the children to their fathers, lest I come and smite the earth with a curse."[10]

The Prophet declared that Obadiah was speaking of salvation for the dead when he said, "And *saviours shall come up on mount Zion* to judge the mount of Esau; and the kingdom shall be the Lord's."[11]

SALVATION IN SPIRIT WORLD

GULF BETWEEN RIGHTEOUS AND WICKED SPIRITS. We hear the objection made, from time to time, that Jesus did not come to save the dead, for he most emphatically declared himself that there was an impassable gulf that separated the righteous spirits from the wicked. In defense of their position they quote the words in Luke: "And beside all this, between us and you there is a great gulf fixed: so that they which would pass from hence

[8]Moses 7:36-39.
[9]*Salvation Universal,* pp. 12-14.
[10]*Era,* vol. 25, pp. 829-831; Mal. 4:5-6.
[11]*Salvation Universal,* p. 18; Obad. 21; Smith, *op. cit.,* p. 223.

to you cannot; neither can they pass to us, that would
come from thence."

These words, according to the story, were spoken
by Abraham's spirit to the rich man who raised his eyes
and asked that Lazarus might go touch his lips and relieve
his torment. Abraham replied that it could not be for
there was a gulf fixed between them that the spirit of no
man could pass. Therefore, say the objectors to the doctrine of universal salvation, "It is quite evident that the
righteous and the wicked who are dead cannot visit each
other, hence there is no salvation for the dead."[12]

CHRIST BRIDGED THE GULF. This was true *before*
the days that Jesus atoned for sin, which is plainly shown
in the passage from the Book of Moses previously
quoted.[13] And it was at this period this event occurred.
However, Christ came and through his death bridged
that gulf, proclaimed liberty to the captives, and the
opening of this prison door to those who sat in darkness
and captivity.

*From that time forth this gulf is bridged so that
the captives, after they have paid the full penalty of their
misdeeds, satisfied justice, and have accepted the gospel
of Christ, having the ordinances attended to in their
behalf by their living relatives or friends, receive the
passport that entitles them to cross the gulf.*

CHRIST PROMISES TO VISIT SPIRITS IN PRISON. The
Lord speaks of this himself: "Verily, verily, I say unto
you, He that heareth my word, and believeth on him that
sent me, hath everlasting life, and shall not come into
condemnation; but is passed from death unto life. Verily,
verily, I say unto you, The hour is coming, and now is,
when *the dead shall hear the voice of the Son of God:*
and they that hear shall live."

And the Jews marveled. Perhaps they thought he
meant those who were "dead in trespasses and sins"

---

[12]Luke 16:19-31; Alma 40:11-14.   [13]Moses 7:36-39.

should hear his voice. At any rate they marveled. He perceived it and said:

"Marvel not at this: for the hour is coming, in the which *all that are in the graves shall hear his voice,* And shall come forth; they that have done good, unto the resurrection of life; and they that have done evil, unto the resurrection of damnation."[14]

Peter tells us that Christ did this very thing: "For Christ also hath once suffered for sins, the just for the unjust, that he might bring us to God, being put to death in the flesh, but quickened by the Spirit: By which also he went and *preached unto the spirits in prison:* Which sometime were disobedient, when once the long suffering of God waited in the days of Noah, while the ark was a preparing, wherein few, that is, eight souls were saved by water."[15]

WHY CHRIST MINISTERED IN SPIRIT PRISON. Why did he preach to these disobedient spirits? Surely not to increase their torments, to taunt them for not accepting of his truth in the days of the prophets! Was it to tantalize them and make them more miserable because of the blessings they had lost! Jesus was a merciful Redeemer, who suffered as no other man suffered that he might save the children of his Father. He would take no pleasure in the suffering of the wicked.

It was his nature to plead for them, to entreat his Father for mercy in their behalf. Therefore, whatever his mission was, it was one of mercy and comfort to those prisoners. Peter tells us that the object of his visit was that the gospel might be preached also to the dead, "that they might be judged according to men in the flesh, but live according to God in the spirit."[16]

The visit of Christ to the spirits in prison was not made in vengeance, to show them that he had power to triumph over the grave, while they, who died without

---

[14]John 5:24-25, 28-29.
[15]1 Pet. 3:18-20.

[16]*Salvation Universal,* pp. 14-16; 1 Pet. 4:6.

the remission of their sins, should remain in that condition of punishment forever. *He took the glorious message of the gospel and proclaimed it to the dead with the promise that they, if they would obey it, should partake of its blessings.*[17]

REPENTANCE ENDS ETERNAL SUFFERING. What good reason can be given why the Lord should not forgive sins in the world to come? Why should man suffer throughout the countless ages of eternity for his sins committed here, if those sins are not unto death? There are many good, honorable men who have wilfully wronged no man, have lived to the best of their opportunities, righteously, yet have not received the gospel, for one reason or another. Where would be the justice in condemning them forever in hell, "where their worm dieth not, and the fire is not quenched?"[18]

We learn from the *Doctrine and Covenants* that eternal punishment, or everlasting punishment, does not mean that a man condemned will endure this punishment forever, but it is everlasting and eternal because it is God's punishment, and he is Everlasting and Eternal.[19] Therefore, *when a man pays the penalty of his misdeeds and humbly repents, receiving the gospel, he comes out of the prison house and is assigned to some degree of glory according to his worth and merit.*[20] . . .

SINS FORGIVEN IN SPIRIT WORLD. That sins are forgiven in the world to come, we need only refer to the words of the Savior: "All manner of sin and blasphemy shall be forgiven unto men: but the blasphemy against the Holy Ghost shall not be forgiven unto men. And whosoever speaketh a word against the Son of man, it shall be forgiven him: but whosoever speaketh against the Holy Ghost, it shall not be forgiven him, neither in this world, *neither in the world to come.*"[21]

[17]*Millennial Star,* vol. 89, pp. 772-773. [20]*D. & C.* 76:38-39, 104-106.
[18]*D. & C.* 76:44; Isa. 66:24. [21]Matt. 12:31-32.
[19]*D. & C.* 19:4-12.

This shows that some sins will be forgiven in the world to come. We are also informed in First Corinthians that, "If in this life only we have hope in Christ, we are of all men most miserable."[22] But we have hope in Christ both in this life and in the life to come.[23]

BAPTISM FOR DEAD

No Salvation Without Baptism. One of the most emphatic and positive statements of our Savior was his saying to Nicodemus: "Verily, verily, I say unto thee, Except a man be born of water and of the Spirit, he cannot enter into the kingdom of God." That to be born of water means to be baptized is so clear it will not admit of successful dispute. To be born of the Spirit is just as positive a statement in relation to the gift of the Holy Ghost, which is received by the laying on of hands.

Nor did the Savior limit his remark by any qualifying clause to refer only to men who are living and with the opportunity of hearing the gospel, or to eliminate from his command those who have passed beyond. The statement is *dogmatic, positive, and without qualification: "Except a man be born of water and of the Spirit, he cannot enter into the kingdom of God!"*[24]

Performance of Vicarious Ordinances. Baptism is an ordinance belonging to this life, as also are confirmation and ordination to the priesthood, and the man who does not receive these blessings here cannot receive them in the spirit world. There he may repent and believe and accept the truth, but he cannot be baptized, confirmed, or ordained, or endowed, for these ordinances belong here. What is to be done in the matter?

We are going to take substitutes who will act vicariously, which means one acting for another, and in the temples they will stand for those who are dead and there, in the behalf of the dead, receive all these blessings for

[22]1 Cor. 15:19.
[23]*Salvation Universal,* pp. 16-17.
[24]*Church News,* Mar. 12, 1932, p. 7; John 3:5.

them. When they do this, *if* the dead accept the labor performed, it is accounted unto them the same as if they had acted for themselves.

The Lord did a great vicarious work for all men, and he has delegated power to us in a lesser degree to perform a vicarious work for the dead. So we, too, may become saviors to our fellow men in this manner, performing work for them that they cannot perform for themselves.

YOUTH OF CHURCH MAY BE BAPTIZED FOR DEAD. Any person in this Church who has been baptized and confirmed and is in good standing may go into the temple to be baptized for the dead. And so these young men and young women, those holding the Aaronic Priesthood and members of the Primary Association, have the privilege of assisting in the saving of the children of our Father in heaven.

What a wonderful privilege this is. How glad we should feel to have the power to help others to salvation in this way and give somebody else a chance to obtain eternal life, which they could not receive without our help. Just think of it, by going to the temples and there being baptized and confirmed for men and women who have died and who have accepted the gospel in the spirit world, we become instrumental in releasing them from the prison house, if they will accept the thing we do for them. What a glorious service to render!

As we grow older, we may perform other labor for the dead in the endowments and sealings in the temple. No man or woman can act for another until he or she has passed through the waters of baptism and obtained the blessings for himself. The young men who hold the lesser priesthood have the authority to be baptized and confirmed, and so this gospel is going forth to the living and also to the dead in the spirit world. In this manner the Lord is reaching out after all his children and is willing to bless them, if they will only obey his work, and not one soul shall be forgotten.[25]

MERIDIAN SAINTS PRACTICED BAPTISM FOR DEAD. Salvation for the dead was understood in the days of the primitive Christian Church, and to some extent baptisms for the dead continued to be performed until A.D. 379, when the Council of Carthage forbade any longer the administration of this ordinance and "holy communion" for the dead. Paul uses baptism for the dead as an argument against the Corinthian Saints, who, even in that day, were falling away from the true gospel. These saints understood the doctrine of baptism for the dead, yet they doubted the general resurrection.[26]

APOSTATE CHURCH SUPPRESSES BAPTISM FOR DEAD. In the *Catholic Encyclopedia*, under the subject of "Baptism," is a statement that baptism for the dead was practiced by some "heretical sects," also that the Jews practiced this ordinance, which, of course, must have been after the resurrection of our Lord. It is intimated also in this article that some early fathers believed that this ordinance was practiced in the early Church.[27] Of course, we have the evidence of this in the words of Paul.

Naturally the Catholic Church would consider all who did practice baptism for the dead as "heretics." It stands to reason that if it was the custom among the Corinthian Saints, then it was also the custom among other branches in the first century. That the practice was suppressed must have been the case, for it certainly was discontinued, and in its stead came the custom of praying people out of "purgatory." I am firmly convinced that this teaching and practice in the Catholic Church is but a *perversion* of the doctrine of baptism for the dead.[28]

---

[25]*Gen. & Hist. Mag.*, vol. 17, p. 149.
[26]*Salvation Universal*, pp. 17-18; 1 Cor. 15:20-30.

[27]*Catholic Encyclopedia*, vol. 2, pp. 271-272.
[28]Pers. Corresp.; 1 Cor. 15:29.

SALVATION FOR DEAD IN VARIOUS AGES

No Work for Dead Before Christ. There is
abundant evidence in the scriptures to show that there
was no work performed for the dead, who died without
the privilege of complying with the principles of the
gospel, until after Christ opened the door, after his crucifixion; but that all ordinances, including the binding or
sealing performed by Elijah, were confined to the living.[29]

After the resurrection of Christ the doors were
opened to the dead, and the vicarious work for the dead
was instituted and the authority of the priesthood held
by Elijah was then *extended* to include blessings for the
dead, who would have received the gospel, if the privilege
had been granted to them on this earth.

Power of Elijah Had in Meridian of Time.
Speaking of Elijah's mission, the Prophet Joseph Smith
has said: *"The spirit, power, and calling of Elijah is that
ye have power to hold the key of the revelations, ordinances, oracles, powers, and endowments of the fulness
of the Melchizedek Priesthood and of the kingdom of
God on the earth; and to receive, obtain, and perform all
the ordinances belonging to the kingdom of God."*[30]

It must have been this authority that was conferred
upon Peter, James, and John, as well as upon Joseph
Smith and Oliver Cowdery. We, therefore, conclude
that the saints in that dispensation had the privilege of
receiving all the keys and authorities that are necessary
for the salvation and exaltation of man. However, these
powers were exercised only for the living, until *after*
the resurrection of Christ, when they were exercised also
in behalf of the dead.[31]

Christ Prepared Way for Salvation for Dead.
There could be no baptisms or endowments or any other
work for the dead before the death of Jesus Christ. He

[29]Moses 7:36-39; Luke 16:19-31; Alma 40:11-14; 1 Pet. 3:18-20; 4:6; Isa. 24:21-22; 42:6-7; 61:1; D. & C. 128:18-25.
[30]Smith, op. cit., p. 337.
[31]Era, vol. 30, pp. 736-737.

it was who carried the message of the gospel to the dead and bridged the gulf spoken of in the parable of the rich man and Lazarus. He it was who, in fulfillment of the prophets, opened the door of the prison house and permitted the prisoners to come free. Until that time the dead were waiting for their salvation or redemption, which should come through the blood of Christ.

The disciples in that day did have the keys for this work. These keys were given to Peter, James, and John on the mount when they received this power from Elias and Moses, the latter conferring the keys of the gathering of Israel. Christ told these three men, who I believe *received their endowments on the mount*, that *they were not to mention this vision and what had taken place until after he was resurrected.* Therefore, the exercise of this authority had to wait until Christ had prepared the way.

VICARIOUS ORDINANCES PERFORMED IN MERIDIAN OF TIME. We do know that in that day they baptized for the dead. What was there to prevent them from giving endowments? Truly it would not be done in the temple at Jerusalem, for that had fallen into apostate hands. But they could, and most likely did, give endowments to the other apostles and many others in some secluded spot or on some mountain.

The first endowments in Utah were given on Ensign Peak. Now it may be argued that the endowments in that day were limited to the living. Perhaps so, but the fact that the Savior said that all the blood of the prophets from Abel to Zacharias, should be required of the generation, because they had greater privileges than any other generation, would imply that they were able to do this work even for the dead under *limited* conditions.[32] . . .

We have no record of any of this work and merely the statement made by Paul.[33] The fact remains, however, that this work has been left almost entirely to this present

---

[32]Matt. 23:34-36; Smith, *op. cit.,* pp.   [33]1 Cor. 15:29.
    222-223.

dispensation. It is our duty to save the dead and that work will continue during the millennium until all are endowed and sealed who are entitled to this blessing.[34]

SALVATION FOR DEAD IN LATTER-DAYS. The work of saving the dead has practically been reserved for the dispensation of the fulness of times, when the Lord shall restore all things. It is, therefore, the duty of the Latter-day Saints to see that it is accomplished. We cannot do it all at once, but will have the 1,000 years of the millennium to do it in. In that time the work must be done in behalf of the dead of the previous 6,000 years, for all who need it. Temples will be built for this purpose, and the labor in them will occupy most of the time of the saints.[35]

By the time Christ comes we are expected to have done all that is within our power to do now for our dead. That does not mean we are going to do all that is to be done, because it will go on during the millennium. The great work of the millennium will be the salvation of the dead, and those who are on the other side will help us, too, by bringing us information. The ordinances for the salvation of the dead are mortal ordinances, because all these ordinances pertain to this life, and immortal beings cannot perform them.[36]

MILLENNIUM: GREAT ERA OF SALVATION FOR THE DEAD. Some people may think that it is impossible for us to do this work for the dead because we have not the names of people who lived in ancient times. We have not the records, we do not know how to reach them from anything we have in this life, and there have been millions of people who no doubt were honest, and did the best they knew, but died without a knowledge of the gospel, whose names it is impossible for us to obtain. How are they going to be saved?

[34]*Church News,* Jan. 13, 1934, p. 8.   [36]*Gen. & Hist. Mag.,* vol. 31, p. 200.
[35]*Salvation Universal,* pp. 18-19.

It is our duty to go to the temple and take our records and work for the dead of our own lineage as far back as we can go, but what about these others? I will tell you. *The great work of the millennium, of 1,000 years, will be for the salvation of these souls.*

Now let us keep it clearly in our minds that we do not enter into exaltation until *after* the resurrection. We do not enter into exaltation in the spirit world. We have privileges there, of course, based upon faithfulness and obedience to the gospel, but during the millennium—and that is the great purpose of the millennium—we will go into the temples.

GENEALOGICAL RECORDS TO BE REVEALED IN MILLENNIUM. Those who will be living here then will be in *daily* communication with those who have passed through the resurrection, and they will come with this information, this knowledge that we do not have and will give it to those who are in mortality saying, "Now go into the temples and do this work; when you get this done, we will bring you other names." And in that way every soul who is entitled to a place in the celestial kingdom of God will be ferreted out, and not one soul shall be overlooked.

The Lord has not overlooked these things. He has seen the end from the beginning. Every name is recorded. Bless your soul, when the Lord says that a sparrow cannot fall without the notice of the Father, do you think he will overlook the people who lived upon this earth, who have tried to the best of their ability to live righteously, but never had the privilege of receiving the gospel? He will give unto them these privileges of salvation and the right, through their obedience to the gospel which shall come unto them, of receiving exaltation in his kingdom.

To think anything less than this would be an evil thought. God is just. He is merciful, and while mercy cannot rob justice, yet in the wisdom of our Father in heaven every soul shall receive blessings according to his merits and according to the mercies of our Heavenly Father, and he will do for the people the best he can.[37]

SALVATION FOR DEAD RESTORED

REVEALED LINE UPON LINE. This work of salvation for the dead came to the Prophet like every other doctrine —piecemeal. It was not revealed all at once. When the Angel Moroni came to the Prophet Joseph Smith, one of the things he told him was that the hearts of the children should turn to their fathers and the hearts of the fathers to the children, so that when the Lord should come the earth should not be smitten with a curse. That is significant. That was the first inkling the Prophet had concerning salvation for the dead, and he did not know just what it meant. He had a very vague idea of the meaning of the words that Elijah would come to "plant in the hearts of the children the promises made to the fathers," and I suppose he pondered over it a good deal.[38]

And then in January of 1836 he received a revelation in which the Lord said, "All who have died without a knowledge of this gospel, who would have received it if they had been permitted to tarry, shall be heirs of the celestial kingdom of God; also all that shall die henceforth without a knowledge of it, who would have received it with all their hearts, shall be heirs of that kingdom"; and, further, that little children who die are heirs of the celestial kingdom.[39]

FULL GLORY OF SALVATION FOR DEAD REVEALED. That was another step in relation to salvation for the dead, and the Prophet still marveled over it and, I suppose, wondered just what that meant and how it would be brought to pass. And then that same year, on the 3rd day of April, Elijah came and restored his keys, and after the restoration of the keys the Prophet received the

---

[37]*Church News,* Jan. 5, 1935, pp. 7-8.   [39]Smith, *op. cit.,* p. 107.
[38]Mal. 4:5-6; *D. & C.* 2:1-3; Joseph Smith, 2:38-39.

inspiration of the work of salvation for the dead and *the full glory of this doctrine was made known.*[40]

After the coming of the angel, and the restoration of these keys, Joseph Smith received further light, and it was made known to him in plainness that *every* principle of truth that pertains to the salvation of man living must be applied to the salvation of those who are worthy of salvation who are dead; and hence, the doctrine of salvation for the dead began to be taught.

In the drivings and persecutions which followed in Missouri, very little was said upon this subject, and the first public discourse upon the question of salvation for the dead was delivered in Nauvoo in the year 1840, at the funeral services of Elder Seymour Brunson.[41]

FIRST MODERN BAPTISMS FOR DEAD. The first baptisms for the dead in this dispensation, of course, were in the Mississippi River at Nauvoo. That was a right granted to the Church under peculiar conditions. Today no baptism for the dead would be valid if performed in a stream of any kind or in a lake or any principal body of water, because the Lord has decreed that the work for the dead—whether baptisms or endowments or sealings—is to be performed in a house that has been built to his holy name, a temple; and he tells us that it is only in the days of poverty that this rite may be performed in some other place than the house of the Lord.[42]

The saints of the primitive Christian Church did not have access to a temple. The temple in Jerusalem was the only temple, and it had fallen into the hands of unbelievers—wicked men—and therefore those members of the Church in that dispensation could not perform this labor for dead in the temple. Therefore all ordinances they performed for the dead had to be performed elsewhere.

---

[40]*Gen. & Hist. Mag.,* vol. 31, pp. 198-199; *D. & C.* 110:13-16.

[41]*Church News,* Jan. 5, 1935, p. 6.
[42]*D. & C.* 124:25-39.

ENDOWMENT OF PETER, JAMES, AND JOHN. Now
under these conditions, when there is no house of the
Lord and the work is urgent, the Lord makes it possible
that not only baptism for the dead but also the ordinances
that pertain to the house of the Lord may be performed
in the wilderness, on a mountain top, or in a lake or a
stream of water. I am convinced in my own mind that
when the Savior took the three disciples up on the mount,
which is spoken of as the "Mount of Transfiguration,"
he there gave unto them the ordinances that pertain to
the house of the Lord and that they were *endowed*. That
was the only place they could go. That place became holy
and sacred for the rites of salvation which were
performed on that occasion.[43]

BAPTISM FOR DEAD IN NAUVOO TEMPLE. This
privilege to baptize in the river continued from the time
they were granted this privilege in 1840 until the con-
ference in October of 1841, and at this October confer-
ence the Prophet declared that there should be no more
baptisms for the dead in the river and there should be
no more baptisms for the dead anywhere until that
ordinance could be performed in the house of the Lord.

Now the Nauvoo Temple was not finished, but the
structure had risen high enough so that the basement
could be covered over, and the basement, of course, is
the place where the font of the temple is. A *temporary*
font was put in that basement; it was dedicated, and on
the 21st of November baptisms for the dead began in the
temple of the Lord in real earnest. President Brigham
Young dedicated that font. Baptisms for the dead continued, under the direction of the Prophet, in the Nauvoo
Temple from the time of the dedication of the font until
our people were driven away from Nauvoo.[44]

TEMPLE WORK CONTINUES IN CHURCH. The spirit
of this work, which had rested so abundantly upon the

---

[43]Matt. 17:1-13.   [44]*Gen. & Hist. Mag.*, vol. 31, pp. 193-
194; D. H. C., vol. 4, pp. 426, 466.

Prophet Joseph Smith, continued with all its power and authority with President Brigham Young. One of the first commandments he received from the Lord, after entering the Salt Lake Valley, was to build a temple to the Lord's name where these ordinances for the salvation of both the living and the dead could be performed. From that day to this, the spirit of temple building and of temple work has continued unabated with the Church.[45]

The first endowments for the dead in this dispensation were performed in the St. George Temple. Endowments for the living were performed in Nauvoo. Even as far back as the days of the Kirtland Temple a *partial* endowment was given for the living.[46]

CHURCH TO BE REJECTED UNLESS TEMPLE WORK DONE. Some of those who would destroy the work of God, have declared that the Church was rejected, with its dead, because the temple at Nauvoo was not finished; and, say they, the Lord, by revelation, declared that he would give the saints sufficient time to build a house (temple) unto him, and if they failed to build it in the sufficient time, they would be rejected with their dead.[47] The fact is, the Nauvoo Temple was built, and many of the saints received their endowments in it and labored for their dead before they were finally driven. from Nauvoo by their enemies.

But the meaning of this revelation is perverted; *the Lord did not say he would reject the Church, with its dead, if they failed to build the temple, but that they would be rejected if they did not perform the ordinances for their dead in the temple when it was prepared for that purpose.*

VICARIOUS ORDINANCES MUST BE DONE IN TEMPLE. Here is the commandment in question: "But I command you, all ye my saints, to build a house unto me;

---

[45]*Era,* vol. 20, p. 198.
[46]Pers. Corresp.; *D. H. C.,* vol. 2, pp 379-380.
[47]"Those who would destroy the work of God" are members of the so-called Reorganized Church of Jesus Christ of Latter Day Saints.

and I grant unto you a sufficient time to build a house unto me, and during this time your baptisms [i.e. baptisms for the dead outside of a temple] shall be acceptable unto me.

"But behold, at the end of this appointment [i.e. the sufficient time] your baptisms for your dead shall not be acceptable unto me [i.e. outside of a temple]; *and if you do not these things [i.e. temple ordinances] at the end of the appointment ye shall be rejected as a church, with your dead,* saith the Lord your God.

"For verily I say unto you, that after you have had sufficient time to build a house to me, wherein the ordinances of baptizing for the dead belongeth, and for which the same was instituted from before the foundation of the world, your baptisms for your dead [i.e. in any other place than in a temple] cannot be acceptable unto me; For therein are the keys of the holy priesthood ordained, that you may receive honor and glory.

"And after this time [when a house is prepared], your baptisms for the dead, by those who are scattered abroad, are not acceptable unto me, saith the Lord."[48]

ORDINANCES GREATER THAN THE TEMPLE. "And if ye do not these things at the end of the appointment," obviously does *not* mean "if ye do not build a temple at the end of the appointment," as our critics infer it does, but it refers to the *ordinances* that were to be performed in the temple; and *the failure on the part of the saints to perform these ordinances for their dead was the thing that would cause their rejection with their dead, not the failure to build the temple,* which was merely the edifice in which the saving principles were to be performed. This is in harmony with the teachings of the Prophet Joseph Smith, who said that if we neglect the salvation of our dead, we do it at the peril of our own salvation! Why? Because we without them cannot be made perfect.[49]

---

[48]D. & C. 124:31-35.   [49]Smith, *op. cit.,* pp. 193, 337-338.

The virtue of salvation for the dead is not in the structure of the temple, but in the ordinances which are performed in the temple. The temple is to the ordinances just what the vessel is to the life-giving nourishment it contains. Those who would reject us on a technicality, because, as they say, "we did not finish the temple," neither build temples nor perform the ordinances for the dead, wherein they prove their rejection by the Lord, according to the revelations of Joseph Smith, the Prophet.[50]

NO SALVATION WITHOUT OUR DEAD

SEALING POWER CONTINUES FAMILY IN ETERNITY. *The doctrine of salvation for the dead, of temple work, holds out to us the glorious prospect of the continuance of the family relation.* Through it we learn that family ties are not to be broken, that husbands and wives will eternally have a claim upon each other and upon their children to the latest generation. However, in order to receive these privileges, the sealing ordinances in the temple of our God must be obtained.

All contracts, bonds, obligations and agreements made by men shall come to an end, but the obligations and agreements entered into in the house of the Lord, if faithfully kept, will last forever. This doctrine gives us a clearer concept of the purposes of the Lord toward his children. It shows his abundant and unlimited mercy and love to all who obey him, aye, even to those who are rebellious, for in his goodness he will grant great blessings even unto them.[51]

MEMBERSHIP IN FAMILY OF GOD. When everything gets finished, we will all be one family—every member of the Church a member of one family, *the family of God.* And we will all be subject to our first progenitor, Adam, Michael, the archangel, who has been appointed and given authority under Jesus Christ to stand at the head

---

[50]*Salvation Universal*, pp. 21-22.   [51]*Era*, vol. 20, pp. 362-363; D. & C. 132:7-17.

and preside over all his posterity.[52] We are one family. And we all have to be joined to that family. So it is not merely enough that we be baptized for our dead or for ourselves, but also we have to be sealed to our parents. We must have the parents sealed to their parents and so on, as far back as we can go, and eventually back to Adam.

There will be cases where some of our ancestors will not be worthy and will drop out, but the links will have to be joined without them. So when the Prophet says we cannot be saved or exalted without our dead, he had this in mind.[53] Suppose we do not do any work for our ancestors. Then where are we? We are out on a limb. We leave ourselves on the side lines. We are not joined into this great family. We may be born under the covenant and thus belong to our parents, but where there are breaks in that lineage we are not united.

SEALINGS ESSENTIAL TO MEMBERSHIP IN GOD'S FAMILY. And, therefore, when the Prophet says we cannot be exalted without them, he is thinking of the family connections—generation to generation. And if we are going to sit down and do nothing and let our ancestors whose history we can obtain go without having their work done, we are just setting ourselves off on the side. We are not members, we do not have the credentials which permit us into that family. You see how important it is that we labor for our dead?[54]

Why do we go into the temples to be sealed, husbands and wives, and children to parents, and why are we commanded to have this work done, not only for ourselves, but also to be sealed to our fathers and mothers, and their fathers and mothers before them, back as far as we can go? Because we want to belong to that great family of God which is in heaven, and, so far as the Church is concerned, on earth. That is why.[55]

---

[52]D. & C. 78:15-16.
[53]Smith, op. cit., 337-338; D. & C. 128:15.
[54]Pers. Corresp.
[55]Conf. Rep., Oct., 1948, p. 154.

No Perfection Without Our Dead. Now, some members of the Church have wondered just what was meant by the words of the Prophet, that we without our dead could not be made perfect. Will not a man who keeps the commandments of the Lord, who is faithful and true so far as he himself is concerned, receive perfection? *Yes, provided his worthy dead also receive the same privileges, because there must be a family organization, a family unit, and each generation must be linked to the chain that goes before in order to bring perfection in family organization.* Thus eventually we will be one large family with Adam at the head, Michael, the archangel, presiding over his posterity. . . .

Perfection Comes Through Celestial Family Organization. We are taught in the gospel of Jesus Christ that the family organization will be, so far as celestial exaltation is concerned, one that is *complete* — an organization linked from father and mother and children of one generation, to the father and mother and children of the next generation, thus expanding and spreading out down to the end of time. If we fail to do the work, therefore, in the temples for our dead, you see our links in this chain—genealogical chain—will be broken; we will have to stand aside at least until that is remedied.

We could not be made perfect in this organization unless we are brought in by this selective or sealing power, and if we have failed to do the work for those of our line, who have gone before, we will stand aside until somebody comes along who will do it for us. And if we have had the opportunity and have failed to do it, then naturally we would be under condemnation, and I think *all through eternity we would regret the fact that we had failed* to do the thing that was placed before us to do and which was our duty to accomplish in the salvation of the children of men.[56]

---

[56]Conf. Rep., Apr., 1942, p. 26.

No Salvation Without Our Worthy Dead. The expression about not being saved without our dead is greatly misunderstood. We will all be saved without *some* of our dead, without any question. The Lord cannot save the wilfully wicked, and they will not be saved, nor will those be who refused to accept the work. This expression means that *we cannot be saved without our dead who prove themselves worthy of salvation.* The Lord will not save all of his family. One third of them rebelled in pre-existence. We are doing the genealogical work for those who died before the gospel was restored and who did not have the chance, not for those who had all the chance in the world and would not receive it.[57]

POLICIES GOVERNING TEMPLE SEALINGS

Ordinances Not to be Performed for All. Some people think we have got to do the work in the temple for everybody. *Temple work belongs to the celestial kingdom, not to the other kingdoms.* There will be millions of people, countless as the sands upon the seashore, who will not enter into the celestial kingdom. That we are told in these revelations.[58] *There will be no need to do temple work for them.*

To be exalted in the celestial kingdom one must be endowed and receive the sealing blessings. There will be many who will enter that kingdom as servants, but only those who comply with all the laws and covenants will be exalted.

No Blessing Will Be Denied the Faithful. *Those who have been faithful members of the Church and could not reach a temple while living will have the work done for them after they are dead.*

We have the assurance that the Lord will reward every soul according to his or her works. He will judge each of us by the intent of the heart. If any worthy person is denied in this life the blessings which so readily come

---

[57]Pers. Corresp.   [58]*Church News,* Jan. 5, 1935, p. 7; D. & C. 76:108-112.

to others, and yet lives faithfully and to the best of his or her ability in striving to keep the commandments of the Lord, then nothing will be lost to him. Such a person will be given all the blessings that can be given. The Lord will make up to him the fulness after this life is ended and the full life has come. The Lord will not overlook a single soul who is worthy, but will grant to him all that can be given which those, apparently more fortunate, received in this life.

No Match-making for the Dead. We never make matches for the dead in the temples. The Lord will bless all who are worthy of the blessings, and they will lose nothing. The work of the millennium will be largely work for the dead who did not have an opportunity when living to obtain the blessings, but who would have accepted the blessings if they had lived. Justice demands this. We need not worry, therefore, because young men or young women die without being married. All who are worthy will be blessed just the same as if they had lived and obtained the blessings. Where, however, a couple is engaged and the woman dies, she may be sealed to her intended husband.

Adjustment of Sealings During Millennium. Children who are legally adopted may, *under proper circumstances,* be sealed into the families who adopted them. It is not possible, however, to rob the dead of their children, if they are entitled to them, even if they are adopted by others.

If a man or a woman who has been sealed in the temple for time and eternity should sin and lose the right to receive the exaltation in the celestial kingdom, he or she could not retard the progress of the injured companion who had been faithful. Everyone will be judged according to his works, and there would be no justice in condemning the innocent for the sins of the guilty.

We may be sure that the Lord is not going to permit any ordinance which we perform incorrectly, through our lack of understanding, to be left binding forever without correction. During the millennium there will be a great deal of adjusting where we, for lack of proper knowledge, have performed sealings ignorantly, but according to our best judgment.

ONLY MORTALS CAN PERFORM TEMPLE ORDI-NANCES. Will resurrected beings during the millennium actually take part in the endowment work of the temple along with mortal beings?

The answer to this question is no! That is, they will not assist in performing the ordinances. Resurrected beings will assist in furnishing information which is not otherwise available, but mortals will have to do the ordinance work in the temples.

Baptism, confirmation, ordination, endowment, and sealings all pertain to this mortal life and are ordinances required of those who are in mortality. Provision has been made for these ordinances to be performed vicar-iously for those who are worthy but who died without the opportunity in this life of receiving these ordinances in person.

You can readily see that it would be inconsistent for a resurrected being to come and be baptized for the dead. The resurrected person has passed to another sphere where the laws and blessings do not pertain to this mortal life. This is equally true of every other ordi-nance. *If it were permissible for resurrected persons to come and do work in the temples, then there would be no reason for us in this mortal life to act vicariously for them, for they would do it for themselves.*

HOW SOON WORK MAY BE DONE AFTER DEATH. How soon after death can the work for a person be done in the temple? It makes no difference as to the length of time when work is done for one who dies without obtaining the blessings in the temple. The Brethren have ruled that some considerable time should elapse because people desired to have the endowment performed for the dead before burial, and this was not deemed to be right.

If a person is in every way worthy of the blessings and was denied them while living, then any time after death the ordinances may be performed. If the person had every opportunity to receive these blessings in person and refused, or through procrastination and lack of faith did not receive them, then he is not entitled to them, and it is doubtful if the work for him will be valid if done within one week or 1,000 years. The Lord has declared that it is he who endures to the end that shall be saved, and he who rejects or neglects these blessings until death, when he has had the opportunity, is not worthy of them.[59]

GET TEMPLE RECOMMENDS WELL IN ADVANCE. A stake president recently complained that he is beseiged at all times and hours, seasonable or unseasonable, by last minute seekers after temple recommends. They approach him in the midst of public meetings; they burst into his office while he is in consultation with clients on important cases; one even solicited his signature while he was in the pool at the Deseret Gymnasium. He pleads that something be done to persuade people desiring recommends to attend the temple to take sufficient forethought so they may know some time in advance when they wish to attend the temple and thus be able to see their bishop and stake president in a proper manner.[60]

PRIESTHOOD BRETHREN NEEDED TO DO TEMPLE WORK. The day has arrived for the priesthood of the Church to take its rightful place in temple service and to set an example to all in the performance of ordinance work for those now in the spirit world, not having had the opportunity of embracing the gospel in life. . . .

Even now there are spirits of numerous men who lived their lives upon earth, and who through no fault of their own await the privileges of the gospel ordinances.

59Pers. Corresp.; Alma 34:31-34; 2 Ne. 27:15-19, 33; D. & C. 132:20-25. 60Era, vol. 48, p. 671.

Perhaps their wives and daughters have years ago been baptized and endowed; they and their sons are forced to wait because no man bearing the priesthood has come to the rescue. None of these families can thus be sealed for eternity in an eternal family union. Delay to them must be disappointing in the extreme.[61]

BLESSINGS COME FROM TEMPLE WORK. I wish to commend all those who have spent their time and means in this worthy cause. There are many good, humble souls who have deprived themselves of the comforts, and at times the necessities of life, in order that they might prepare the records and perform the labor for their dead that the gift of salvation might be taken unto them. These labors of love shall not go for naught, for all those who have worked in this goodly cause shall find their treasure and riches in the celestial kingdom of God. Great shall be their reward, yea, even beyond the power of mortals to understand.[62]

---

[61]*Church News*, Mar. 27, 1949, p. 21.   [62]*Gen. & Hist. Mag.*, vol. 26, p. 6.

CHAPTER 10

SALVATION FOR THE LIVING

NO SECOND CHANCE FOR SALVATION

NOW IS DAY OF OUR SALVATION. Our scriptures are very explicit in their declaration in relation to the requirements made of sons and daughters of God. *They who overcome all things are to be crowned as sons and daughters of God and be members of the Church of the Firstborn.*[1]

We are taught in the *Book of Mormon:* "For behold, *now is the time and the day of your salvation; . . . this life is the time for men to prepare to meet God; yea, behold the day of this life is the day for men to perform their labors.*"[2] These people to whom Amulek was speaking had heard the truth and were not altogether ignorant of the plan of salvation, because they had gone out of the Church by apostasy. So he declared unto them that this is the day for them to repent and turn unto God or they would be lost.[3]

The Lord, in his mercy, grants to every soul the privilege of repentance and the blessings of the gospel. If men do not receive this privilege here, they will receive it in the spirit world, for it must come to all. *If they reject it here, they may not receive the fulness in eternity.*[4]

THOSE WHO HAVE A FUTURE DAY OF SALVATION. On January 21, 1836, Joseph Smith received the following revelation: *"All who have died without a knowledge of the gospel, who would have received it if they had been permitted to tarry, shall be heirs of the celestial*

---

[1]Rev. 21:7; *D. & C.* 76:51-60.   [3]*Rel. Soc. Mag.*, vol. 6, p. 466.
[2]*Church News*, Feb. 1, 1936, p. 5;   [4]*Church News*, Feb. 1, 1936, p. 5.
   Alma 34:31-32.

*kingdom of God; also all that shall die henceforth without
a knowledge of it, who would have received it with all
their hearts, shall be heirs of that kingdom, for I, the Lord,
will judge all men according to their works, according to
the desire of their hearts."*[5]

What a wonderful ray of light is here thrown on
the question of man's redemption! If Joseph Smith had
made no other contribution to the world than to restore
this divine truth, it would have stamped him as one of
the greatest benefactors of the race.

One very significant thing in this revelation, which
should be remembered, is the fact that the Lord did *not*
say that all who are dead are entitled to these blessings
in the celestial kingdom, if they hear the gospel in the
spirit world, but all who would have received the gospel
had they been given the opportunity in this mortal life.
*The privilege of exaltation is not held out to those who
have had the opportunity to receive Christ and obey his
truth and who have refused to do so.*

OFFER OF SALVATION MADE EITHER NOW OR IN
SPIRIT WORLD. The justice of the Lord is manifest in
the right he grants to all men to hear the plan of salvation and receive it. Some have that privilege in this life;
if they obey the gospel, well and good; if they reject it,
then in the spirit world the same opportunities with the
same fulness do *not* come to them.

If they die without that opportunity in this life, it
will reach them in the world of spirits. The gospel will
there be declared to them, and if they are willing to
accept, it is counted unto them just the same as if they
had embraced it in mortality. In this way justice is meted
out to every man; all are placed on an equality before
the bar of God.[6]

*Those who have the opportunity here, those unto
whom the message of salvation is declared, who are*

---

[5]Joseph Fielding Smith, *Teachings of*   [6]*Millennial Star*, vol. 89, pp. 771-772.
the Prophet Joseph Smith, p. 107;
D. & C. 128:5.

*taught and who have this truth presented to them in this
life—yet who deny it and refuse to receive it—shall not
have a place in the kingdom of God. They will not be
with those who died without that knowledge and who
yet accepted it in the spirit world.*

SOME NOT ELIGIBLE FOR VICARIOUS SALVATION.
There are too many people in this world, who have heard
the message of the gospel, who think they can continue
on to the end of this mortal life, living as they please, and
then accept the gospel after death and friends will perform the ordinances that they neglect to perform for
themselves, and eventually they will receive blessings in
the kingdom of God. This is an error.

It is the duty of men in this life to repent. *Every
man who hears the gospel message is under obligation
to receive it.* If he fails, then in the spirit world he will
be called upon to receive it, but he will be *denied* the
fulness that will come to those who in their faithfulness
have been just and true, whether it be in this life or in
the spirit world.[7]

SECOND CHANCE LEADS TO TERRESTRIAL KINGDOM.
Moreover, we learn that those who *rejected* the gospel
when it was offered them in ancient times, but afterwards
accepted the "testimony of Jesus" in the spirit world
when it was declared to them, and who were honorable
men of the earth, are assigned to the terrestrial glory,
not the celestial.[8]

Then again, we are informed that the wicked of the
earth who do not repent in this life and who do not receive the gospel, shall be assigned to the telestial kingdom. In that kingdom they will become "servants of the
Most High; but where God and Christ dwell they cannot
come, worlds without end."[9]

---

[7]*Church News,* Aug. 5, 1939, p. 5.   [9]*D. & C.* 76:112.
[8]*D. & C.* 76:73-75; 1 Pet. 3:18-21;
    Moses 8:19-30.

All of these, however, will be called upon to repent. They will have to suffer the torments of the damned until they do, and through that suffering they will be brought to repentance and to acknowledge Jesus Christ as their Redeemer and the Son of God. Every knee must bow and every tongue confess, no matter which kingdom the inhabitants of the earth enter.[10]

FALSE NOTIONS ABOUT SALVATION FOR DEAD. Salvation for the dead is grossly misunderstood by many of the Latter-day Saints. It is due to the justice of our Eternal Father that *a chance* for salvation and exaltation is given to every soul. Some of the spirits rejected their privilege and rebelled in the former existence and had to be punished. All the others were granted bodies and the privilege of abiding in covenants here that would give them salvation, with the provision that any of the number coming to earth who, for causes over which they had no control, were denied the privileges of obedience to gospel covenants in the mortal life should have that privilege in the spirit world after death. But the Lord did *not* offer to those who had *every* opportunity while in this mortal existence the privilege of *another* chance in the world of spirits.

The endowment and sealing work for the dead is for those who died without having had the opportunity to hear and receive the gospel; also, for those who were faithful members of the Church who lived in foreign lands or where, during their life time, they did not have the privilege to go to a temple, yet they were converted and were true members of the Church. The work for the dead is not intended for those who had every opportunity to receive it, who had it taught to them, and who then refused to receive it, or had not interest enough to attend to these ordinances when they were living.

So many of the members of the Church have the

---

[10]*Church News,* Feb. 1, 1936, p. 5;
    D. & C. 76:109-112.

thought that if they do not do the work for dead friends, they are sure to be neglected and the opportunity will never come to them. We should remember that in his justice the Lord will never permit one soul to be lost who is worthy of salvation. Every person who is entitled to the blessings will receive them.[11]

TEMPLE WORK NOT FOR REBELLIOUS

CANNOT FORCE TEMPLE BLESSINGS ON DEAD. This idea that some of us have that we can go into the temple and perform the ordinances for the people who have been bitter against the truth, have known the truth and had every opportunity to receive the gospel and have refused to receive it, this idea that when they die we can go to the temple and do the work for them, is not in keeping in any sense with the revelations the Lord has given us.[12]

We may be sure that the Lord is just, and no man will be denied any blessing to which he is entitled. *Neither will any man receive that to which he is not entitled, even though we should endeavor to give it to him by the ordinances of the house of the Lord.* It is far better for us to leave some matters in the hands of the Lord, especially in the case of those who turn away from the Church and die unrepentant.[13]

We are not going to save and exalt in the celestial kingdom all the children of our Heavenly Father through our vicarious labors. Only those will enter into celestial glory who are worthy of it, and if we perform labor in the temples for those who are unworthy, they shall not be entitled to those blessings simply because we have worked for them.

JUDGMENT OF DEAD IS ACCORDING TO THEIR WORKS. It is our duty to perform the ordinance work for the dead, and then *the Lord will do the adjusting.* I believe that every accountable man, if he is to gain sal-

---

[11]Pers. Corresp.
[12]*Gen. & Hist. Mag.,* vol. 31, p. 197.
[13]Pers. Corresp.; 3 Ne. 12:20; 28:34-35.

vation, must receive a remission of sins by baptism, either in this life, or by proxy if he is dead. It behooves us to perform baptisms and all other ordinances for those who are dead.

Not all who are baptized for will be entitled to the blessings of the endowment. Not all will be entitled to the sealing ordinances, but that is in the hands of the Lord, and he will judge whether a man is worthy or not. We will perform the work, and the Lord will determine the final result.

There is an expression given by John in the Book of Revelation as follows: "And I saw the dead, small and great, stand before God; and the books were opened: and another book was opened, which is the book of life: and the dead were judged out of those things which were written in the books, according to their works."[14]

From this we learn that the dead are to be judged according to their works, out of the things that are written in the books, and the judgment will be just. *If the life of an individual has been such that he is unworthy of celestial glory, all that we can do for him by our vicarious labors will not place him there. Salvation will be based on merit.*

REBELLIOUS DEAD DENIED SALVATION. It was revealed to the Prophet Joseph Smith in a vision in the Kirtland Temple, January 21, 1836, that "all who have died *without a knowledge of this gospel,* who would have received it if they had been permitted to tarry, shall be heirs of the celestial kingdom of God; also all that shall die henceforth *without a knowledge of it,* who would have received it *with all their hearts"*; also, that little children "who die before they arrive at years of accountability, are saved in the celestial kingdom of heaven."[15]

He did not see, however, the rebellious, the ungodly, the corrupt and filthy, and those who love and make a lie, as heirs of that kingdom. There is another place pro-

---

[14]Rev. 20:12.   [15]Smith, *op. cit.,* p. 107.

vided for them.[16] *Men cannot be thrust into the kingdom of God, irrespective of their worthiness or unworthiness, just because their relatives or friends perform labor for them after they are dead.*

VICARIOUS ORDINANCES NOT FOR REBELLIOUS. I have known of cases where individuals have died who were bitterly opposed to the Church, and had denied the faith and left the Church, and hardly had they died when relatives have appealed to the First Presidency for the privilege of having their work done for them in the temple. Such appeals have been made at times so that relatives of the person, who passed away under such unfavorable circumstances, might be able to give the deceased a burial according to the rites and customs of the Latter-day Saints. Now, all this is wrong.

What good is it going to do for us to perform in the temples ordinances for those who die with an unrepentant attitude of this kind? If they had the opportunity and would not receive the truth while living, can we force it upon them when they are dead? Is it within our power, because we labor in the vicarious work as proxies for them, to make them heirs of the celestial kingdom? No, it is not!

But, one will say: "Perhaps they will not receive these blessings now, but later they may do so, and therefore our labors will not be in vain." Let me ask you these questions: Where in the scriptures, or where in the revelations from the Lord, is it found written, that the man who dies in rebellious opposition to the gospel, who has once had the light and through transgression turned from it, or who rejected it after it was presented to him and who has been familiar with it all his life, shall become an heir of the celestial kingdom *even though he repents in the world of spirits?* Has the Lord promised that the rebellious, the wicked, these who reject this truth shall eventually, after repentance, become heirs of the celestial

---

[16]*D. & C.* 76:98-112; *Rev.* 22:14-15.

kingdom? I do not gather any such conclusion from my reading of the scriptures.[17]

APOSTATES EXCLUDED FROM SALVATION FOR DEAD. Oh, I wish we could destroy the idea that is in the minds of some that we can live in unrighteousness and actually turn against the truth, and then our children will come along after we are dead and have the work done for us, and all will be lovely, and we will receive the blessings. The Lord is the judge of all men, and if such a person is entitled to receive *any* blessings, he will get them. But read section 76 of the *Doctrine and Covenants* in regard to those who enter into the terrestrial kingdom and see what it says.[18]

Why, if the honorable men of the earth who receive not the gospel in this life when they have the chance, are consigned to that kingdom, are we going to have it within our power to act for the apostate—the man who is bitter in his soul, who has known the truth but has turned away from the light and rejected the gospel—and go into the house of the Lord and pull him into the celestial kingdom? That doctrine actually prevails in the minds of some. . . .

APOSTATE CHURCH AND SALVATION FOR DEAD. They have in the Catholic Church the doctrine of indulgences, and you will remember you have read in history how, during the Middle Ages particularly, a man by paying the price could receive the privilege, so far as the church could give it—there was no power in it!—to go out and sin. Even before the sin was committed, he could have promise of forgiveness.

They sold these indulgences. That is one of the main things that took Martin Luther out of the Catholic Church. He began to realize that the practice was wrong; it was not possible, not just or right for a person to sell forgiveness of sins for a price, either before or after the sin; and they used to do that. If a man wanted to go out

[17]*Rel. Soc. Mag.*, vol. 5, pp. 678-680.   [18]*D. & C.* 76:71-80, 86-87.

and sin, they had a schedule of prices, so Motley tells in his *Rise of the Dutch Republic*.[19] In the Catholic Church they offer prayers for the dead to get them out of purgatory. And people pay the priests to pray for the dead. Now that is a *corruption* of the doctrine of salvation for the dead.

TREND TOWARD APOSTATE CONCEPTS OF SALVATION FOR DEAD. I can see confronting us a danger, and a very serious danger, because some of our people are of the opinion that the work can be done for them or their relatives after they are dead, so it is not so necessary for them to be righteous here. They think when they die, they shall receive that work in its fulness and the necessary ordinances will be performed for them in the temple, which will entitle them to the full reward of the faithful. This false belief causes men and women to live lives of unrighteousness, with indifference to the gospel, with the idea in their minds that when they are gone their children will do the work, and they shall receive the blessing. *This is pernicious doctrine!*

I heard a man say, "I am not good enough to go into the temple of the Lord. I have my faults, I have my appetites that I acquired before I ever heard of the gospel. I am not good enough to go into the temple, but when I am dead, then my children can go in and do the work."

Now I have read to you the scripture.[20] I believe it is the word of God "with the bark on it," where the prophet of the Lord declared unto apostates and those who have heard the gospel that if they did not repent and come into the Church now, in this day of repentance, but continued to procrastinate their repentance unto the end, that the night would come when no work could be done for them, and their souls would be lost. I think that is pretty good scripture. I do not know how the Lord could do otherwise in justice.

[19]J. L. Motley, *Rise of the Dutch Republic*, vol. 1, pp. 71-72.   [20]Alma 34:30-35.

Now, mark you, I am not saying that there are not people who have come into the Church and gone out of it again, who did not understand the truth, and for whom the Lord will make allowances. He, of course, is going to judge every case! I cannot judge. I am speaking now generally; I have no individual case in mind. But the fact is, nevertheless, the Lord has declared what we must do to receive the fulness of the gospel and become sons and daughters. He has told us which class of people will enter into his kingdom. He has told us which people will enter into the third kingdom, and we have the privilege of choosing which kingdom it will be.[21]

SALVATION FOR WORTHY DEAD ONLY

GOSPEL ORDINANCES FOR CELESTIAL KINGDOM ONLY. I want to correct an idea that prevails very largely in the minds of many members of the Church. I know that this is discussed in our Gospel Doctrine classes, in our Mutuals, and in other places, because the question is brought to me frequently and they contend on it—the question whether or not the temple work will have to be performed for everybody upon the earth. I want to say to you *no*, absolutely *no*.

Now let us get this plainly in our minds. I think it is a self-evident truth that ought to impress us without any argument whatever. All of the ordinances of the gospel—baptism, laying on of hands for the gift of the Holy Ghost, the work in the temples for the salvation of the living and the dead—these ordinances, everything else, *all of the ordinances of the gospel pertain to the celestial kingdom of God.*[22]

We are not preaching the gospel with the idea of trying to save people in the terrestrial world. *Ours is the salvation of exaltation.* What we are trying to do with the gospel of Jesus Christ is to bring people back again, through the power of the priesthood and the ordinances

[21]*Rel. Soc. Mag.*, vol. 6, pp. 469-472.   [22]Smith, *op. cit.*, p. 12; *D. & C.* 76:51-52, 70; 84:74-75; 2 Ne. 9:23-24.

of the Church, as sons and daughters of God, receiving a fulness of the Father's kingdom. That is our endeavor.

VICARIOUS ORDINANCES NOT FOR ALL. *We are not going to do the temple work for everybody because it does not pertain to them. We are going to do the temple work for those who are entitled, through their faith and their repentance, to enter into the celestial kingdom.* But somebody says, "How do we know? We search our records for hundreds of years and do the work for all of them." Of course we do, because we cannot judge. I do not know whether one man is worthy and another is not.

The Lord has given us the privilege of doing the work for all of *our kindred,* with the hope, of course, on our part that all of them will receive the truth. Since we are of the house of Israel, our parents, generation by generation as they go back, also would be of the house of Israel, and hence they would be more likely to receive the gospel than would those who are pure gentiles.

Now if there are any in our lines we do work for in the temple who are unworthy or unwilling to receive the ordinances of the house of the Lord, then the Lord will be the judge. He will set that ordinance aside and it will not be accounted as done. That is in his hands. Our duty is to do the work the Lord has required at our hands for the salvation of our dead.[23]

SALVATION FOR RIGHTEOUS DEAD ONLY. The Lord has given us the opportunity to perform in the temples the necessary labor for the *righteous and repentant dead.* The Lord is not going to save all the world in the celestial kingdom. But all who would have received the gospel had it been declared to them in the flesh, shall receive it in the spirit world, and they become heirs of the celestial kingdom. So the Prophet Joseph Smith has taught us. Millions will enter into the other kingdoms. The Lord said the telestial kingdom will be filled with people as

---
[23]*Gen. & Hist. Mag.,* vol. 31, p. 196.

innumerable as the sands upon the shore, or the stars of heaven.[24]

MURDERERS DENIED VICARIOUS ORDINANCES. We are called upon to assist in saving our *own families*. This is the great duty the Lord has given to us. It is our privilege to go back and trace *our ancestors* as far as we can and then go to the temple and do the work for all of them. The Lord will judge whether they are worthy or not to receive what we have done. Remember, though, we do not have the privilege of performing the ordinances for murderers who shed innocent blood, nor for those who take their own lives. These are left in the hands of the Lord. If we find in our record one of this kind, we should pass him by and not attempt to do work for him. . . .

I cannot imagine a murderer like Nero, for example, having the work done for him and being entitled to the blessings of the celestial kingdom along with Isaiah who laid down his life for the truth. Men are to be graded, and every man will receive all that he is entitled to receive according to the laws of justice and mercy. It is for this purpose the Lord has prepared several glories, or kingdoms, and as Paul saw it, there will be glories as diversified as the magnitude of the stars. No one who is entitled to salvation or exaltation will be neglected.[25]

TEMPLE WORK AND ENDURING TO END

FOLLOW AVAILABLE LIGHT TO BE SAVED. Those who die without law will be redeemed, because they will be judged without law. But *all who have received law and who have known the truth in a degree will be judged according to the truth that they have known, and if they have not lived up to that which they have known, or which they have been taught or had the privilege of receiving, then they cannot enter into the celestial kingdom.*[26] It is, however, our duty to save the world, the dead as well

---

[24]D. & C. 76:109.
[25]*Gen. & Hist. Mag.*, vol. 21, pp. 152-153; 1 Cor. 15:40-41.

[26]2 Ne. 9:25-27; Mosiah 2:32-51; 3:11-12, 20-27; 4:5-7; 15:25-27; Alma 34:30-35; Moro. 8:22-26.

as the living. We are saving the living who will repent by preaching the gospel among the nations and gathering out the children of Israel, the honest in heart. We are saving the dead by going into the house of the Lord and performing these ceremonies—baptism, the laying on of hands, confirmation, and such other things as the Lord requires at our hands—in their behalf.[27]

TEMPLE BLESSINGS LOST THROUGH INDIFFERENCE. If you are slipping, if you are careless and indifferent and you violate the covenants you made when you went through the temple and you continue to do that, remember the Lord has said repeatedly that it is he who endures to the end who shall be saved. And if that is what you have been doing, that leaves you out. You will not gain salvation.

I will read you these words of our Savior himself as he stood before his disciples on this continent. He answered their questions, gave them instructions, and told them he came into the world to die, that he might draw all men unto him, *but not in the celestial kingdom:* "And my Father sent me that I might be lifted up upon the cross; and after that I had been lifted up upon the cross, that I might draw all men unto me, that as I have been lifted up by men even so should men be lifted up by the Father, to stand before me, to be *judged of their works,* whether they be *good* or whether they be *evil*—And for this cause have I been lifted up; therefore, according to the power of the Father I will draw all men unto me, that they may be judged according to their works."

UNFAITHFUL NEVER TO GAIN SALVATION. "And it shall come to pass, that whoso repenteth and is baptized in my name shall be filled; and *if he endureth to the end,* behold, him will I hold guiltless before my Father at that day when I shall stand to judge the world. And *he that endureth not unto the end, the same is he that is also hewn*

---

[27]Conf. Rep., Oct., 1911, p. 120.

*down and cast into the fire, from whence they can no more
return, because of the justice of the Father.* And this is
the word which he hath given unto the children of men.
And for this cause he fulfilleth the words which he hath
given, and he lieth not, but fulfilleth all his words."

"Oh," someone says, "the Lord is just and merciful.
He is a merciful God and when man repents, God will
give him these privileges. The Lord will reinstate him
after he is dead when he repents." Every man has to
repent eventually and every knee has to bow, even those
going into the telestial kingdom.

Now, it says here that this is the word which he
had given unto men and that he lieth not but fulfilleth
his word. I quote further: *"And no unclean thing can
enter into his kingdom; therefore nothing entereth into
his rest save it be those who have washed their garments
in my blood, because of their faith, and the repentance
of all their sins, and their faithfulness unto the end."*[28]

Now, every knee must bow, the Lord has said, and
every tongue confess that Jesus is the Christ; but that
does not mean the bowing or bending of the knee and
confessing Jesus as the Son of God is going to put people
in the celestial kingdom. The devils recognized him when
he was on the earth, and they cried out and called him
the Holy One. Think of it; they knew why he had come.
They recognized him as the Son of God.[29] But they did
not repent. They cannot repent.

WILFULLY REBELLIOUS DENIED REPENTANCE AND
SALVATION. It is possible for people to get so far in the
dark through rebellion and wickedness that the spirit of
repentance leaves them. It is a gift of God, and they get
beyond the power of repentance. How well Mormon
speaks of that, in reference to the people who turned
away with their eyes open, who turned against the truth
some 200 years following the coming of Christ. The

---

[28]3 Ne. 27:14-19.   [29]Matt. 8:28-31; Mark 5:6-10; Luke
                                       8:28-31; Acts 19:13-16.

people rebelled; Mormon speaks about them and their condition beyond the power of redemption because of their wickedness and the hardness of their hearts, which the Spirit of the Lord could not penetrate.

They sinned wilfully, and therefore salvation cannot come to them. It was offered to them, and they would not have it. They rejected it. They fought it and preferred to take the course of rebellion; and the Lord on one occasion said to Mormon, "You shall not preach to these people; they have turned against me and you shall not preach to them." He had a right to say that. Now why did he say that? Because they had every opportunity and would not receive the truth. They mocked at it, and so the Lord said, "You don't have to talk to them; there is no need to cry repentance to them any longer." And after a while Mormon still pleaded with the Lord to let him try again. It was useless.[30]

President Brigham Young said, "People who fight the truth don't stop fighting it after their death." Do not get the idea that everybody is going to repent and be saved. The Lord is going to do for every soul just the best that he can. But justice demands that each be placed where he fits himself, according to his works, and mercy cannot rob justice.[31]

AWFUL DESTINY OF REBELLIOUS. There can be no salvation without repentance. A man cannot enter into the kingdom of God in his sins. It would be a very inconsistent thing for a man to come into the presence of the Father and to dwell in God's presence in his sins.

. . .

I think there are a great many people upon the earth, many of them perhaps in the Church—at least some in the Church—who have an idea they can go through this life doing as they please, violating the commandments of the Lord and yet eventually they are going to come

---

[30]Morm. 1; 2; 3; 4; 5; Moro. 9; Hela.   [31]Pers. Corresp.; *Discourses of Brig-*
13:24-39.   *ham Young,* 2nd ed., pp. 576-583.

into his presence. They think they are going to repent, perhaps in the spirit world.

They ought to read these words of Moroni: "Do ye suppose that ye shall dwell with him [Christ] under a consciousness of your guilt? Do ye suppose that ye could be happy to dwell with that holy Being, when your souls are racked with a consciousness of guilt that ye have ever abused his laws?

"Behold, I say unto you that ye would be *more miserable to dwell with a holy and just God, under a consciousness of your filthiness before him, than ye would to dwell with the damned souls in hell.* For behold, when ye shall be brought to see your nakedness before God, and also the glory of God, and the holiness of Jesus Christ, it will kindle a flame of unquenchable fire upon you."[32]

Do you think that a man whose life has been filled with corruption, who has been rebellious against God, who has not had the spirit of repentance, would be happy or comfortable should he be permitted to come into the presence of God?[33]

---

[32]Morm. 9:3-5.   [33]*Church News*, Apr., 29, 1939, pp. 3, 6.

CHAPTER 11

THE DIVINE LAW OF RECORD KEEPING

PLACE OF HISTORY IN PLAN OF SALVATION

HISTORY: A GUIDE TO PROGRESS. History is the record of human progress and the accumulation of the experiences of the past. This may apply to every fact in life, whether it is the history of nations or individuals, the history of the earth, or the history of scientific research. Of course, in speaking of history we usually confine our thoughts to the annals of the human race.

History is obtained through written records and through tradition. *All records are history,* no matter what they are. All that deals with science, literature, art, or anything that pertains to the actions or welfare of man, his research, his study, his actions—all is circumscribed by history. However, we are dealing with the activities of men and nations.

The importance of written records of the lives of men and the activities of nations is apparent to everyone, because through them we have advanced in knowledge and power. We profit by the thoughts and actions of those who have gone before, because their experiences become ours as we put them into action. We profit by their mistakes and by their successful achievements. We accept the actions of the ages past, and thus, using our judgment, we gather out from that which has been recorded that which will be of benefit to us, and so we incorporate it in our lives.

HISTORY: AN AID TO CIVILIZATION. Without history and our knowledge of lands and peoples, we would be no better than the savage, or in an uncivilized condition. This is very clearly shown in the *Book of Mormon* by Nephi in his writings. He tells the story of how the Lord gave commandment to his father to send him and his brothers back to Jerusalem that they might bring the brass plates with them from Jerusalem to the land of promise. That record contained the genealogy of Lehi's family; it contained the five books of Moses and the prophecies of the prophets of old down to Isaiah and even some of the words of Jeremiah. This record was obtained under difficulties, and it was the foundation for the Nephite civilization in this new world.[1]

On the other hand we have the experiences of the Mulekites, who also came from Jerusalem, but without any record. Instead of increasing in knowledge and wisdom the opposite was the case, and when they were discovered by the Nephites, they were found in a semi-civilized condition. They had to be taken by the Nephites and taught in knowledge and wisdom. The Nephite people were outnumbered by their Mulekite relatives, but being wiser and having more knowledge they absorbed the less fortunate nation.[2]

FALSE SLANTING OF HISTORY. In regard to the recording of history, the thing that is most important is accuracy. *If history is not accurate, it is harmful.* It has been said that history is what historians declare it shall be, and many historians write with that thought in mind. Of course this is a deplorable situation, which we cannot help.

If you take history written 50 years ago by some writers of the North in relation to the Civil War and compare it with the writings of someone from the southern states, you will find a vast difference. If you go back 100 years and take histories of the United States and read the account in them of the struggles for independence and compare them with histories published by the British, you will find many differences, because men's minds are prejudiced, and their prejudice enters into their writings.

---

[1] Ne. 3; 4; 5.   [2] Omni. 1:12-18.

So when you read history, you do not always know whether you are reading the truth or not. . . .

FALSE NON-MORMON HISTORIES OF CHURCH. Articles have been published in eastern magazines purporting to be the history of President Brigham Young, but which are the embodiment of miserable rot, yet they continue to be read and believed by many.

For instance, one writer says that a man who had lost his leg came to President Young having faith and desiring to be healed and have his leg restored, and President Young said, "Yes, I can do it. I can give you a new leg, but if I do you will come up in the resurrection with three legs, and it is better to go through life with one than to come forth in the resurrection with three." That is the kind of rubbish that men put out as history, and many people are gullible enough to believe it. So when you read alleged history, you do not always know when you are reading the truth.

I could take you in the library of the Historian's Office in Salt Lake City and show you whole rows of books written by enemies of the Latter-day Saints, with scarcely a true statement in one of them. When you read of Rome, Greece, or any of these old countries, do you know if you are reading actually the events that took place? Well, you do not. You are reading what was reported by this historian and *some of it may be false.* This should not be the case with the Latter-day Saints, and it is not the case with the records written by inspiration of the Lord.

JUDGMENT OUT OF CHURCH BOOKS AND HISTORIES. *The most important history in the world is the history of our Church, and it is the most accurate history in all the world.* It must be so. It is the most important to us because that history contains the hand dealings of God direct to us through revelation as it has come in the *Doctrine and Covenants,* in the *Book of Mormon,* and in any revelation that comes to us through the servants of the Lord for our guidance.

Do you know that the time is coming when *we are going to be judged out of the books that are written?* Therefore we should make these records accurate; we should be sure of the steps we take. We are going to be judged out of the things written in books, out of the revelations of God, out of the temple records, out of those things which the Lord has commanded us to keep and have on file concerning the records of the people.[3]

There will be other records, of course, because if we happen to make mistakes, there will be the record in heaven which is a perfect record.[4] In our history, if there are mistakes, we can say as did Moroni in the *Book of Mormon,* "They are the mistakes of men."[5]

PLACE OF CHURCH IN RECORD KEEPING

ADAM COMMANDED TO KEEP GENEALOGICAL REC-ORDS. The Lord has always impressed upon his people the necessity of keeping records. In Adam's day, we are informed by Moses, the Lord commanded that records be kept. We read in the *Pearl of Great Price* that a *Book of Remembrance* was kept in the language of Adam and that his children were taught to read and write, having a language which was pure and undefiled. "Now this same Priesthood, which was in the beginning, shall be in the end of the world also. Now this prophecy Adam spake, as he was moved upon by the Holy Ghost, and *a genealogy was kept of the children of God.* And this was the book of the generations of Adam, saying: In the day that God created man, in the likeness of God made he him."[6]

And so they were commanded to keep records. They were not only commanded to keep a record of important

[3]2 Ne. 29:11; 3 Ne. 27:23-26; Rev. 20:12-13.
[4]D. & C. 128:6-8.
[5]Gen. & Hist. Mag., vol. 16, pp. 52-55, 58-59; Morm. 8:17.
[6]Moses 6:5-8, 46; Abra. 1:28, 31; Mal. 3:16; 3 Ne. 24:16; Ether 8:9; D. & C. 85:9.

events, but they were also to keep a record of their *families* and preserve it that it might be of benefit in time to come.

Right here I want to say just a word or two in regard to the thought which is so prevalent in the world today that in the beginning man had no written language—such teaching is false. It was through transgression and by turning from this channel of truth that men lost the power to record their thoughts and properly express them, and it is not the fault of God nor does it show any defect in his work.

LORD COMMANDS KEEPING OF HISTORIES AND REC-ORDS. Now coming down to our day, we have some of the words of the Lord given to us, recording our duty in relation to record keeping. The very day the Church was organized the Lord gave a revelation in which he said: "Behold, there shall be *a record kept among you;* and in it thou shalt be called a seer [referring to Joseph Smith], a translator, a prophet, an apostle of Jesus Christ, an elder of the church through the will of God the Father, and the grace of your Lord Jesus Christ."[7] From the very beginning, the first day of the organization of the Church, this commandment was given.

On the 8th day of March, 1831, the Lord gave an-other revelation in which he said: "Behold, it is expedient in me that my servant John [Whitmer] should *write and keep a regular history,* and assist you, my servant Joseph, in translating *all things* which shall be given you, until he is called to further duties."[8]

Oliver Cowdery was the first one appointed to assist Joseph in transcribing and keeping a history of the Church; John Whitmer took his place, when Oliver Cowdery was given something else to do. We have on file in the Historian's Office the records written in the hand writing of Oliver Cowdery, the first historian, or recorder of the Church.[9]

---

[7]*D. & C.* 21:1.
[8]*D. & C.* 47:1.

[9]*Gen. & Hist. Mag.,* vol. 16, pp. 53, 55-56.

INSPIRED HISTORIES AND RECORDS ARE ACCURATE. When you read the *Book of Mormon,* you know you are reading the truth. Why? Because God directed men to write events as they occurred, and he gave them the wisdom and inspiration to do this. Thus records were written by men who believed in God. These records never fell into the hands of apostates, but the historians wrote and spoke as they were moved upon by the Holy Ghost, and we know that *what they wrote is true, because the Lord has put his stamp of approval upon it.*[10]

How is it with the history of the Hebrews? We know that which Moses wrote is true because the Lord gave him inspiration. The five books of Moses, beginning with the creation of this earth, is a record we can rely upon as being true because it was done under the supervision, if you please, of our Father in heaven.

In the Historian's Office we gather a good many things which are not true. We have to take notice of the expressions and statements of the enemies of the people; we put them in our library and save them as the Lord has commanded us to do.[11] However, what shall remain as the history of the Church when that history is compiled, will be accurate, and if errors creep in it, the Lord himself will bring to pass means whereby they will be eliminated.

You pick up a record of the history of the Church and that record is *accurate.* It fell to my lot to prepare a volume of history,[12] and because I did not regard as true what our enemies have said, I have gone in for a little criticism myself. You may as well say that the *Book of Mormon* is not true because it does not give credence to the story the Lamanites told of the Nephites.

Nothing has had an influence upon the human race all down through the ages that the Hebrew record has had. It is the foundation of the civilizations of modern

---

[10]*Book of Mormon,* "Preface" and "Testimony of Three Witnesses"; Moro. 10:4-5; *D. & C.* 1:29; 6:17; 17:6; 18:2-3.

[11]*D. & C.* 123:1-17.
[12]Joseph Fielding Smith, *Essentials in Church History,* pp. 1-696.

times. Some men ridicule the *Bible;* they make fun of the prophets of old, and yet the *Bible* is the foundation upon which our civilization is built.

RESPONSIBILITY OF CHURCH OFFICERS FOR RECORD KEEPING. There are a great many duties in regard to keeping records and one is the duty of the clerk or historian to make accurate records, recording not only events that take place, but the biographies of the people, their faith, their works, and their diligence in keeping the commandments of the Lord, and these things we are doing in this Church.

We have a very good system of keeping records in the Church, and it is because of the commandments which have been given us by the Lord.[13]

Now I want to impress upon those who are keeping records in this Church the importance of record keeping. We are trying to get the clerks to follow the instruction which has been given them and send to us a detailed history of the stakes. We want the clerks in the wards to keep a detailed history of the wards and furnish information to us quarterly, that we may file it in the archives of the Church.

We are asking presidents of stakes, and bishops of wards, also mission presidents, carefully to supervise and scrutinize these prepared histories of the missions, and stakes, and wards and then sign with their own names the history before it comes to be filed in the archives of the Church, stating that to their best knowledge and understanding that which is written is correct. We want them to see that everything of importance is recorded. We are under the necessity very frequently of sending letters out to a great many of the stakes and some of the missions and asking them to see that the historical records which are delinquent are forwarded. We would like to have these records sent to us on time. . . .

---

[13]*Gen. & Hist. Mag.,* vol. 16, pp. 55-57.

QUALIFICATIONS OF CLERKS AND RECORDERS. Now, brethren, I am appealing to the presidents of stakes and bishops to see that these records are properly kept. Let me say further that the choosing of a clerk and recorder is a very important thing. Sometimes we think that anybody can keep a record. It requires intelligence to do so. A man ought to have keen discernment; he ought to be able to segregate facts; he ought to be able to choose and record the things that are important and separate them from the things that are perhaps unimportant and make a record of them.

Our custom in recording is to take more than we need rather than less. We can always eliminate if something is recorded that we do not need, but it is sometimes a very difficult thing to find something that we have overlooked.[14]

LAW OF PERSONAL RECORD KEEPING

INDIVIDUAL RESPONSIBILITY FOR RECORD KEEPING. Now what is our duty in regard to records? Is it necessary for each one of us individually to keep a daily journal? I would say not. *It is necessary for us to keep an accurate record of our families and record accurately the dates of births, marriages and deaths, and ordinances and everything that is vital. Every important event in our lives should be placed in a record, by us individually.* We do not do it. Some people keep a daily record; about like this: "Got up in the morning, made the beds, washed the dishes, went to the picture show, came home, went to bed"; and so it goes. That means nothing. If you have accomplished *something worth while* during the day, put it down; it may be of use to posterity. If our fathers had only done this, it would have been a great help to us today in gathering records of our dead.

In the days of Adam, genealogy was kept. In the days of Nephi how glad the people were when they received the records of their fathers, and hundreds of years

---

[14]Conf. Rep., Apr., 1934, pp. 17-19.

after Lehi came to the promised land, men could rise up and say, "I am a descendant of Nephi, or Jacob, or Zoram," because they kept these records.

It is just as important for me to know the date of my baptism as it is to know the date of my birth. Why? Because it is a vital thing in my life.

WHAT RECORDS WE SHOULD KEEP. What do we mean by *vital* records? We mean those records containing the dates of *births, marriages,* and *deaths,* the three great events in the life of the individual. Other vital things in the life of members of the Church are to know the dates of *blessing, baptism, ordinations* and other matters that pertain to our welfare and may be of benefit to our posterity.

I wonder, if I were to ask the question here, who could rise up and tell me the date of his baptism, who confirmed him a member of the Church, who ordained him to the priesthood? Birth into this Church is nearly as vital as birth into this world, and yet we do not pay much attention to it. People come to the temple to do work and do not know when they were baptized, and they have to make a guess that it was such and such a time and it was perhaps in such and such a place, but they do not know. We should not depend on the records of the Church too much, for some records may be lost, some may accidently be destroyed.

When the pioneers crossed the Mississippi River coming to this land under distressing circumstances, some of the records of branches were lost. One of the reasons why, when the people came here, President Young instituted baptism was that people claimed that they were members of the Church and had no records to show for it; but that was not the only reason. These records are important and while the Church has the duty upon it to keep an accurate record of the members of the Church, individually, their birth, blessing as a child, baptism, ordinations and so on, yet each member should keep it *also*, because he may want that information sometime when it cannot be obtained from the records of the Church.[15]

PATRIARCHAL RECORDS AND PRIVATE JOURNALS. All patriarchal records belong to the Church and not to the patriarchs who gave the blessings. Neither do they belong to the families of the patriarchs. When a patriarch has completed his record, or when he dies, the record should be sent to the Historian's Office to be filed. Many of these records have not been received, and in some instances the descendants of the patriarchs have claimed them as personal property; this is wrong.

Moreover, there are many important private journals scattered about which we would like to obtain for preservation and for historical purposes. We discover that when these are left in the keeping of the descendants of the pioneers, they frequently are lost, or lose their value by the time they reach the third or fourth generation, and are thrown away. If they are given to us, we will file them away where they will be preserved.[16]

GENEALOGICAL RESEARCH

PURPOSE OF GENEALOGICAL RESEARCH. Now the duty of a man in his own family is to see that he and his wife are sealed at the altar. If married out in the world before they joined the Church, or if they have been in the Church and have been unable to go to the temple, it is that man's duty to go to the temple, have his wife sealed to him and have their children sealed, so that the family group, that unit to which he belongs, is made intact so that it will continue throughout all eternity. That is the first duty that a man owes to himself, to his wife, and to his children. He receives this blessing by virtue of the priesthood.

Then it is his duty to seek his record as far back as he can go and do the same thing for each unit. He should begin with his father and mother and their children, and

_____
[15]*Gen. & Hist. Mag.*, vol. 16, pp. 57-58.   [16]Conf. Rep., Apr., 1934, p. 20.

his grandfather and his children, great-grandfather and his children, and have the work done in like manner, linking each generation with the one that goes before. That is the responsibility resting upon every man who is at the head of a household in this Church.

Now the Lord has not placed upon any man in this Church the responsibility of doing the temple work for his neighbor. If you want to help your neighbor, there is no objection. If he needs help and you can help him, he will appreciate it. But your responsibility is to do your own work for your *own* line, going from son to father, going clear back as far as you are able to carry this record. When you do that, then you place yourself in line, through the fulness of the priesthood, eventually to receive the fulness of the glory of God.[17]

LIMIT RESEARCH TO OWN KINDRED. No person has a right to select names promiscuously of any family and go to the temple to perform the work for them. This cannot be tolerated, for it would lead to *confusion* and *duplication* of work. Let each family do the work for their *own* dead kindred, as they may have the right, and if they do work for others, it must be *at the instance* and *with the consent* of the living relatives who are immediately concerned.

A few individuals have desired to do the work for men of renown, generals, presidents, magistrates, and others who have risen to prominent stations in the world. One object they apparently have in view is that they may say they have done the work for such and such persons. But there is an order in this work, as in all things pertaining to the gospel, and in no case should work be done in this manner, unless the circumstances are such that proper sanction of the temple authorities can be given.[18]

Some of us get so enthusiastic over this temple work that we are not willing to abide by the rules and the reg-

---

[17]*Gen. & Hist. Mag.*, vol. 30, pp. 1-3.   [18]*Salvation Universal*, pp. 31-32.

ulations and to *confine ourselves to our own line,* but we want to spread out into the other fellow's line, and we want to do the work because we readily find names that belong to somebody else, and that method of work for the dead is not permissible. It is all right to *help* others do their work, if we do that with *proper consent,* but each family group is *entitled* to do the work for its particular line.

LIMITATION ON DOING TEMPLE WORK FOR FRIENDS. A great many people are very anxious to do work for friends, and this thing has been carried to an extreme. We do not need to worry ourselves very much about friends. A man came to me a few days ago and presented two lists and said he wanted to do the work for these people because they were his friends. The oldest man of the group was born in 1710, and his children were born between 1730 and 1740, yet he called them his friends.

Now we should confine our activities to our own line. *If* there is a good reason for doing the work for somebody who had befriended us, somebody who would have accepted the gospel but did not have the opportunity and who has no relatives in the Church, that is a different matter, and we may be privileged to do the work, but we need not be overanxious to work for those not of our own lineage whom we list as friends.[19]

DO TEMPLE WORK IN AN ORDERLY WAY. The kingdom of God is a house of order because all things therein obey the law. The temples of the Lord on earth should also be orderly for the same reason. Temple work should not be done in a haphazard or disorderly way. Those who labor for the dead should endeavor to prepare their records in an orderly and systematic manner.

When names are copied in an improper way and incomplete records are sent to the temples, but one thing will be the result—*confusion.* The compilers of records

19Conf. Rep., Apr., 1942, pp. 26-27.

should try to find the information so that records can be made in family groups with all the necessary data for correct identification. When names are taken out of books without any accompanying information that will identify them, or show relationship to parents and other members of the family, little, if any, good can follow.

If work in the temples is done for such individuals, it is very incomplete and questionable. When the temple work is limited to baptizing and endowing because other ordinances cannot be performed for lack of information, it will more than likely have to be done *over again*. In this way the records are burdened with unnecessary matter which cannot be properly arranged.

Genealogical researchers will make fewer mistakes and in the end save time and means by giving more attention to their recording. It is the disposition of many of the people to hurry their work along in an unorganized fashion because of their zeal for temple work. Patience, accompanied by prayer and thorough research, will prove best in the end.[20]

PREPARE AND SUBMIT RECORDS WELL IN ADVANCE. The utmost care and intensive scrutiny should be given each family record submitted for baptism and endowment. This requires time. Those planning to come to the temple from a distance, whenever possible, should *think ahead several months* and submit their records to the index office well in advance of their visit, naming the date when the names will be required at the temple.

Numerous cases occur almost every day of persons arriving at the temple, bringing with them the names of those whose ordinances they wish to administer that very day, expecting that by some magic process the names can be cleared and in readiness for them in the course of an hour or so. Such people certainly have no conception of the care and time required to check names to avoid duplications, to type them upon cards and family

[20]*Gen. & Hist. Mag.*, vol. 20, pp. 41-42.

group sheets in duplicate, to proofread every card and family record so typed, and transmit the cards to the temple.

Some emergency cases are unavoidable, and marvels have been accomplished to accommodate patrons in such cases. But usually there is no need for unseemly rushing through of names, for a little careful pre-planning would have made all this unnecessary.

IMPORTANCE OF ACCURACY IN GENEALOGICAL RECORDS. One of the chief causes of delay in checking names for temple work is the prevalence of faulty records. Hundreds and hundreds of sheets must be returned because they cannot be read and properly interpreted. Errors are committed in the grouping of parents and children, children often being assigned to the wrong parents, and names of some children being omitted. Incorrect or incomplete statements of names, dates, places, and relationships are far too common. The Genealogical Society must therefore utilize the full time of many employees in straightening out poorly-compiled records.

If all family groups submitted were accurate, the time required for checking could be reduced tenfold. A censor can quickly scrutinize a *true* record and pass it on to the attendants in the index bureau to check for duplications, but one that is palpably erroneous and incomplete may require that the censor go to the library and refer to each of the records from which the data on the sheet was obtained, properly evaluate what is found and determine its proper interpretation. Such procedure has in some cases required a day and a half of the censor's time, and several hours attention from a supervisor also. A number of similar delays, of course, greatly extend the time required for passing upon all family group sheets received.

PURPOSE OF GENEALOGICAL SOCIETY. The Genealogical Society is doing far more than ever before to insure that every record approved for temple work shall be one hundred percent accurate. Our people should be aware of and appreciate this fine assistance being given and do all in their power to speed up the process by doing their part efficiently and well. They should take thorough pains in preparing every record for temple work and should send with the sheets clear instructions as to which temple the records when approved should be sent.[21]

The Society was organized for the following purposes:

1. To assist the saints to obtain genealogies of their ancestors.

2. To secure from all nations and peoples, so far as possible, genealogical records and deposit them in suitable quarters where they may be preserved for the perusal and benefit of members of the society.

3. To provide a place where the saints may be instructed in the best methods of keeping accurate and intelligent records of their temple work and be assisted in the clerical labor.

4. To increase the interest of the Latter-day Saints in the important work of salvation for the dead.

GENEALOGICAL SOCIETY NOT AN AUXILIARY ORGANIZATION. This organization came into existence shortly after the opening of the Salt Lake Temple in the spring of 1893. In the fall of 1894 President Wilford Woodruff, together with his counselors and a number of other leading brethren, one of whom was Franklin D. Richards, organized the Genealogical Society. This organization is very closely connected with the temples. *It is not an auxiliary.* Get that firmly fixed in your minds. The Sunday School, Primary, Mutuals and Relief Society, these are auxiliary organizations, but this organization is a part of the great temple work system of the Church. This organization is an aid to the temples and an aid to the Latter-day Saints in performing their labors in the temples. It has a place which is unique, peculiar to itself. It

---

[21]*Era,* vol. 48, p. 671.

has a position which is absolutely necessary in this Church and kingdom.[22]

BEWARE OF GENEALOGICAL "LINK-MEN." We are also troubled at times by what are known as *link-men,* individuals in the world who manufacture names so that they can complete unbroken a family line. This is done for the purpose of making money, and is, of course, *knavery* of the *worst kind.* Those who are guilty of this trickery do not understand salvation for the dead and may not fully realize the wickedness of such a course.[23]

QUALIFICATIONS OF WARD GENEALOGICAL WORKERS. The first thing in order to qualify as a worker in the genealogical work in the ward is to have a thorough knowledge of the principles of the gospel, a testimony of the mission of the Redeemer and of the mission of the Prophet Joseph Smith, and a firm faith in the efficacy of the work of salvation for the dead. This is the foundation on which to build.

Unless we are converted ourselves to any principle or to any truth, it will be impossible for us to teach it successfully to others. No person can understand temple work unless he has the abiding testimony of the Spirit of the Lord that the gospel is true, unless he is convinced in his heart that the principle of salvation reaches out and embraces every soul who is dead who is entitled to receive the remission of sins, and that the dead just as the living have that opportunity.

Next, a person in order to be a successful worker, whether it be in the ward or elsewhere in this work, should have the knowledge which is gained in the temple of the Lord. No person can fully qualify as a teacher or instructor or worker in genealogical work until he himself has been to the temple and received of the blessings there for himself. Then he will understand the necessity of these ordinances in behalf of the dead.

---

[22]*Gen. & Hist. Mag.,* vol. 13, p. 75.   [23]*Salvation Universal,* p. 32.

CHOOSE ENDOWED PERSONS AS GENEALOGICAL WORKERS. I realize that a person may be enthusiastic and may be converted to this work and may sense to some extent the necessity of it without having received the blessings of the house of the Lord himself, but he will not be fully equipped because he lacks knowledge and understanding, if he has not been to the temple and made himself familiar with the ordinances to be obtained therein.

Many times good sisters are interested in this work who are not privileged to go to the temple because, perchance, they have married outside of the Church, which is a regrettable thing. And yet realizing the importance of this labor, to some extent, they become interested and desire to labor in this work. But I would suggest that only those who have had the privilege of going through the house of the Lord should be called upon to act as workers to visit the people and teach them in regard to these important duties.

I would not discourage anyone else, rather I would encourage them to do all that they can in the gathering of records, in compiling them properly and other detailed matters concerning the preparation of work for the temple. But I maintain that in the wards as well as in the stakes, in order to be fully equipped and qualified, that persons acting in these capacities should receive the blessings of the house of the Lord.

CAPABLE PERSONS NEEDED AS GENEALOGICAL WORKERS. The ward genealogical worker should have some initiative, should be full of suggestions, should understand how, more or less, to read character, to discern the spirits of men and know how to approach individuals in order to impart unto them the message of salvation. All people cannot be approached alike; tact should be used. If a person is not converted to temple work, it would be impossible to go into his home and teach him temple work in the same manner that it would be possible to teach somebody who is already converted. A different approach would be necessary.

I regret to say that the idea has prevailed very largely in some quarters that a person who is good, but perhaps has never done anything very much, is suitable to act as a worker in genealogical work, either in the stake or in the ward. That idea, of course, is being overcome. But we have had to contend with that, more or less, in some stakes and some wards, because the presiding officers, perhaps the bishop, has felt that this was an honorary position only, and therefore he could call into this organization someone merely to give him a little honor, where there would be no labor attached to it. Therefore they have chosen individuals along in years who otherwise might be capable, but because of old age were not in a condition of health to visit among the people and to take this message of salvation to them.[24]

CHOOSING GENEALOGICAL RESEARCH CONSULTANTS. The Church does not approve of the solicitation of research orders in Sunday School classes or other Church meetings. It is the recommendation of the officers of the society that before a person is employed as a genealogical consultant that due consideration be given to his qualifications.

Some record gatherers have proffered to furnish our people with names for temple work at a definite price for each name. Such a method of procedure should act as a warning to anyone with the slightest degree of experience that accuracy and thoroughness would be a secondary matter in this method of research. We know of no reputable genealogist who would consent to do research on such a basis.[25]

DUTY TO PERFORM ORDINANCES FOR DEAD. The great responsibility resting upon the members of the Church today is to gather the records, which are now

---

[24]Gen. & Hist. Mag., vol. 13, pp. 66-67.   [25]Era, vol. 48, p. 408.

being published in the world by those who have partaken of this spirit and whose hearts have been turned toward their fathers, and perform the saving ordinances for those whose names can thus be obtained.[26]

---

[26]*Era*, vol. 20, p. 363.

CHAPTER 12

SPIRITUAL LIFE AND DEATH

THE SECOND DEATH

NATURE OF TEMPORAL OR PHYSICAL DEATH. What is spiritual death? This question has disturbed the peace of mind of many good people and has been a subject for discussion in religious bodies where the testimony of the Spirit of the Lord does not control. Yet, the answer to this question is not a difficult one and should be readily found by any member of the Church who is familiar with the scriptures.

Death, according to the accepted definition of the word, when applied to mortal man, *is a state of total and permanent cessation of all the vital functions, and it is followed by the dissolution of the body, which returns to the various elements of which it is composed.* "For dust thou art, and unto dust shalt thou return,"[1] was the decree of the Lord to Adam after his fall. When death takes place the spirit which is released finds its way into the realm prepared for departed spirits, there to await the resurrection when again spirit and body will be united to continue inseparably in the state of immortality throughout eternity.

PHYSICAL DEATH A TEMPORARY STATUS. The fact that after death the body decays and crumbles into dust has led many to reason, falsely, that the second or spiritual death will be the dissolution of the spirit as well as of the body and that this death will be pronounced upon all the wicked. This, however, is an error. The physical death, or the death of the mortal man, is not a permanent

---
[1]Gen. 3:19.

separation of the spirit and the tabernacle of flesh, not-withstanding the fact that the body returns again to the elements. It is only a temporary separation which shall cease at the resurrection day, when the body shall be called forth from the dust, animated by spirit, to live again.

This blessing comes to all men through the atone-ment of Christ, irrespective of their goodness or wicked-ness while in mortality. Paul said there should be a resurrection of both the just and the unjust,[2] and the Savior said that all who were in their graves should hear his voice and should come forth, "they that have done good, unto the resurrection of life; and they that have done evil, unto the resurrection of damnation."[3]

NATURE OF SPIRITUAL OR SECOND DEATH. *Spiritual death is defined as a state of spiritual alienation from God—the eternal separation from the Supreme Being; condemnation to everlasting punishment is also called the second death.* In other words, the second or spiritual death, which is the final judgment passed upon the wicked, is the *same as the first death, banishment from the presence of the Lord.*[4]

NATURE OF SPIRITUAL OR ETERNAL LIFE. The greatest gift of God is the gift of eternal life.[5] Eternal life is the reward a man shall receive who is obedient to all the laws and covenants of the gospel, and who has, because of his faithfulness, been sanctified through the blood of Jesus Christ. He who receives this great gift shall be *like Jesus Christ,*[6] not only in bodily form, but also a son of God; he "shall *inherit all things,"* and the Father has said, "I will be his God, and he shall be my son."[7] *Eternal life is God's life.* It is that gift by which the righteous not only dwell in his presence, but by which they become *like him.*

---

[2]Acts 24:15.
[3]John 5:29.
[4]*Era*, vol. 21, pp. 191-192; *D. & C.* 29:41.

[5]*D. & C.* 6:13; 11:7; 14:7; 1 Ne. 15:36; Rom. 6:23.
[6]1 John 3:1-3.
[7]Rev. 21:7.

Paul has said: "For as many as are led by the Spirit of God, they are *the sons of God*. For ye have not received the spirit of bondage again to fear; but ye have received the Spirit of *adoption*, whereby we cry, Abba, Father. The Spirit itself beareth witness with our spirit, that *we are the children of God: And if children, then heirs; heirs of God, and joint-heirs with Christ;* if so be that we suffer with him, that we may be also *glorified together.*"[8]

All who attain to this glory have the privilege of *eternal increase* and shall be blessed with knowledge, power, and dominion until they shall receive a *fulness.* "They are they who are priests and kings, who have received of his fulness, and of his glory. . . . Wherefore, as it is written, *they are gods,* even the sons of God— Wherefore, *all things are theirs,* whether life or death, or things present, or things to come, all are theirs and they are Christ's, and Christ is God's. And they shall overcome *all things.* . . . These shall dwell in the presence of God and his Christ forever and ever."[9]

SPIRITUAL OR ETERNAL DEATH OPPOSITE OF ETERNAL LIFE. As all things have their opposites, there is *a punishment which is the opposite to eternal life,* which punishment is the *"heaviest of all cursings."*[10] This is the second or spiritual death, which is banishment from the presence of God and from his light and truth forever. In speaking of the *second death* as *eternal death,* we do not mean that those who partake of it are doomed eternally to the dissolution of the body and also of the spirit. *The spirit of man is eternal and cannot die in the sense of ceasing to exist.*

THE SONS OF PERDITION

REBELLION OF LUCIFER IN PRE-EXISTENCE. We learn from the scriptures that Lucifer—once a son of the morning, who exercised authority in the presence of God

---

[8]Rom. 8:14-17.   [10]D. & C. 41:1.
[9]D. & C. 76:56-62.

before the foundations of this earth were laid—rebelled against the plan of salvation and against Jesus Christ who was chosen to be the Savior of the world and who is spoken of as the "Lamb slain from the foundation of the world."[11]

In this rebellion, in which Lucifer attempted to destroy the free agency of the spirits of men, he enticed one-third of the spirits to follow him. He and his followers were cast out of heaven, and when the earth was prepared, they came to it as spirits, being denied the privilege of birth and of receiving tabernacles of flesh in the world.

It was of this casting out of Satan to which Christ made reference when he said to his disciples, "I beheld Satan as lightning fall from heaven."[12] This is the same "dragon" spoken of by John in the Revelation, whose tail drew one-third of the stars of heaven, and who fought against Michael and his angels and was cast out of heaven, and who came to the earth to continue the fight against the Church of Jesus Christ and the priesthood.[13]

Two Classes of Sons of Perdition. The great punishment received by these rebellious spirits is that they are to *remain without bodies eternally* and are *denied the redemption* through the atonement of Jesus Christ. *They are banished forever from the presence of God because they have lost the power of repentance, for they chose evil by choice after having had the light.* While dwelling in the presence of God they *knowingly entered into their rebellion.* Their mission on earth is to attempt to destroy the souls of men and make them miserable as they themselves are miserable. *These spirits are known as sons of perdition.*[14]

There is *another* class of sons of perdition. This class is composed of all those who have known the power of God in this mortal life and then, having *full knowledge*

---

[11]Rev. 13:8; Isa. 14:12-20; Moses 4:1-4; Abra. 3:22-28.
[12]Luke 10:18.
[13]Rev. 12:7-9; D. & C. 76:25-31.
[14]2 Ne. 9:8-9.

of the power and purposes of God, rebel against him, putting Jesus Christ to open shame.

The Lord has defined this class as follows: "Thus saith the Lord concerning all *those who know my power, and have been made partakers thereof*, and suffered themselves through the power of the devil to be overcome, and to *deny the truth* and *defy my power*—They are they who are the sons of perdition, of whom I say that it had been better for them never to have been born; For they are vessels of wrath, doomed to suffer the wrath of God, with the devil and his angels in eternity; Concerning whom I have said *there is no forgiveness in this world nor in the world to come*—Having denied the Holy Spirit after having received it, and having denied the Only Begotten Son of the Father, having crucified him unto themselves and put him to an open shame.

"These are they who shall go away into the lake of fire and brimstone, with the devil and his angels—And the only ones on whom the second death shall have any power; Yea, verily, the only ones who shall not be redeemed in the due time of the Lord, after the sufferings of his wrath."[15]

PUNISHMENT OF SONS OF PERDITION. The extent of this punishment none will ever know except those who partake of it.[16] That it is the most severe punishment that can be meted out to man is apparent. *Outer darkness* is something which cannot be described, except that we know that it is to be placed beyond the benign and comforting influence of the Spirit of God—banished entirely from his presence.

This extreme punishment will not be given to any but the sons of perdition. Even the wicked of the earth who never knew the power of God, after they have paid the price of their sinning—for they must suffer the excruciating torment which sin will bring—shall at last come forth from the prison house, repentant and willing to

---

[15]*D. & C.* 76:31-38.   [16]*D. & C.* 29:27-29; 76:44-48.

bow the knee and acknowledge Christ, to receive some influence of the Spirit of God in the telestial kingdom.

"For they shall be judged according to their works, and every man shall receive according to his own works, his own dominion, in the mansions which are prepared; And they shall be servants of the Most High; but where God and Christ dwell they cannot come, worlds without end."[17]

With the sons of perdition, however, even this blessing is denied. *They have wilfully made themselves servants of Satan and servants to him shall they remain forever. They place themselves beyond the power of repentance and beyond the mercies of God.*

NATURE OF THE SIN THAT BRINGS SECOND DEATH. It is of this class that Jesus spoke when he said: "Wherefore I say unto you, All manner of sin and blasphemy shall be forgiven unto men: but the *blasphemy against the Holy Ghost shall not be forgiven unto men.* And whosoever speaketh a word against the Son of man, it shall be forgiven him: but whosoever speaketh against the Holy Ghost, it shall not be forgiven him, neither in this world, neither in the world to come."[18]

This sin is also spoken of by John as "a sin unto death,"[19] and by the author of the Hebrews as one which cannot be forgiven, in these words: "For it is impossible for those who were once enlightened, and have tasted of the heavenly gift, and were made partakers of the Holy Ghost, And have tasted the good word of God, and the powers of the world to come, If they shall fall away, to renew them again unto repentance; seeing *they crucify to themselves the Son of God afresh, and put him to an open shame.*"[20]

RESURRECTION OF SONS OF PERDITION. All men who are on the earth, blessed with bodies of flesh and bones, are here because of obedience to law in their first

---

[17]D. & C. 76:111-112.
[18]Matt. 12:31-32.
[19]1 John 3:16-17.
[20]Heb. 6:4-6.

estate. This first estate was the world of spirits where we dwelt before earth life commenced. All who were obedient to law there and did not rebel with Lucifer, were entitled to come to this earth and receive tabernacles of flesh, and since men are not punished for Adam's transgression, the Lord has redeemed all men from the mortal death brought to pass through Adam's fall. "For as in Adam *all* die, even so in Christ shall *all* be made alive,"[21] that is, they shall come forth in the resurrection, their spirits and bodies again uniting never again to be divided.

We learn from the scriptures that *"this restoration shall come to all,* both old and young, both bond and free, both male and female, *both the wicked and the righteous;* and even there shall not so much as a hair of their heads be lost." But "the wicked remain as though there had been no redemption made, *except* it be the loosing of the bands of death; for behold, the day cometh that *all shall rise from the dead* and stand before God, and be judged according to their works."[22]

THE FIRST AND SECOND SPIRITUAL DEATHS COMPARED. This second death is not, then, the dissolution or annihilation of both spirit and body, but banishment from the presence of God and from partaking of the things of righteousness.

In speaking of the transgression of Adam, the Lord has said: "Wherefore, I, the Lord God, caused that he should be cast out from the Garden of Eden, from my presence, because of his transgression, *wherein he became spiritually dead, which is the first death, even that same death which is the last death, which is spiritual,* which shall be pronounced upon the wicked when I shall say: Depart, ye cursed."[23]

The second death is spiritual; it is banishment from the presence of the Lord. It is similar to the first spiritual death, which has passed upon all men who have remained

[21]1 Cor. 15:22.
[22]Alma 11:41-44.
[23]D. & C. 29:41.

unrepentant and who have not received the gospel. Those who have suffered the first spiritual death or departure, which is a shutting out from the presence of God, have the privilege of being redeemed from this death through obedience to the principles of the gospel. Through baptism and confirmation they are *born again* and thus come *back into spiritual life,* and through their continued obedience to the end, they shall be made partakers of the blessings of eternal life in the celestial kingdom of God.

Those who partake of the second death are those who have had the spiritual light and have rebelled against it. These *remain* in their sins in their banishment.

RESURRECTION WITHOUT REDEMPTION FOR SONS OF PERDITION. Alma in the *Book of Mormon* has clearly and forcefully depicted their status in the following words: "And now behold, I say unto you then cometh a death, even a second death, which is a spiritual death; then is a time that whosoever dieth in his sins, as to a temporal death, shall also die a spiritual death; yea, *he shall die as to things pertaining unto righteousness.*

"Then is the time when *their torments shall be as a lake of fire and brimstone,* whose flame ascendeth up forever and ever; and then is the time that they shall be chained down to an everlasting destruction, according to the power and captivity of Satan, he having subjected them according to his will.

"Then, I say unto you, they shall be *as though there had been no redemption made;* for *they cannot be redeemed* according to God's justice; and *they cannot die, seeing there is no more corruption.*"[24]

From this we learn that the resurrection shall come unto all who have received tabernacles of flesh and this because they kept their first estate which entitled them to this mortal existence in the flesh. Since they are not

---

[24]Alma 12:16-18.

to be punished for Adam's transgression, *they will be entitled to the resurrection* through the mercy and justice of God and the shedding of the blood and the resurrection of Jesus Christ, for they were not responsible for the temporal or mortal death.

However, because they have failed utterly to keep their second estate, when they are raised in the resurrection with their bodies and spirits inseparably connected, they still remain, as the prophets have said, *as though there had been no redemption made for them, "Except it be the loosing of the bands of death,"*[25] that is the mortal death. Then shall the final sentence be passed upon them, and with Lucifer and those who served him in the beginning, shall they be cast out into outer darkness.

NATURE OF TORMENT OF ETERNAL FIRE. These are the words of Samuel, the Lamanite prophet, in respect to this death: "Yea, behold, this death [of Christ] bringeth to pass the resurrection, and redeemeth *all mankind* from the first death—that spiritual death; for all mankind, by the fall of Adam being cut off from the presence of the Lord, *are considered as dead,* both as to things temporal and to things spiritual. But behold, the resurrection of Christ redeemeth mankind, yea, even all mankind, and bringeth them back into the presence of the Lord.

"Yea, and it bringeth to pass the condition of repentance, that whosoever repenteth the same is not hewn down and cast into the fire; but whosoever repenteth not is hewn down and cast into the fire; and *there cometh upon them again a spirtual death, yea, a second death, for they are cut off again as to things pertaining to righteousness."*[26]

This fire and brimstone, we are informed, is a representation of the torment which shall be suffered by the wicked. It is not actual fire, but it is the *torment of the mind;* in other words, it is the punishment which the

---

[25]Alma 11:41; *D. & C.* 76:42-48.   [26]Hela. 14:16-18.

Savior speaks of as being the worm that dieth not and the fire that is not quenched,[27] which shall endure forever.

Let us be thankful that there will be but few who partake of this dreadful punishment.[28]

LUCIFER BECAME PERDITION BY REBELLION. If Lucifer had not known the effects of his rebellion, how would he ever become perdition? If he were ignorant, he could not have become perdition. He was not ignorant, and therefore *he became perdition,* and they who followed him were *sons of perdition,* because he and *they sinned knowingly.* They did what they did with their eyes open, and were in rebellion against God. However, Lucifer did not know all the purposes of the Father as we learn from the *Pearl of Great Price, Moses 4:6.* Therefore the Lord used Satan's evil acts to accomplish his own purposes.[29]

GOSPEL BRINGS SPIRITUAL LIFE

GOSPEL SAVES FROM SPIRITUAL DEATH. It was necessary, after the expulsion from the garden, for the Lord to place within the reach of Adam and his posterity the means of escape from the spiritual death. The gospel plan was presented to them for that purpose so that they could again be brought back in touch with the Lord through his Holy Spirit.

But it was not expedient for them at that time to be redeemed from the mortal death, for the probationary state was given for them to prepare for their eternal reward. For this preparatory state was a proving time for all mankind, that they (through their agency) might work out their salvation, through obedience, or their condemnation, through disobedience, to the laws of the gospel.[30]

SPIRITUAL REGENERATION BY OBEDIENCE TO GOS-PEL. When men sin, they must comply with certain laws

---

[27]Mark 9:44; 2 Ne. 9:16.
[28]*Church News,* Oct. 7, 1933, p. 1, 6, 8.

[29]*Church News,* Mar. 9, 1935, p. 8.
[30]*Era,* vol. 21, p. 193.

in order to get relief from the sin. We read that Adam was tempted by Satan and yielded to the temptation, and through that sin he became spiritually dead, and that meant banishment from the presence of the Lord. There was only one way he could come back again into the presence of God, and that was by *spiritual regeneration,* from the condition of spiritual death to a condition of spiritual life again.

The Lord sent an angel to Adam to make known to him the plan of redemption by which he could come back again into the presence of the Father, and in this way was made known to him the mission of Jesus Christ as our Redeemer. So the Lord has provided for all men— through faith, and repentance, and the waters of baptism, and the gift of the Holy Ghost—a spiritual regeneration, by which men may come back into his presence, even as many as will. For these conditions of death were inherited by all of Adam's children, and *all who reach the age of accountability are banished from the presence of God, or partake of spiritual death, unless they are redeemed from this spiritual death by obedience to the principles of the gospel.*[31]

PASSING FROM DEATH TO LIFE THROUGH GOSPEL. In the teachings of the Savior, he said that those who would accept his doctrines should pass from death unto life;[32] that he came to give them life, "and that they might have it more abundantly";[33] and that if they would believe in him they should never die,[34] that is, the spiritual death. "He that despiseth his ways shall die,"[35] for it is decreed that spiritual death shall come to all those who refuse to live in spiritual life.[36]

"Verily, verily, I say unto you, He that heareth my word, and believeth on him that sent me, hath everlasting

---

[31]*Gen. & Hist. Mag.,* vol. 17, pp. 145-146; *D. & C.* 29:36-45.
[32]John 5:24.
[33]John 10:10.
[34]John 11:25-26.
[35]Prov. 19:16.
[36]*Church News,* May 8, 1937, p. 5.

life, and shall not come into condemnation; but is passed from death unto life."[37]

Of course Christ does not mean by this that man is not going to die and his body be put into the tomb. He is referring to spiritual death. Every man that believes on him, and will accept his commandments, is brought back from that spiritual death, *through the waters of baptism,* unto eternal life. And he shall die no more if he remains true and faithful to his covenants for he has passed from death unto life. *We have passed from death to life because we have accepted the gospel of Jesus Christ.*[38]

DAMNATION

WHAT IT MEANS TO BE DAMNED. What is damnation? *It is being barred, or denied privileges of progression, because of failure to comply with law.* All who fail to enter into the celestial kingdom are damned, or *stopped in their progression,* but they will enter into some other glory which they are entitled to receive.

The Lord does not delight in the punishment of men. He is kind enough to grant to each his freedom to merit blessings or punishment according to his free will or pleasure. It never was the intention of the Lord to destroy, in the sense of annihilation, any of the souls of his children. His great object is to save them all, if they will freely partake of the blessings of salvation.[39]

MEANING OF DESTRUCTION OF SOUL. Here is another thought we hear a great deal about, "The elements are the tabernacle of God; yea, man is the tabernacle of God, even temples; and whatsoever temple is defiled, God shall destroy that temple."[40] Now, *destruction does not mean annihilation.* We know, because we are taught in the revelations of the Lord, that *a soul cannot be destroyed.*

---

[37]John 5:24.
[38]*Gen. & Hist. Mag.,* vol. 17, p. 147.
[39]*Era,* vol. 19, pp. 427-428.
[40]*D. & C.* 93:35.

Every soul born into this world shall receive the resurrection and immortality and shall endure forever. Destruction does not mean, then, annihilation. When the Lord says they shall be destroyed, he means that they shall be *banished from his presence,* that they shall be cut off from the presence of light and truth, and shall not have the privilege of gaining this exaltation; and that is destruction.[41]

MEANING OF ETERNAL PUNISHMENT. *Eternal punishment, or endless punishment, does not mean that those who partake of it must endure it forever.* "It is not written that there shall be no end to this torment, but it is written *endless torment.* Again, it is written *eternal damnation;* wherefore it is more express than other scriptures, that it might work upon the hearts of the children of men, altogether for my name's glory. . . . Behold, the mystery of godliness, how great is it! For, behold, *I am endless, and the punishment which is given from my hand is endless punishment,* for *Endless is my name.* Wherefore—*Eternal punishment is God's punishment. Endless punishment is God's punishment.*"[42]

The laws of God are immutable, and from this explanation we learn that the same punishment always follows the same offense, according to the laws of God who is eternal and endless, hence it is called, *endless punishment,* and *eternal punishment,* because it is the punishment which God has fixed according to unchangeable law. A man may partake of endless torment, and when he has paid the penalty for his transgression, he is released, but *the punishment remains and awaits the next culprit, and so on forever.*[43]

PARADISE AND HELL

REBELLIOUS GO TO SPIRIT PRISON. There is an expression that the Lord made to Enoch in regard to those who should be destroyed in the flood, in the days of Noah.

---

[41]*Church News,* Mar. 30, 1940, p. 4;   [42]*D. & C.* 19:6-12.
      Matt. 10:28.   [43]*Era,* vol. 19, pp. 197-198.

He said he had prepared a prison for them, because of their disobedience, and would shut them in it. There they would remain until the time when they should be visited by the Son of God, when he should again carry to them that message which they rejected from Noah.[44]

We read in the scriptures that the Son of God, after his death, went to the spirits in prison and taught them the principles of the gospel, that they might live according to God in the spirit and be judged according to men in the flesh. Those very same spirits, who were disobedient in the days of Noah, heard the voice of the Son of God when he went to them, while his body was in the tomb, and all who were willing to receive his testimony and obey his commandments received relief from their torment.[45]

But from the time of their death in the flood until the time of the crucifixion of the Savior, they were shut up in the prison house in torment, suffering the penalty of their transgressions, because they refused to hear a prophet of the Lord—and so it will be with every man who rejects the gospel, whether he lived anciently or whether he lives now; it makes no difference. *Every man who rejects the testimony of Jesus, who denies the truth, who refuses to receive the testimony as it is declared unto him by the elders of Israel, shall be punished and shall be placed in the prison house, and there he shall stay until he has paid the penalty of his transgressions.*[46]

RIGHTEOUS GO TO PARADISE. It is the righteous who go to paradise. It is the righteous who cease from those things that trouble. Not so with the wicked. They remain in torment. They have their anguish of soul intensified, if you please, when they get on the other side, because they are constantly recalling to mind their evil deeds. They are aware of their neglected opportunities, privileges in which they might have served the Lord and received a reward of restfulness instead of a reward of

---

[44]Moses 7:37-39.   [46]*Gen. & Hist. Mag.,* vol. 9, p. 18.
[45]1 Pet. 3:18-20.

punishment. And so they remain in torment until the time comes for their deliverance. . . .

The righteous, those who have kept the command-ments of the Lord, are not shut up in any such place, but are in happiness in paradise. They cease from all this trouble, and trial, and tribulation, and anguish of soul. They are free from all these torments, because they have been true and faithful to their covenants.[47]

DIVISIONS IN THE SPIRIT WORLD. All spirits of men after death return to the spirit world. There, as I under-stand it, *the righteous—meaning those who have been baptized and who have been faithful*—are gathered in one part and all the others in another part of the spirit world. This seems to be true from the vision given to President Joseph F. Smith and found in *Gospel Doc-trine*.[48]

What the Lord really said to the thief was that he would be with him in the world of spirits and there he would be taught the truth, as this seemed to be his desire while upon the cross.

I understand that the righteous may *now* go among the other spirits, and there the gospel is being taught, but the spirits barred from the association of the righteous cannot go where the righteous are.[49]

According to the story of Lazarus and the rich man, there was a gulf which separated the righteous from the unrighteous *(which included all the spirits not baptized),* and neither class could pass into the other *until the Savior bridged the gulf,* so those holding the priesthood then could cross over to teach the others.[50]

[47]*Gen. & Hist. Mag.,* vol. 29, pp. 11-12; Alma 40:11-14.
[48]Joseph F. Smith, *Gospel Doctrine,* 4th ed., pp. 596-602.
[49]Joseph Fielding Smith, *Teachings of the Prophet Joseph Smith,* pp. 309-311; Luke 23:39-43.
[50]Pers. Corresp.; Luke 16:19-31.

CHAPTER 13

THE LAW OF TEMPLE BUILDING

TEMPLES: THEIR NATURE AND ANTIQUITY

WHAT IS A TEMPLE? *Temples, according to the revelations of the Lord, are sanctuaries specially dedicated for sacred rites and ceremonies pertaining to exaltation in the celestial kingdom of God.* They are separate and distinct in their purpose from the ordinary houses of worship. A church building, no matter how magnificent and costly, if its purpose is for the general gatherings of the people, is not a temple. *Temples are sanctified for the purpose of performing rites for and making covenants with the pure in heart, who have proved themselves by faithful service worthy of the blessings of exaltation.*[1]

A vital principle of the gospel is the building of temples and the performing of ordinances therein pertaining to the salvation and exaltation of both the living and the dead. A temple is not a house designed for public worship, like a cathedral, chapel, meetinghouse, or synagogue; neither do the congregations of the people assemble in temples to receive general instruction. A temple is a holy sanctuary built to the name of the Lord.

JACOB'S TEMPLE AT BETH-EL. The Latin *Templum* and the Hebrew *Beth-el* have virtually the same meaning — *The House of the Lord.* When Jacob was fleeing from his enraged brother, he tarried at a certain place called Luz. Here he took some stones for a pillow and lay down to sleep. In the night the Almighty appeared to him and renewed upon him the promises made to Abraham. So

[1]*Gen. & Hist. Mag.*, vol. 21, p. 53.

greatly was Jacob impressed that when he arose, he set up the stones as a monument and called the place *Beth-el,* because said he, *"The Lord is in this place, and this is the gate to heaven."* So, he called the place *the House of God.*[2]

TEMPLE SANCTUARIES WITHOUT TEMPLE BUILD-INGS. When the first temples were built, we do not know, because of the limitations of history. Sacred sanctuaries may have been built by the inspired patriarchs before the flood. Whether this be true or not, this we do know, that the principles and ordinances of the gospel were the same then as now; and all men who seek eternal life are required to receive the *same covenants* and *obligations.*

The Lord has revealed that, under conditions of poverty and at times when a sacred sanctuary to his name cannot be had, he will reveal his purposes in the wilderness, a selected grove, or on the mountain top.[3]

Many covenants pertaining to exaltation were revealed to the ancients according to decrees made before the world was. Under peculiar and special privileges these covenants and obligations may be revealed in the open spaces. Sanctuaries on the mountain top, the wilderness, or the grove, when necessity required it, have been consecrated, but only when a regularly constructed temple was not available. . . .

SANCTUARIES ON MOUNTAIN TOPS. Of necessity the first sanctified temples were the mountain tops and secluded places in the wilderness. If we are correctly informed, Adam built his altar on a hill above the valley of Adam-ondi-Ahman. At that place the Lord revealed to him the purpose of the fall and the mission of the Savior.[4]

As Enoch stood in the place Mahujah, "There came a voice out of heaven, saying—Turn ye, and get ye upon

[2]Gen. 28:10-22; 35:1-15.
[3]*Era,* vol. 39, p. 204; *D. & C.* 124:28-36.

[4]*D. & C.* 107:53-57; 116; 117:8, 11; Moses 5:5-8; Joseph Fielding Smith, *Teachings of the Prophet Joseph Smith,* pp. 122, 158.

the mount Simeon." Upon this mount Enoch beheld the heavens open, he was clothed upon by the glory of the Lord, he saw the Lord and spoke to him face to face. On this mount the Lord revealed to him the fulness of the plan of salvation, and he saw the peoples of the earth unto the latest generations.[5]

It was upon the great mountain Shelem, which was sanctified and made holy, that the brother of Jared was commissioned and received one of the greatest revelations ever given unto man, for he was shown all things from the beginning to the end of time. This vision the Lord has promised to reveal to men when wickedness shall cease upon the earth.[6]

Jacob named the place where the Lord appeared to him, *Beth-el*, which interpreted means *the House of God*.[7]

It was at the holy sanctuary on Horeb, called *the mountain of the Lord*, that Moses received his commission to deliver Israel.[8] On Sinai, another consecrated spot, Moses spoke with the Lord face to face and received the law for the guidance of Israel.[9] Moreover, it was on "an exceedingly high mountain," the name of which is unknown, that Moses saw in vision the creation and was told to write it.[10] In such consecrated places Moses conversed with the Lord *until* the tabernacle was completed in the wilderness.

REVELATION ON MOUNT OF TRANSFIGURATION. The Savior took Peter, James, and John upon a high mountain and there he, with Moses and Elias, conferred upon these apostles the keys of the priesthood.[11] At that time many things pertaining to the earth and its inhabitants were revealed to these apostles, for *the earth was transfigured* before them as it will appear when it receives its glory.[12] The Lord consecrated and made holy the

---

[5]Moses 7:2-69.
[6]Ether 3:1-28; 4:1-8.
[7]Gen. 28:10-22; 35:1-15.
[8]Ex. 3:1-22; 4:1-22.

[9]Ex. 19; 20; 21; 22; 23.
[10]Moses 1:1-42.
[11]Smith, *op. cit.*, p. 158.
[12]*D. & C.* 63:20-21.

mountain top, instead of taking the apostles to the temple in Jerusalem, because the temple had become a "den of thieves," having fallen into the hands of apostate Jews who did not worship the true and living God.[13]

LATTER-DAY SANCTUARIES. The Lord sent Michael and Gabriel to Daniel with important revelations, which were made known on the banks of the rivers Ulai and Hiddekel.[14] These places became consecrated because there was no temple on the earth at that time. Joseph Smith prayed in the grove near his father's house, and that spot was made holy by the vision of the Father and the Son.[15] John the Baptist restored the Aaronic Priesthood on the banks of the Susquehanna River, and the Melchizedek Priesthood was restored by Peter, James, and John, in the wilderness, for there was no house of the Lord on the earth where they could come.[16]

Shortly after the organization of the Church and when the membership was small, the Lord commanded the Saints to build a temple in which he could reveal the keys of authority and where the apostles could be endowed and prepared to prune his vineyard for the last time.[17] This temple was built, and on the 3rd day of April, 1836, the Savior came to it. The same day Moses restored the keys of the gathering of Israel from the four parts of the earth and the leading of the 10 tribes from the land of the North. Elias committed the keys of the dispensation of Abraham, and Elijah restored the keys of the sealing power, by which the ordinances in the temple are bound in heaven as well as on earth, for both the living and the dead.[18]

Had there been such a house when John the Baptist, and Peter, James, and John came, they would have delivered their authority in it. Necessity made it expedient for them to come in the wilderness.

---

[13]Matt. 21:12-13.
[14]Dan. 7; 8; 9; 10; 11; 12.
[15]Joseph Smith 2:16-20.
[16]D. & C. 13; 128:20.
[17]D. & C. 88:119-120; 95:3-17; 109.
[18]D. & C. 110.

TEMPLES IN ANCIENT ISRAEL. The Lord required haste in the building of the tabernacle by Moses so that he might reveal himself therein. It was in this portable, but costly sanctuary, that the Lord instructed Moses after it was built. For several centuries the tabernacle served the people of Israel and was known as the *temple of God*.[19]

In the days of Solomon the most magnificent and costly temple ever reared was built, and in it *the ordinances of salvation for the living were administered*.[20] This continued until, through the wickedness of the people of Israel, the temple was destroyed. This was replaced by the temple of Zerubbabel, after the return from captivity,[21] which temple was plundered and desecrated by Antiochus Epephanes and partly destroyed by him.

Shortly before the birth of the Savior, Herod commenced the restoration of the temple, and the construction continued for many years. This temple was destroyed by the Romans in the year 70 A.D., so that not a stone remained upon another. From that time until the year 1836, so far as we know, there was no temple built to the name of the Lord on the Eastern Hemisphere.

TEMPLES PROVE DIVINITY OF CHURCH. It is probable that the saints of the primitive Church of Jesus Christ had no temples because of their scattered condition and the persecutions they had to suffer. Such ordinances as they observed for the living and for the dead, which properly belong to the house of the Lord, were performed in such places as the Lord designated, in their inability fully to comply with his decree to build a house.

It is rather strange, and significant, that there were no sacred temples on the Eastern Hemisphere, after the meridian of time, where ordinances were performed for the living and for the dead. That there were no such

---

[19]Ex. 35; 36; 37; 38; 39; 40; 1 Sam. 1:9; 3:1-18.
[20]2 Chron. 3; 4; 5; 6; 7.
[21]Ezra 1; 2; 3; 4; 5; 6; 7; 8.

edifices and no ceremonial endowments given, bears striking evidence that the people had departed from the revealed gospel of Jesus Christ. It is also very significant that among the so-called "factions" which have broken away from the Church of Jesus Christ of Latter-day Saints, there is not one which performs such ordinances or believes in them.

The Lord commanded the Church to perform these rites, including baptism for the dead, in a house built and consecrated to his name, saying that if the Church did not perform such ordinances, it would be rejected with its dead.[22] These "factions" bear judgment against themselves in the fact that they neither build temples nor believe in the essential endowments therein. *Temple building and the ordinances of the house of the Lord for the living and the dead set a distinctive mark on the true Church of Jesus Christ.*

KIRTLAND AND NAUVOO TEMPLES COMPARED. The Kirtland Temple was but a *preparatory temple* which was built before the nature of temple ordinances was revealed. The primary purpose of its erection was to provide a sanctuary where the Lord could send messengers from his presence to restore priesthood and keys held in former dispensations, so that the work of gathering together all things in one in the dispensation of the fulness of times might go on.

In the Kirtland Temple no provision was made for the ordinances in behalf of the dead, although some endowment was given in it, in part, for the living. When the Nauvoo Temple was built, it was perfected in all details according to the vision given to the Prophet Joseph Smith. This is also true of all the temples constructed since that time in the Church.[23]

NEPHITE TEMPLES. The Nephites built temples and worshiped in them until about 200 A.D., when they too fell into apostasy, and there remained on the earth no

---

[22]*D. & C.* 124:25-48.   [23]*Gen & Hist. Mag.,* vol. 21, pp. 53-56.

sanctuary recognized by the Lord to which he could come.[24]

TRUE AND FALSE TEMPLES. When the first temples were built by command of the Lord, we do not know. It is well known that among the heathen nations temples and altars were built as places of worship and for the offering of sacrifice to their gods.

It is also known that the fulness of the gospel was given to Adam and by him taught to his children, and that the Lord renewed his covenants with Noah and his sons. From Noah the truth went forth, and the law of sacrifice, in which certain animals were offered in the similitude of the sacrifice of Jesus Christ, was also practiced and taught. As men began to spread over the earth they carried with them these principles which were first revealed to Adam.

In time men departed from the truth and holy ordinances were perverted. Human sacrifice was substituted for the sacrifice of goats and lambs. May we not rightfully conclude that these *heathen temples grew out of the knowledge first given regarding temple building, and that the ceremonies performed in them were perverted forms also based on the true temple ordinances?*[25]

KIRTLAND TEMPLE

LORD COMMANDS TEMPLE BUILDING. It was only a few brief months after the organization of the Church when the doctrine of temple building and ceremonial ordinances therein was partly revealed. The saints were told that there should stand a sacred house of the Lord in Jackson County, Missouri.[26] The site was selected and dedicated, but because of the hatred and open hostility of the people in that land, no temple was built there, although that day will come in the due time of the Lord.

---

[24]*Era*, vol. 39, p. 205; 2 Ne. 5:15-16; Jac. 1:17; 2:2, 11; Mosiah 1:18; 3 Ne. 11:1.

[25]*Gen. & Hist. Mag.*, vol. 21, p. 53.
[26]*D. & C.* 57:1-5; 58:57; 84:2-5, 31-32; 97:10-20; 124:51.

The first temple erected in this dispensation was at
Kirtland, Ohio. December 27, 1832, the Lord commanded that a house be built there, "even a house of
prayer a house of fasting, a house of faith, a house of
learning, a house of glory, a house of order, a house
of God."[27]

KEYS AND ENDOWMENTS PROMISED SAINTS. It was
further stated in the revelations that the Lord had *keys*
and *endowments* to bestow upon his elders requiring the
building of such a house. In December, 1830, the Lord
gave commandment that the saints move their headquar-
ters from the state of New York to "the Ohio."[28] One
reason given for this change of location was that the Lord
desired to give to the Church his law. Moreover, he
desired to *endow* the elders of the Church.

The Lord said in a subsequent revelation given in
January, 1831: "Wherefore, for this cause I gave unto
you the commandment that ye should go to the Ohio;
and there I will give unto you my law; and there *you
shall be endowed with power from on high;* And from
thence, whosoever I will shall go forth among all nations,
and it shall be told them what they shall do; for I have
a great work laid up in store, for Israel shall be saved,
and I will lead them whithersoever I will, and no power
shall stay my hand."[29]

SAINTS COMMANDED TO BUILD KIRTLAND TEMPLE.
In May, 1833, the Lord gave by revelation the dimensions
of this house. It was to be "fifty-five by sixty-five feet
in the width thereof and in the length thereof, in the
inner court." There were to be a lower court and an
upper court, and the building was to be dedicated "from
the foundation thereof," according to the order of the
priesthood.

The Lord also said: "And ye shall not suffer any
unclean thing to come into it; and my glory shall be there,

---

[27]D. & C. 88:119.   [29]D. & C. 38:32-33.
[28]D. & C. 37:1-4.

and *my presence shall be there.* But if there shall come into it any unclean thing, my glory shall not be there; and my presence shall not come into it."[30]

June 1, 1833, the Lord rebuked the saints for inactivity. The necessity for such a building was urgent and the Lord said: "For ye have sinned against me a very grievous sin, in that ye have not considered the great commandment in all things, that I have given unto you concerning the building of mine house." And again he endeavored to impress upon the Church the necessity for such a building, for in it were to be given keys, "For the preparation wherewith I design to prepare mine apostles to prune my vineyard for the last time, that I may bring to pass my strange act, that I may pour out my Spirit upon all flesh."[31]

SAINTS BUILT KIRTLAND TEMPLE IN THEIR POVERTY. It is doubtful if the leading elders realized the importance of making haste and the urgent necessity for the bestowal of keys so that they could go forth with greater power to preach among the nations of the earth. Nevertheless, following this rebuke they went to with their might to complete the sanctuary. A building committee consisting of Reynolds Cahoon, Jared Carter, and Hyrum Smith was appointed, and these brethren proceeded at once to erect the temple.

June 5, 1833, George A. Smith hauled the first load of stone for the temple, and Hyrum Smith and Reynolds Cahoon commenced digging the trench for the walls and finished the same with their own hands. July 23, 1833, the same day that the saints were murderously driven from their homes in Jackson County, the corner stones of the temple were laid. The work progressed rapidly from that time on.

Be it remembered that the saints were at that time few in number and very poor, yet they were called upon to make almost super human efforts to erect a building to

---

[30]*D. & C.* 94:3-9.   [31]*D. & C.* 95:3-4.

the name of the Lord, which was worthy of his name.
In due course of time, the edifice was completed. The
time for the dedication was set for the 27th day of March,
1836.

The dimensions of the temple were 80 by 59 feet
and the walls 50 feet high. There was a tower 110 feet.
The two main halls, "the lower and the upper courts,"
were in keeping with the dimensions given in the revelation. The building had four vestries in front, and five
rooms in the attic, which were used for school purposes
and for the quorums of the priesthood.

At each end of the main auditorium there were four
rows of pulpits one above another. At the east end the
pulpits were for the Melchizedek Priesthood and at the
west for the Aaronic. It was so constructed that veils
or curtains could be lowered, thus dividing the auditorium
into four compartments or rooms for special and separate
services.

PENTECOSTAL MANIFESTATIONS IN KIRTLAND TEM-
PLE. At the dedication there were given to the saints
some wonderful manifestations. The house was filled
with heavenly beings, who were seen only by part of
the congregation. Some had the privilege of a vision of
the Savior. The spirit of prophecy rested upon a number
of the leading brethren, and it was a feast of Pentecost
to all who were assembled there.[32] The prayer of dedication was given to the Prophet Joseph Smith by revelation and is found as section 109 in the *Doctrine and
Covenants*.

While the temple at Kirtland was in course of construction and as soon as provisions would allow, sections
of the building were used for class instruction and for
other purposes. Ordinances were revealed, and important revelations pertaining to the restoration were given,
before the temple was dedicated.

---

[32]*History of the Church,* vol. 2, pp.
    410-428.

It was in December of 1833, that the patriarchal priesthood was revealed, and Joseph Smith, Senior, was ordained as the first patriarch in the Church. On this occasion the Prophet Joseph Smith said: "Blessed of the Lord is my father, . . . and blessed, also, is my mother, . . . and blessed, also, are my brothers and sisters, for they shall yet find redemption in the house of the Lord, and their offsprings shall be a blessing, a joy, and a comfort to them."[33]

This blessing, given by the Prophet to members of his father's family, was indicative of the blessings which were in store for *all* who should receive covenants and obligations to salvation in this house of the Lord.

NATURE OF ENDOWMENT IN KIRTLAND TEMPLE. In January, 1836, over two months before the dedication, the first ceremonies of endowment were given in the temple. They were not as complete as are the ceremonies today, but nevertheless, it was the beginning of the re- vealing and bestowing of the heavenly blessings in this dispensation. Washings and anointings were given, and the Prophet saw wonderful visions of the celestial kingdom.[34] . . .

The greater manifestations and endowment came, however, after the dedication of the temple. At that time all the elders who were out preaching the gospel were ordered to come to Kirtland to receive their endowment. The Lord said in June, 1834: "Verily I say unto you, it is expedient in me that the first elders of my church should receive their *endowment from on high in my house*, which I have commanded to be built unto my name in the land of Kirtland."[35] For this reason they were assembled at Kirtland at the dedication.

This prophetic utterance about the elders obtaining an endowment in the temple at Kirtland is of *double meaning*. First, there were to come from on high essen-

---

[33]Smith, *op. cit.*, pp. 38-39.
[34]Smith, *op. cit.*, pp. 107-108.
[35]D. & C. 105:33.

tial blessings for the saints, which up to that time had not been revealed. Second, the elders were to receive greater powers that they might be better qualified to teach. It was made known by many manifestations of divine power at the dedication that the temple had been accepted as the house of the Lord.

PURPOSE OF KIRTLAND TEMPLE. The Kirtland Temple holds a *peculiar place* in the annals of temple building. It is *not* like other temples. It was built *primarily* for the restoration of keys of authority. *In the receiving of these keys the fulness of gospel ordinances is revealed.* The keys of salvation and exaltation for both the living and the dead were given within its sacred walls. An endowment, such as was necessary at the time, was also given. This was not as complete as the endowment later revealed.

In the Kirtland Temple there was no provision made for the salvation of the dead. It had no baptismal font, for it was only a *preparatory temple*. It had no provision for the endowment ordinances which were later revealed. It was a temple, however, and *fully* answered the purpose of its creation.

The Kirtland Temple filled its mission shortly after the time of its dedication. The Lord revealed line upon line and precept upon precept in relation to the eternal exaltation of his children. When the knowledge in the fulness came, it was essential that other temples be erected with the facilities for that perfection which the Kirtland Temple lacked. The Nauvoo Temple was built according to the perfected pattern, as it was revealed to the Prophet Joseph Smith.

POLLUTION OF KIRTLAND TEMPLE. Like the Temple of Solomon and those which succeeded that grand structure in Jerusalem, the Kirtland Temple was polluted and ceased to be a sanctuary to the name of the Lord. Even today, if it had remained undefiled it could hardly be used for the performance of the essential ordinances which are received in temples, for it was not built for them.

Though its day as a sacred and holy house of God was short, yet that day was glorious while it lasted. In it the Savior appeared and the keys of dispensations were revealed, in preparation for the complete salvation and exaltation of all who will receive the truth.[36]

Today that temple stands in the place of an ordinary meetinghouse and in the hands of those who know little, if anything, of the sacred ordinances for which temples are built.[37]

It is not a sacred temple today—not by any means. It is no more a temple than an adobe building, and is not recognized by the Lord any more. *It filled the measure of its creation*, then fell into the hands of wicked men, and the Lord ceased to consider that building as a house built unto his name, and in the 124th section of the *Doctrine and Covenants* he says so.[38]

LATTER-DAY TEMPLES

PURPOSES OF TEMPLES. Why do we build temples? It is because the Lord commands it. For what purpose are they built? In order that sacred ordinances and covenants necessary to the exaltation in the celestial kingdom may be bestowed upon all those who are *worthy* of the exaltation.[39] . . .

According to the letter of the commandment, none is entitled to enter the temple and receive these ordinances except those who have prepared themselves for exaltation by the keeping of all of the commandments and have prepared themselves by faith and faithfulness to be so endowed. This strictness is not always followed, and many are privileged to receive some of these ordinances on the promise of faithfulness thereafter.[40]

[36]D. & C. 110.
[37]Era, vol. 39, pp. 206-208.
[38]Gen. & Hist. Mag., vol. 31, p. 199;
    D. & C. 124:25-42.
[39]D. & C. 76:52-56.
[40]Era, vol. 56, pp. 294-295.

The responsibility resting upon the members of the Church in this dispensation is far greater than that given to any other dispensation. This being the last dispensation, it is our responsibility to labor, not only for ourselves, but also for *all the righteous dead of all other dispensations* for whom the work has to be done. Moreover, the Lord has revealed to us things which no other dispensation had relating to the kingdom of God.[41]

LATTER-DAY TEMPLES FORETOLD. That temples and temple ordinances are essential to the Christian faith is well established in the *Bible*. Malachi predicted the coming of the Lord suddenly to his temple, in the day of vengeance, in the latter times, as a refiner and purifier.[42] Ezekiel predicted the building of a temple in Jerusalem which will be used for ordinance work *after the gathering of Israel* from their long dispersion and when they are cleansed from their transgressions.[43] John the Revelator saw the day when, after the earth is sanctified and celestialized, the presence of the Father and the Son in the New Jerusalem would take the place of the temple, for the *whole city,* due to their presence, would become a temple.[44]

CONSTRUCTION AND DEDICATION OF NAUVOO TEMPLE. The Nauvoo Temple was publicly dedicated May 1, 1846, by Elder Orson Hyde, and the following day about 3,000 saints met in the building in a public service. It is most likely that the greater number of these saints were also at the dedication. It is not reasonable to suppose that this building was dedicated until it was finished for *each part* had been dedicated as it was finished, and the dedication on the 1st of May, 1846, was of the entire structure. . . .

That structure cost more than one million dollars. The saints were poor, and during a great deal of the time

[41]*Gen. & Hist. Mag.,* vol. 21, p. 57;   [43]Ezek. 37:26-28.
        D. & C. 121:26-32.   [44]*Church News,* Feb. 6, 1932, p. 4;
[42]Mal. 3:1-6.   Rev. 21:21-23.

the temple was in course of erection they were harassed by their enemies. The Prophet Joseph was forced into exile to avoid his enemies who tried to drag him to Missouri, and therefore he could not devote his personal attention to the building of the temple, as he otherwise would have done; and in this way the work was retarded to some degree by the enemies of the people.

Moreover, the building of that structure was not like building one today. The saints could not order their timber from the lumber yard in a state of preparation for the temple. There were no iron foundries from which they could obtain the required metal properly prepared, but on the contrary, every detail had to be performed by the saints. The timber had to be hewed in the far off forests of Wisconsin, carried to Nauvoo, and cut into boards and for the various uses of the temple. The stone had to be cut and polished from the quarries, and the whole work had to be supplied out of the tithing of the people.[45]

ENDOWMENT HOUSE: A TEMPLE. One of the first things that the brethren did when they arrived here in the Salt Lake Valley was to build a temple. They called it the *Endowment House*. It stood on the northwest corner of the temple block. In that building they performed the sacred ordinances which we now perform in the Salt Lake Temple and these other temples.

That building was dedicated as a house of the Lord and was just as holy, just as sacred, as is the Salt Lake Temple; just as holy and just as sacred as was the tabernacle, or temple—for it was a temple—which Moses built and which was carried by the children of Israel in their travels in the wilderness.

ISRAEL'S TABERNACLE: A TEMPLE. In the day of Moses the Lord commanded them to build a house to his name. It was portable. It was made of very costly

---

[45]*Origin of the "Reorganized" Church,*
   pp. 31-32, 37.

material, nevertheless they could take it apart and set it up again so they could travel; and that was the temple that served the purposes of the ordinances which were performed in those days, until the building of the temple of Solomon.

It was in this temple that Samuel resided as a little child. It was in this temple that his mother came to pray and ask the Lord for a blessing, for she wanted a son. When a son was born according to the promise the mother had made, he was taken to this temple, not to Solomon's, because that had not been built.[46]

MISSOURI TEMPLE

SAINTS TO BUILD TEMPLE IN JACKSON COUNTY. The Latter-day Saints are building temples and believe that the time will come when they will be called on to build the great temple which shall grace the New Jerusalem, or City of Zion, the capital city of God on this continent.[47]

The Lord will not call upon those who are cut off from his people to accomplish his holy work. The temple will not be built by those who say that Joseph Smith was a fallen prophet and who have failed to accept the fulness of the word of the Lord as it came through him.

No people will be commanded and directed by revelation from the Lord to build his temple, when they know nothing of temple building and the ordinances performed in temples. The Latter-day Saints may be assured that when the time comes for the building of the house of the Lord, he will call upon his people who have remained true and have been faithful in the purposes of the Lord in bringing to pass the salvation of the living and of the dead.

APOSTATE FACTIONS WILL NOT BUILD TEMPLE. We may be doubly sure that the Lord did not send Elijah

---

[46]*Gen. & Hist. Mag.*, vol. 31, pp. 194- [47]*Church News*, Feb. 6, 1932, p. 4.
195; 1 Sam. 1:9; 3:1-18.

the prophet with the keys of the sealing ordinances—which are performed in the temple, so that the earth will not be smitten with a curse when the Redeemer shall come—and then call into favor a people who *rejected* the coming of Elijah, and all the authority and keys he was sent to bestow, and ask them to build the temple of the Lord.

Those who hold the portion of the temple site where the dedication took place in 1831 are without divine authority. We may say of them as the Lord said of those of old: "Woe unto you, . . . for ye shut up the kingdom of heaven against men: for ye neither go in yourselves, neither suffer ye them that are entering to go in."[48]

When the Lord shall speak, the way shall be opened for the accomplishment of his purposes, and all opposition will melt like the hoar frost before the rising sun. "For thus saith the Lord, I will cut my work short in righteousness, for the days come that I will send forth judgment unto victory."[49] "Behold, I will hasten my work in its time."[50]

LATTER-DAY LAMANITE WORK MISUNDERSTOOD. My attention has been called to statements in the *Book of Mormon* which some interpret to mean that the Lamanites will take the lead in building the temple and the New Jerusalem in Missouri. But I fail to find any single passage which indicates that this is to be the order of things when these great events are to be fulfilled.

Most of the passages used as evidence, in an attempt to prove that the Lamanites will take the lead and we are to follow, seem to come from the instruction given by our Lord when he visited the Nephites after his resurrection. Chapters 20 and 21 of Third Nephi are the main sources for this conclusion. But I fail to find in any of the words delivered by our Savior any declaration out of which

---

[48]Matt. 23:13.
[49]D. & C. 52:11.
[50]*Era*, vol. 33, p. 469; D. & C. 88:73.

this conclusion can be reached. It all comes about by a misunderstanding and an improper interpretation.

REMNANT OF ISRAEL IN ALL NATIONS. In these chapters the Lord is speaking throughout of the *remnant of Jacob*. Who is Jacob whose *remnant* is to perform this great work in the last days? Most assuredly *Jacob is Israel*. Then again, when he speaks of the seed of Joseph, who is meant? Those who are descendants of Joseph, son of Israel, and this includes, of course, the Lamanites as well as the *Ephraimites* who are now being assembled and who are taking *their place*, according to prophecy, *at the head to guide and bless the whole house of Israel.*[51]

In his discourse the Savior states that the gentiles who are upon this land will be blessed, if they will receive the gospel, and they will be numbered with the house of Israel. The gentiles were to be a scourge to the remnant upon this land. Again, they were to be nursing fathers to them and this they are beginning to be in these latter-days, after the terrible scourging in former days.

The gentiles were promised that they would be entitled to have all the blessings which were given to Israel, if they would repent and receive the gospel. All of this was seen in vision by Nephi and was stated by the Savior on the occasion of his visit to the Nephites.

He also said that if the gentiles, *not only upon this land, but also of all lands,* did not repent he would bring the fulness of the gospel from among them. The remnant of the house of Israel spoken of in First Nephi, chapter 13, and Third Nephi, chapters 16, 20, and 21, does not have reference only to the descendants of Lehi, but to *all* the house of Israel, the children of Jacob, those upon *this land* and those in *other lands*. Reference to the gentiles also is to *all the gentiles* on *this land* and in *other lands*.

---

[51]*D. & C.* 133:30-34; Gen. 48:15-20;
  Deut. 33:13-17.

WORLD-WIDE MISSION OF REMNANT OF ISRAEL. When the Lord is speaking of his covenants, he is not confining them to the descendants of Lehi, but applies them to *all* the house of Israel. "And verily, verily, I say unto you, that when they [the covenants as recorded by Isaiah] shall be fulfilled then is the fulfilling of the covenant which the Father hath made unto his people, O house of Israel. And then shall *the remnants,* which shall be scattered abroad *upon the face of the earth,* be gathered in from the east and from the west, and from the south and from the north; and they shall be brought to the knowledge of the Lord their God, who hath redeemed them. And the Father hath commanded me that I should give unto you this land, for your inheritance."

Much of our misunderstanding, however, seems to come out of the interpretation placed upon the succeeding verses: "And I say unto you, that if the Gentiles do not repent after the blessing which they shall receive, after they have scattered my people—Then shall ye, who are a remnant of the house of Jacob, go forth among them; and ye shall be in the midst of them who shall be many; and ye shall be among them as a lion among the beasts of the forest, and as a young lion among the flocks of sheep, who, if he goeth through both treadeth down and teareth in pieces, and none can deliver. Thy hand shall be lifted up upon thine adversaries, and all thine enemies shall be cut off. And I will gather my people together as a man gathereth his sheaves into the floor."[52]

Are we justified in applying this merely to the Lamanites and saying that they are to go forth as a young lion pouring out vengeance upon the gentiles? Also does the phrase, "Ye who are a remnant of the house of Jacob," in verse 16, have reference just to the Lamanites? The verses which follow indicate that it has reference to *the remnants of Israel, which had been scattered in all lands.* To apply it to the Lamanites in face of the entire theme

[52]3 Ne. 20:12-18.

of this discourse, in my judgment, narrows it too greatly. Then again, *this prophecy was also given to Micah and has reference to "many people,"* not merely to the gentiles on this land.[53]

GENTILES MAY ASSIST IN BUILDING OF ZION. Here is another part of this discourse which, in my judgment, is misinterpreted: "For it shall come to pass, saith the Father, that at that day whosoever will not repent and come unto my Beloved Son, them will I cut off from among my people, O house of Israel; And I will execute vengeance and fury upon them, even as upon the heathen, such as they have not heard. But if they will repent and hearken unto my words, and harden not their hearts, I will establish my church among them, and they shall come in unto the covenant and be numbered among this remnant of Jacob, unto whom I have given this land for their inheritance; And they shall assist my people, the remnant of Jacob, and also as many of the house of Israel as shall come, that they may build a city, which shall be called the New Jerusalem."[54]

I think this is the stumbling block. This has been interpreted to mean that the remnant of Jacob are those of the descendants of Lehi, but there is nothing in the passage as I read it which should convey this thought. Remember that all through the Lord has been speaking of the remnant of Jacob or Israel, and of the great promises made to the gentiles who are on *this land* and in *all other lands,* if they will only come into the Church and be numbered with the house of Israel. Their privileges would be to assist in building the New Jerusalem, and if they refuse, then shall the punishments come upon them.

EPHRAIM PRESIDES OVER ALL ISRAEL. I take it we, the members of the Church, most of us of the tribe of Ephraim, are of the remnant of Jacob. We know it to be the fact that the Lord called upon the descendants

53Micah 5:4-15; 3 Ne. 21:12-20.   543 Ne. 21:20-24.

of *Ephraim* to *commence his work* in the earth in these last days. We know further that he has said that he set Ephraim, according to the promises of his birthright, at the head. Ephraim receives the *"richer blessings,"* these blessings being those of *presidency* or *direction.* *The keys are with Ephraim.* It is Ephraim who is to be endowed with *power to bless* and *give to the other tribes, including the Lamanites, their blessings.* All the other tribes of Jacob, including the Lamanites, are to be crowned with glory in Zion *by the hands of Ephraim.*

Now do the scriptures teach that Ephraim, after doing all of this is to abdicate, or relinquish his place, and give it to the Lamanites and then receive orders from this branch of the "remnant of Jacob" in the building of the New Jerusalem? This certainly is inconsistent with the whole plan and with all that the Lord has revealed in the *Doctrine and Covenants* in relation to the establishment of Zion and the building of the New Jerusalem.

Father Lehi made one promise to his son Joseph and that was that from his seed should arise one who should do "much good, both in word and in deed, being an instrument in the hands of God, with exceeding faith, to work mighty wonders, and do that thing which is great in the sight of God, unto the bringing to pass much restoration unto the house of Israel, and unto the seed of thy brethren."[55]

That the remnants of Joseph, found among the descendants of Lehi, will have *part* in this great work is certainly consistent, and the great work of this restoration, the building of the temple and the City of Zion, or New Jerusalem, will fall to the lot of the descendants of Joseph, but it is *Ephraim* who *will stand at the head and direct the work.*[56]

TEMPLE WORK DURING MILLENNIUM. During this time of peace, when the righteous shall come forth from

[55]2 Ne. 3:24.   [56]Pers. Corresp.; Ether 13; *D. & C.* 133:30-34.

their graves, they shall mingle with mortal men on the
earth and instruct them. The veil which separates the
living from the dead will be withdrawn and mortal men
and the ancient saints shall converse together. Moreover,
in perfect harmony shall they labor for the salvation and
exaltation of the worthy who have died without the
privileges of the gospel.

The great work of the millennium shall be performed
in the temples which shall cover all parts of the land and
into which the children shall go to complete the work for
their fathers, which they could not do when in this mortal
life for themselves.

In this manner those who have passed through the
resurrection, and who know all about people and conditions on the other side, will place in the hands of those
who are in mortality, the necessary information by and
through which the great work of salvation for every
worthy soul shall be performed, and thus the purposes of
the Lord, as determined before the foundation of the
world, will be fully consummated.[57]

TEMPLE BLESSINGS, COVENANTS, AND ENDOWMENTS

ENDOWMENTS A PROTECTION IN THIS LIFE. The
endowment received now is greater than that given in
Kirtland, for the Lord has revealed additional covenants
and obligations for us to keep. If we go into the temple,
we raise our hands and covenant that we will serve the
Lord and observe his commandments and keep ourselves
unspotted from the world. If we realize what we are
doing, then the endowment will be a protection to us all
our lives—a protection which a man who does not go to
the temple does not have.

I have heard my father say that in the hour of trial,
in the hour of temptation, he would think of the promises,
the covenants that he had made in the house of the Lord,
and they were a protection to him. He was but 15 years

---

[57]*Church News*, May 14, 1932, p. 6.

of age when he received his endowments and went forth into the mission field. This is exceptional, I know, and I do not recommend that our sons and our daughters go to the temple as young as that, but that they go as soon as they are prepared.

This protection is what these ceremonies are for, in part. They save us now, and they exalt us hereafter, if we will honor them. I know that this protection is given for I, too, have realized it, as have thousands of others who have remembered their obligations.

And yet mothers and fathers will say: "Oh, let the children have a good time; let them do as the world does, and when their charms are gone, then they can go to the temple." Therefore many procrastinate the day of their repentance, which is a very dangerous thing to do.

ENDOWMENTS ESSENTIAL FOR EXALTATION HEREAFTER. These blessings insure to us, through our faithfulness, the pearl of great price the Lord has offered us, for *these are the greatest blessings we can receive in this life*. It is a wonderful thing to come into the Church, but you cannot receive an exaltation until you have made covenants in the house of the Lord and received the keys and authorities that are there bestowed and which cannot be given in any other place on the earth today.

You have read what the Prophet has written in the *Pearl of Great Price*. He has given us some of the interpretations of the Egyptian characters in the writings of Abraham, and we learn that Abraham wrote things and sealed them up that they cannot be read. They cannot be revealed unto the world, but are to be had in the holy temple of God. *They are certain keys and blessings that are obtained in the house of the Lord that we must have if we are to obtain exaltation.*[58]

YOUTH OF ZION SHOULD SEEK ENDOWMENTS. Having put this matter before you in this way, endeavoring to impress you with the importance of these blessings

---

[58]Book of Abraham, fig. 2, pp. 34-35.

obtained in the temples, I would like to ask you a question: "Are these blessings to be desired?" The question answers itself.

Now let me ask another. "When the Lord offers us these great blessings, are we justified in saying, 'It is all right, we want them, but we want to put them off just as long as we can before we receive them, so that we can live as the world lives'?"

Is there any sincerity in that? Is there any spirit of humility, or repentance, or faith in such an attitude? I have known of mothers saying to their daughters, "I do not want you to go to the temple now. Wait a little while. When you get older, you may go to the temple, but now have a good time while you are young."

Well, of course, *if* a girl is going to enter into covenants in the temple which she does not intend to keep, it is better for her not to go there, far better for her to stay out. But *is there any blessing the Lord offers us that we are justified in postponing because we feel that it will interfere with our having a good time, or indulging in the customs and fashions of the world?* Is it right for us to feel that we are justified in seeking the things of the world until we are along in years and then we will repent and turn unto the Lord? Should we not *seek to obtain these important blessings just as soon as we can, consistently and in reason?*

FAITH AND RIGHTEOUSNESS TO PRECEDE ENDOWMENTS. Children should not go to the temple until they are old enough to understand the purpose of their going. They should be taught the principles of the gospel, and to have faith in God, and in the mission of Jesus Christ, and should gain a testimony of the truth *before* they receive the blessings of the temple.

I believe that a young man or a young woman should seek after these blessings in the temple, and just as soon as they are old enough to understand the meaning of temple ordinances, they should have them. Moreover, *they should not go to the temple until they do have a testimony of the truth and a knowledge of the gospel,* no matter how old they may be. It is not intended that these sacred covenants should be given to those who do not have faith and who have not proved themselves worthy by obedience to the gospel.

ENDOWED PERSONS SHOULD KEEP THEIR COVE-NANTS. After we have received these covenants we should observe them sacredly, even if it should cost us the association and good will of all the world. Why? *Because we have found the pearl of great price, the kingdom of God.* We are on the road to receive all that the Father has, all that he can give—exaltation. If others are not willing to receive these blessings, let them take their course, but for us, let us walk in the light of the truth and forsake the world.

I think that just because girls go through the temple they need not necessarily be ostracized socially by friends and companions. I know of mothers, however, who have made their daughters feel that they would be and that they could not make themselves attractive if they went to the temple and kept the covenants made there, for they would not be able to dress according to the fashion. Such a doctrine may mean the damnation of that precious daughter, in whose welfare you have such an interest, if you feel that way.

MISSIONARIES TO BE ENDOWED. The Lord has not offered us these blessings that we might receive them just before we die or when we are old or crippled. What are these blessings for? Not only for eternity, but also to be a guide to us and a protection through the struggle of life.

Do you understand why our missionaries go to the temple before they are set apart for their mission fields? This is a requirement made of them no matter what their age, because the Lord has said it should be done. He called all the missionaries to Kirtland in the early day of the Church to receive endowments in the temple erected there. He said this was so that they could go out with greater power from on high and with greater protection. Zion was not to be redeemed until endowments were given.[59]

OBLIGATION TO KEEP TEMPLE COVENANTS. When you go to the house of the Lord, and make covenants, and enter into ordinances, and receive the blessings of that house, it is expected that you observe and keep those instructions and commandments as they are given unto you; and it is not within your power when you come out to alter or change. . . .

Do you think for one minute that we can go through the temple and make covenants that we will do certain things, with the promise made to us that if we will do these things the Lord will receive us into his kingdom — not as aliens, not as strangers, not as servants, but he will receive us into that kingdom with open arms, as sons and daughters in very deed — and then we can go off, after receiving these covenants from the house of the Lord, and alter and change and break those covenants to suit our fancy and what we consider our convenience because we desire to follow the customs and fashions of a sinful world, and then expect the promised blessing? . . .

CONDEMNATION FOR BREAKING TEMPLE COVENANTS. Now these people go into the temple; instruction is given them there that these ordinances are sacred, and holy, and must be kept. They raise their hands, and they enter into a covenant that they will observe and keep these covenants which they receive in the house of the Lord. Then straightway they go out, and, like the man that James speaks of who looked into the glass, saw his face, and then went away and forgot what manner of man he was, so do they.[60]

I say unto you *the Lord is not bound, unless you keep the covenant.* The Lord never breaks his covenant.

[59]*Gen. & Hist. Mag.,* vol. 21, pp. 101-   [60]Jas. 1:22-25.
104; *D. & C.* 95:8-9; 105:9-12.

When he makes a covenant with one of us, he will not break it. If it is going to be broken, we will break it. But when it is broken, he is under no obligation to give us the blessing, and we shall not receive it. There are people who go into the house of the Lord and receive covenants which are based on faithfulness, who go out and are unfaithful, shall they not receive their reward?[61]

[61]*Rel. Soc. Mag.*, vol. 6, pp. 467-468.

CHAPTER 14

LAW OF THE RESURRECTION

CHRIST AND THE RESURRECTION

QUESTIONS ABOUT THE RESURRECTION. By what power and authority does the resurrection come?

How many resurrections have there been, and how many are yet to come?

Who is privileged to come forth in each?

Is the resurrection now going on?

Are there any who have lived on the earth who will be denied the resurrection?

Will any who receive the resurrection die again, that is, suffer the separation of the spirit and the body the second time?

Will any creatures, other than mankind, partake of the resurrection?

Will the same body be restored, or will it be a different body?

RESURRECTION NEEDED BECAUSE OF FALL. Our Savior, Jesus Christ, is the Author of the resurrection. *He came into the world to redeem it and all upon its face from mortality and give immortality to every creature.* The coming of our Savior to accomplish this end is due to the fact that death was brought into the world through the fall of Adam. If Adam had not partaken of the fruit of the tree of the knowledge of good and evil, he would not have died. . . .

Had such a condition prevailed, Adam would still be in the Garden of Eden, and all things would have continued as they were, and under such conditions, there would have been no need for a Redeemer.[1] . . .

We know the true reason for the coming of Jesus Christ into the world. It was, first, to redeem *all* men from the physical or mortal death, which Adam brought into the world; and second, to redeem all men from spiritual death, or banishment from the presence of the Lord, on conditions of their repentance, and remission of sins, and endurance to the end of the mortal probation.

Had there been no fall, there would have been no resurrection. Since there was a transgression which brought death, the atonement had to be made by the Son of God, who was always the master over death. His sacrifice was an infinite atonement.

He declared himself to be the "resurrection and the life," and that he had power in himself to lay down his life and take it up again. Such power has never been the possession of any other creature upon the earth. All other creatures were under the curse of death, and Christ alone could free them.[2]

CHRIST HAD POWER OVER DEATH. The means provided for our redemption from death were prepared in the plan of salvation before Adam and Eve were sent to the earth. Jesus Christ volunteered to come and atone for Adam's transgression and thus gain the victory over the devil.[3] Therefore, he is called the *Lamb of God,* who was chosen to be slain "from the foundation of the world."[4]

The only way this atonement could be made was for Jesus, who was chosen to pay the debt to justice and redeem us from the grasp of Satan, to come into the world with power over death, for no one who was under the bondage of death could pay the debt and restore us to live forever.

---

[1]Moses 3:16-17; 6:57-59; 2 Ne. 2:22-26.
[2]*Era,* vol. 45, pp. 780-781; 2 Ne. 2:6-10; 9:6-9; John 10:11-18; 11:23-26.

[3]Moses 4:1-4; Abra. 3:22-28.
[4]1 Pet. 1:19; Rev. 13:8.

260 DOCTRINES OF SALVATION

Jesus was the *only person* who ever came into this world who had *power over death*, and having that great power, by the shedding of his blood on the cross, he could redeem us and get the power of the resurrection. After he came forth from the tomb, he had all power to call every other person forth from the grave. And after he came forth, on the third day after his crucifixion, he opened the graves of the righteous saints who had lived from the days of Adam to the time of his crucifixion.

He had declared to Martha that he is the resurrection and the life, and this he taught to his disciples.[5] Jacob, the brother of Nephi, has given us a very clear understanding of the mission of Jesus Christ and how he came to redeem us from *death* and from *Satan*. He explains how we would have been *angels to the devil*, without the death and resurrection of Jesus Christ; and now because of the mercies of our Heavenly Father and his beloved Son Jesus Christ, we have escaped from the grasp of this great monster.[6]

ATTAINING FELLOWSHIP WITH GOD THROUGH RESURRECTION. Jesus Christ arose from the dead and was the first fruits of the resurrection.[7] The witnesses of this wonderful occurrence cannot be impeached. In this day the tendency of the religious world is away from this fundamental truth, and ministers and teachers are denying that Jesus is the Christ, the Only Begotten Son of God.

The Savior taught that no man can testify of God and reject his Son, and that no man can deny that Jesus Christ is the Redeemer of the world and believe in the Father who sent him. We must honor the Father through the Son, and he who rejects the Son and denies the power of the resurrection, knows not God.[8]

Again, as John the Baptist taught: "He that believeth on the Son hath everlasting life: and he that believeth

---

[5]John 11:23-26.   [7]1 Cor. 15:23.
[6]*Era*, vol. 57, p. 559; 2 Ne. 9:6-26.   [8]John 5:19-30; Luke 10:22.

not the Son shall not see life; but the wrath of God abideth on him."[9] This does not mean that those who reject the Son shall not come forth in the resurrection, for *all* shall be raised from the dead, but the unbeliever shall not partake of eternal life in the kingdom of God where dwell the Father and the Son.

It is, however, the purpose of the Father to extend the power of the resurrection to all men, through the atonement of the Son, and thus give immortality to all his children. The fact remains, however, that *we cannot be in fellowship with God if we do not accept the Sonship of Jesus Christ and believe in his power to redeem us from the grave.* Therefore, all who reject the authority of the Son have the wrath of God abiding on them. . . .

CHRIST DESTROYS DEATH. When men deny the resurrection of Christ and the coming forth from their graves of all mankind, it is a confession on their part that they are ignorant of the work of the Lord regarding the destiny of man. Our existence in mortality is most important; it is not accidental. It was never intended that we should pass through this life without coming in contact with sin—without temptation, without mortality.

Adam was sent into the world to perform a mission, including the bringing to pass these very things, that we in the mortal state might obtain experiences by coming in contact with all the vicissitudes of mortal life. In this way we receive an education that could not be obtained in any other way. So mortality came through the will of God, and through the fall of man, death has passed upon all men Through the atonement of Jesus Christ, life is restored again, and death is overcome and destroyed.

Immortality and eternal life constitute the great work of the Father, and the last enemy to be destroyed, we are informed, is death. When Christ has destroyed death by bringing to pass the resurrection of all mankind from

[9]John 3:36.

the grave, he will have finished his work, and then he will deliver up the kingdom to his Father.[10]

CHRISTIANITY SURVIVED BECAUSE OF RESURRECTION. If Christ had not risen from the dead, do you think that Peter, James, and John, and the other disciples would have gone into the city of Jerusalem immediately following his crucifixion, and that there they would have begun to preach Christ and him crucified, boldly declaring unto the populace that he had been raised from the dead?

Is that reasonable? Is it reasonable to believe that Paul who started as a persecutor of the saints would suddenly change and accept Christ as the Son of God, that he too would go into those same communities to preach that Christ was the Son of God, if he had not been raised from the dead?

I will tell you what is reasonable, and it is set forth right here in these scriptures. After the crucifixion of the Savior the disciples scattered. They were disappointed, they thought the end of all had come, so they were about to go back to their fishing nets.

Two of the disciples on the evening of that first day of the resurrection were walking along the street towards a small city outside of Jerusalem, when a stranger, apparently, came along and asked them why they were sad, and they, thinking him to be a stranger in Jerusalem, said: "Art thou only a stranger in Jerusalem, and hast not known the things which are come to pass there in these days?"

And then, after answering other inquiries, they referred to the story of Christ's crucifixion, and they added: "But we trusted that it had been he which should have redeemed Israel: and beside all this, today is the third day since these things were done."[11] Then Christ revealed himself to them.

---

[10]Conf. Rep., Apr., 1926, pp. 40-43;   [11]Luke 24:13-48.
   1 Cor. 15:24-28.

*If Christ had not come forth from the tomb, Peter,
James, and John would have gone back to the sea of
Galilee to their nets, the other disciples would have gone
back to their various occupations, and Christianity would
have come to an end abruptly.*

RESURRECTION PUT LIFE INTO CHRISTIANITY. Instead, immediately following the resurrection the disciples
took on new life. They began boldly to declare that
Christ had been raised from the dead. They bore that
witness to the people. On the day of Pentecost when
Peter was preaching, he said this:

"Ye men of Israel, hear these words; Jesus of Nazareth, a man approved of God among you by miracles
and wonders and signs, which God did by him in the
midst of you, as ye yourselves also know: Him, being
delivered by the determinate counsel and foreknowledge
of God, ye have taken, and by wicked hands have crucified and slain: Whom *God hath raised up,* having
loosed the pains of death: because it was not possible that
he should be holden of it."[12]

There he bore witness on the day of Pentecost to
that assembly of the mission of Christ and how he had
been raised from the dead.

A little later, after Peter and John had healed the
lame man at the gate of the temple, Peter boldly spoke to
the Jews who were assembled. More emphatically were
his remarks delivered.

He said to them: "But ye denied the Holy One and
the Just, and desired a murderer to be granted unto you";
—He was at this time speaking to those, right to their
teeth, who had been responsible for the death of Christ!
—"And killed the Prince of life, whom God hath raised
from the dead; whereof we are witnesses."[13]

That was his testimony to those very men. Peter
would not have dared to do a thing like that if Christ
had not been raised from the dead.

---

[12]Acts 2:22-24.   [13]Acts 3:14-15.

PRIMITIVE CHURCH PROSPERED BECAUSE OF RES-
URRECTION. And so it is unreasonable for Mr. Joseph
McCabe or anyone else to say that the evidence is over-
whelming in regard to the life of Christ, that he lived, that
he gathered around him a following, that he was taken
and crucified—and then stop.

To be consistent, Mr. McCabe should have continued. He ought to have said that when Paul joined the
Church, he also declared—as did Peter and others in
the city of Jerusalem and throughout Palestine where
Christ was known—that Jesus was raised from the dead.
And he ought to have accepted it, because there were no
better witnesses than Peter and the other apostles and
the followers of Christ, who went around bearing witness
of Jesus' resurrection.

Moreover, that little handful of Christians—and it
was only a handful at the time of the death of Christ—
immediately began to *increase* in numbers. In the course
of a very short time they numbered thousands. Three
thousand were added to the Church after that memorable
meeting on the day of Pentecost, and all of these people
were instructed in the resurrection by eye witnesses who
had been companions of the Lord Jesus Christ during
his ministry.[14]

We read that Christ after his resurrection labored
among the disciples for 40 days.[15] He was seen, Paul
tells us, by upwards of 500 people upon one occasion,
or perhaps upon more than one occasion.[16] The author
of the book of Luke, in the commencement of that history,
has this to say: "Forasmuch as many have taken in hand
to set forth in order a declaration of those *things which
are most surely believed among us.*"[17]

DOCTRINE OF THE RESURRECTION

RESURRECTION EASY TO BELIEVE. The resurrection
is not a hard thing to believe. There are many things

---

[14]Acts 3:41.   [16]1 Cor. 15:6.
[15]Acts 1:3.   [17]Luke 1:1.

harder than that to believe. *Life itself is a mystery.* What do we know about it? Where does it come from? *Is there anything more wonderful than the creation of the body?* Why, bless your soul, that is more wonderful than to call together the elements that compose the body after death and cause life to come into them again.

In my judgment that is nothing to be compared as a miracle with the creation of that body in the beginning, putting life into it. Yet we see that every day; that is common. We see it, so we acknowledge it to be a fact. It is no more a miracle, it is no more wonderful, to have some body raised from the dead. They have come back; they have made their appearances; they have given commandments to men.

It is not the purpose of the Lord to reveal himself to every individual, but he does reveal himself to his servants, and he sends them forth with the message. Blessed is he who believes, but has not seen.[18]

MODERN PHILOSOPHIES DENY RESURRECTION. It has become quite popular, in these days of modern philosophy and materialism, for men of wisdom to deny the literal resurrection of the body. The doctrine of the resurrection, however, is fundamental to the Christian religion. It cannot be spiritualized or dissolved into thin vapor. It was taught by Christ and his disciples and was true in their day. It is just as true today, and equally important.

The burden of the message and ministry of Jesus Christ was to bring to pass the immortality and eternal life of man. In fact, we are taught by modern revelation that this is the very thing which constitutes the great work and glory of God.[19]

This doctrine may be peculiar to the Latter-day Saints, but let it be remembered it was taught and believed with equal confidence by the early Christian Saints. It is because men have departed from the revealed word

---

[18]*Church News,* June 3, 1933, pp. 5, 7.   [19]Moses 1:39; *D. & C.* 29:43-44.

of the Lord that these modern ideas in relation to the future life prevail today.

How Christ Is the Resurrection and the Life. Christ declared himself to be the One sent by the Father to bring to pass the redemption from the grave of all men. To Martha's pleading at the tomb of Lazarus, the Lord said: *"I am the resurrection, and the life: he that believeth in me, though he were dead, yet shall he live: And whosoever liveth and believeth in me shall never die."*[20]

Here are *two thoughts* expressed which have appeared confusing to many, yet his meaning is plain. As the resurrection and the life, he had power to bring forth from their graves all the children of Adam.

In giving to those who believed on him the power that they should never die, he had no reference to the mortal or physical dissolution, but to the second death, which is banishment from the presence of God. *This second death,* from which the righteous are freed, is the condemnation of those who are consigned to *immortality outside of the kingdom of God.*

Ezekiel and Daniel Teach Resurrection. In the Old Testament, as well as in the New, the doctrine of the literal resurrection is emphatically declared. Many have tried to spiritualize those scriptures. The Lord taught Ezekiel in vision how the literal resurrection would be brought to pass. "Behold, O my people, *I will open your graves, and cause you to come up out of your graves,* and bring you into the land of Israel. And ye shall know that I am the Lord, when I have *opened your graves,* O my people, and *brought you up out of your graves.*"[21]

Daniel, also, saw the vision of the resurrection and declared: "And many of them that sleep in the dust of the earth shall awake, some to everlasting life, and some to shame and everlasting contempt."[22]

---

[20]John 11:25-26.
[21]Ezek. 37:12-13.

[22]Dan. 12:2.

CHRIST TEACHES RESURRECTION. What could be more definite, or come with greater authority, than this statement of Jesus Christ, who holds the keys of the resurrection? "Verily, verily, I say unto you, The hour is coming, and now is, when the dead shall hear the voice of the Son of God: and they that hear shall live. . . . Marvel not at this: for the hour is coming, in the which *all that are in the graves* shall hear his voice, And *shall come forth;* they that have done good, unto the *resurrection of life;* and they that have done evil, unto the *resurrection of damnation.*"[23]

AMULEK TEACHES RESURRECTION. In this dispensation, by way of the *Book of Mormon,* the Lord has made it known that there shall be such a resurrection. "The spirit and the body shall be reunited again in its perfect form; both limb and joint shall be restored to its proper frame, even as we now are at this time; and we shall be brought to stand before God, knowing even as we know now, and have a bright recollection of all our guilt. Now, this restoration shall come to *all,* both old and young, both bond and free, both male and female, both the wicked and the righteous; and even there shall not so much as a hair of their heads be lost."[24]

REASON FOR THE RESURRECTION. *Why the resurrection?* That it is a fact we know, that is, we who are Latter-day Saints, for the Lord has revealed it unto us, and the scriptures on this truth are clear. We know that Christ appeared to his disciples after his resurrection, and they have testified of his appearance unto them. Now, why should there be a resurrection and the promise made that all men shall come forth from their graves?

A great many people believe that the mortal body has served its purpose in this life and will not come forth from the dead, but that the spirit rises to dwell with God. Then why did Jesus Christ come into the world to die?

[23]John 5:25, 28-29.   [24]*Church News,* Apr. 9, 1932, p. 6; Alma 11:43-44.

Was it because the plan that the Father had arranged in the beginning had been frustrated, or destroyed, through the fall of man?

Adam had a body before death came upon him, and his fall was a part of the great plan of man's salvation. Mortality, and consequently death, is due to the fall, and *Jesus Christ came into the world to make reparation and to give man, through the resurrection, immortality and eternal life.*

In the *Book of Mormon* we are informed that man partakes of mortality that he may obtain experiences that could not come to him in any other way and that through his obedience to the gospel of Jesus Christ, which is based on the infinite sacrifice of the Son of God, he may obtain salvation and exaltation in the presence of the Father and the Son.[25]

Surely the Lord understood the end from the beginning, and it was perfectly understood in the councils in the heavens before the world was made, that *Jesus Christ was to come into this world to die* and thus repair a broken law and again restore life to mankind, that they might have it more abundantly.[26]

LITERAL NATURE OF RESURRECTION. The world today is discarding the doctrines of the Church. Many men no longer accept Jesus Christ as the Son of God; they do not believe in his atonement. They have rejected the resurrection. They no longer accept it as being essential to salvation, and yet it is one of the fundamental doctrines of the Church.

Christ, the prototype, the example, came forth from the dead, as he said he would. After he had laid down his life and had taken it again on the third day, he presented himself to his disciples and told them to handle him and see, for a spirit had not a body of flesh and bones as they saw that he had. And so they came, and they handled him.

---

[25]2 Ne. 2:6-10; Alma 12:22-37; 42:1-31.   [26]Conf. Rep., Apr., 1926, pp. 41-42.

Further to convince them, he partook of the fish and honeycomb. He ate in their presence and convinced them by a practical demonstration that it was he himself, that the uneducated may read and understand; and yet the wise men in all their learning, close their eyes against these truths.[29]

CHRIST GAINED ALL POWER THROUGH RESURRECTION. Moreover, he taught them that all power, both in heaven and in earth, had been given unto him *through his obedience* to his Father and *through the resurrection* which he had received.[28]

He was the first fruits of the resurrection; he came forth and taught mankind that as he came forth from the dead so all men should come forth from the dead, both the good and the bad, and that men should be judged according to their works and receive their reward according to merit. That is the gospel of Jesus Christ in its simplicity. It is so plainly set forth in these scriptures that the fool may read and understand; and yet the wise men in all their learning, close their eyes against these truths.[29]

LATTER-DAY EVIDENCE OF RESURRECTION

ANCIENT APOSTLES: WITNESSES OF RESURRECTION. We know that Christ has risen from the dead, that he has ascended on high, taking captivity captive, and has *become the Author of salvation* unto all who will believe, who will repent of their sins and accept him as the Redeemer of the world. Latter-day Saints are not left in doubt regarding these things.

There were many witnesses who testified of the resurrection of the Savior at the time he came forth from the dead. He appeared first unto Mary at the tomb, later unto the Twelve, or to the eleven, one of them having lost his apostleship, and afterwards unto a multitude of the saints. He labored among his disciples for some time,

---

[27]Luke 24:36-43.
[28]Matt. 28:16-18.

[29]*Era*, vol. 27, pp. 1149-1150; 2 Ne. 9:28-29.

confirming their faith and strengthening them in the gospel of which he is the Author. Of this they have borne record and have given their testimony to the world.[30]

But after the falling away from the truth, the world was in darkness and *without living witnesses* of the resurrection of Christ, *until* the restoration of the gospel in the dispensation of the fulness of times. At the present time upon the face of the earth there are many who can testify that Jesus is the Christ, for the Spirit of God has revealed unto them this truth; and no man can know that Jesus is the Christ unless the Holy Spirit reveals it unto him.

JOSEPH SMITH: WITNESS OF THE RESURRECTION. The Prophet Joseph Smith was raised up as a witness of the resurrection of Christ and was given power and authority to institute his gospel anew among the children of men. Others, also, beheld him, in our own generation, conversed with him, and were instructed by him and were taught the principles of truth which make us free. They also have borne record to the world of these things. We know that he hath risen from the dead, that he might bring all men unto him, on conditions of repentance.[31]

MATTHEW: WITNESS OF THE RESURRECTION. Matthew testified that at the time of the resurrection of Christ there was also a resurrection of the saints who had died in earlier times. Matthew is very particular in giving details in his writing. He speaks as an *eye witness* with full authority to testify.

He says: "And the graves were opened; and many bodies of the saints which slept arose, And came out of the graves after his resurrection, and went into the holy city, and appeared unto many."[32]

Latter-day Saints believe the testimony of Matthew. Moreover, they do not depend solely upon the testimony of the disciples of Christ who were with him in his min-

---

[30]Acts 2:29-36; 1 Cor. 15:3-9; Luke 24:30-43; John 20:14-23.

[31]Conf. Rep., Apr., 1912, pp. 67-68.

[32]Matt. 27:52-53.

istry, but they have the testimony of witnesses who have lived in our own day.[33]

BOOK OF MORMON: A WITNESS OF RESURRECTION. How fortunate we are as Latter-day Saints. We have all of this evidence, we have all of this knowledge that is given to us in the New Testament, the testimonies of the witnesses who were with Christ. In addition to that we have the testimonies of the elders and those who were associated with Christ in his ministry upon this continent among the Nephites as recorded in the *Book of Mormon*.[34]

And in addition to that, we have the testimonies of men of our own day and time. There are many here in this congregation who have, perhaps, lived and conversed, as I have myself, with men who lived in the days of the Prophet Joseph Smith and who heard from his own lips his story.

I have heard President Wilford Woodruff many times speak of these things; I have heard others, who were associated with the Prophet Joseph Smith, tell the story of how he had taught them in relation to the opening of the heavens and the coming of messengers from the presence of God in this day in which we live.

FIVE MODERN WITNESSES OF RESURRECTION. We have the testimony of Joseph Smith, of Oliver Cowdery, David Whitmer, Martin Harris, and Sidney Rigdon. There is no need to discuss any others. There are others. We have the testimony of these five men who all bore witness, solemnly to the world, that in this dispensation of the fulness of times Christ appeared, that he sent messengers from his presence to them. These five men are witnesses. Joseph Smith and Oliver Cowdery stood in the presence of the Lord Jesus Christ in the Kirtland Temple on the 3rd day of April, 1836. They stood in the presence of John the Baptist on the 15th day of May, 1829. They stood in the presence of Peter,

James, and John, a short time later in 1829. They also received keys of authority from Moses, Elias, and Elijah on that 3rd day of April, 1836.[35]

Oliver Cowdery, David Whitmer, and Martin Harris stood in the presence of an angel of God some time about June, 1829, and there they conversed with him, and they heard the voice of God speaking unto them from the heavens. They have given us their testimony; it is recorded in every edition of the *Book of Mormon.* We have that testimony. Sidney Rigdon has given us his testimony, both while he was in the Church and after he left it, that he with Joseph Smith in 1832, on the 16th day of February, saw the heavens opened, and they saw the Lord Jesus Christ sitting upon the right hand of God, and they have recorded for us that wonderful vison.[36]

Can we dispute these facts? Shall we put all that aside and say that these witnesses were deceivers, that they lied, or that they presented these things under hallucination? Is it consistent for us to do a thing of that kind? I say no. I say that when a man stands out in the face of all this evidence and says that nobody has ever returned from the dead, he is either ignorant or a fool; maybe he is both. The fact remains that *these witnesses spoke the truth,* and they are witnesses for God.

The Lord said he would raise up certain witnesses to testify of the restoration of the gospel, and of the coming forth of the *Book of Mormon,* and that, "Wo be unto him that rejecteth the word of God!"[37]

THE HOLY GHOST: WITNESS OF THE RESURRECTION. It is either due to *ignorance* or to *wickedness,* when all this evidence is presented to them, and they push it aside and say we have no evidence. I say it will stand at the last day as a testimony against them, and they will have to face it. I accept it as being true. I do not accept it as being true merely because Joseph Smith said it, be-

---

[35]*D. & C.* 13:110.   [37]2 Ne. 27:14.
[36]*D. & C.* 76:19-25.

cause Oliver Cowdery said it, because David Whitmer, Martin Harris and Sidney Rigdon have said it.

I say it is true because *the Spirit of the Lord himself has borne that testimony upon my soul.* I know that as they knew it—not because I have been in the presence of those holy messengers, but because the Lord has fulfilled his promise with me, as he has no doubt with many of you.[38]

I know that Jesus Christ lives. I know that he is the Son of God, the Redeemer of the world; that through his ministry, through his death and the shedding of his blood, all men may receive the remission of sins, through obedience to the gospel, and through their faithfulness and obedience to the end they will receive exaltation in the kingdom of God.

That is just as true as it is that we are here in this building today. Wo be unto the men who close their eyes and their ears against this knowledge. Nephi knew. As he was writing about these things, he knew what would happen, and he said: "Wo unto the deaf that will not hear; . . . Wo unto the blind that will not see."[39]

The truth is here, the evidence is here, overwhelmingly. We ought to know these things. We ought not be in doubt. No man should wonder whether or not men can come forth from the dead. It has been done. It will be done. The Lord shall give every soul his body back in the resurrection; the spirit and body shall be reunited inseparably never again to be divided, according to the plans of our Father in heaven.[40]

SONS OF PERDITION AND THE RESURRECTION

UNIVERSAL NATURE OF RESURRECTION. It has been taught by some that the resurrection would not be universal among those who have received mortal bodies, that some known as sons of perdition would be denied the privilege of the resurrection. It is very strange that such

[38]Matt. 7:7-11; John 7:15-17; Jas. 1:5-7; 1 Cor. 2:1-16.
[39]2 Ne. 9:31-32.
[40]*Church News,* June 3, 1933, p. 7.

a doctrine could be entertained in the face of the many instructions and revelations coming from the Lord and his holy prophets. They universally testify that *all* shall come forth from the dead. Justice demands this because men are not responsible for death and hence are entitled to redemption from its grasp.

In his great mercy, love, and justice, our Father in heaven has provided that *all* his children who have gained mortality shall live again. *The soul cannot be destroyed.* The spirits of all men are eternal. They lived before this mortal life came, and through the atonement of Jesus Christ, they shall live after this mortal life is ended.[41]

Our Redeemer came into the world to obtain the mastery over death. If one soul born into this world, no matter how wicked he may be, were denied the resurrection, then Jesus Christ would not have the victory. It is imperative, therefore, that *all* must receive the resurrection.[42]

ALL MEN TO BE RESURRECTED. No person who has lived and died on this earth will be denied the resurrection. Reason teaches this, and it is a simple matter of justice. Adam alone was responsible for death, and therefore the Lord does not lay this to the charge of any other person. Justice demands that no person who was not responsible for death shall be held responsible for it, and therefore, as Paul declared, "As in Adam *all* die, even so in Christ shall *all* be made alive."[43]

Again the Lord has said: "But, behold, verily I say unto you, before the earth shall pass away, Michael, mine archangel, shall sound his trump, and then shall *all the dead awake*, for their graves shall be opened, and they shall come forth—*yea even all*. And the righteous shall be gathered on my right hand unto eternal life; and the wicked on my left hand will I be ashamed to own before the Father."[44]

---

[41]*Church News,* Feb. 15, 1941, p. 7.   [43]1 Cor. 15:22.
[42]*Era,* vol. 57, p. 16.   [44]*D. & C.* 29:26-27.

This passage should be enough for any member of the Church, to set him right, but strange to say, there are those who misconstrue it and say it does not mean what it says.

Then we have the clear statement of Jacob in the *Book of Mormon:* "And he cometh into the world that he may save all men if they will hearken unto his voice; for behold, he suffereth the pains of all men, yea, the pains of every living creature, both men, women, and children, who belong to the family of Adam. And he suffereth this that *the resurrection might pass upon all men,* that *all* might stand before him at the great and judgment day."[45]

What could be stronger and more convincing than these words of our Redeemer: "Marvel not at this: for the hour is coming, in the which *all* that are in the graves shall hear his voice, And *shall come forth;* they that have done good, unto the resurrection of life; and they that have done evil, unto the resurrection of damnation."[46]

JOSEPH SMITH TEACHES RESURRECTION OF SONS OF PERDITION. Let us consider now some of the sayings of later prophets. This is from the Prophet Joseph Smith: "There have been remarks made concerning all men being redeemed from hell; but I say that those who sin against the Holy Ghost cannot be forgiven in this world or in the world to come; they shall die the *second death.* Those who commit *the unpardonable sin* are doomed to *Gnolom* —to dwell in hell, worlds without end. As they concoct scenes of bloodshed in this world, so *they shall rise to that resurrection which is as the lake of fire and brimstone.* Some shall rise to the everlasting burnings of God; for God dwells in everlasting burnings, and *some shall rise to the damnation of their own filthiness* which is as exquisite a torment as the lake of fire and brimstone."[47]

---

45 2 Ne. 9:21-22.
46 John 5:28-29.

47 Joseph Fielding Smith, *Teachings of the Prophet Joseph Smith,* p. 361.

JOHN TAYLOR TEACHES UNIVERSAL RESURRECTION.
This is from President John Taylor: "What, will everybody be resurrected? Yes, *every living being!* 'But every
man in his own order: Christ the firstfruits; afterward
they that are Christ's at his coming. Then cometh the
end.'[48] The saints shall live and reign with Christ a
thousand years. One of the apostles says, 'But the rest
of the dead lived not again until the thousand years were
finished.'[49] But *all* must come forth from the grave, some
time or other, in the selfsame tabernacle that they possessed while living on the earth. It will be just as Ezekiel
has described it—bone will come to its bone, and flesh
and sinew will cover the skeleton, and at the Lord's bid-
ding breath will enter the body, and we will appear, many
of us, a marvel to ourselves."[50]

JOSEPH F. SMITH TEACHES UNIVERSAL RESURREC-
TION. And this is the testimony of President Joseph F.
Smith: "*Every creature* that is born in the image of God
will be resurrected from the dead, just as sure as he dies;
you can write that down if you please, and never forget
it, nor allow yourself to have any unbelief on that account.
'As in Adam *all* die, even so in Christ shall *all* be made
alive.'[51] . . .

"It matters not whether we have done well or ill,
whether we have been intelligent or ignorant, or whether
we have been bondmen or slaves or freemen, *all men will
be raised from the dead;* and, as I understand it, when
they are raised from the dead, they become immortal
beings, and they will no more suffer the dissolution of the
spirit and body."[52]

GEORGE Q. CANNON TEACHES UNIVERSAL RESUR-
RECTION. These references should be enough, but there
may be some who will rise up and say that the Lord has
spoken otherwise, and they will base their contention on

[48]1 Cor. 15:23-24.   [51]1 Cor. 15:22.
[49]Rev. 20:5.   [52]*Era,* vol. 19, p. 386.
[50]*Journal of Discourses,* vol. 18, p. 333;
     Ezek. 37:1-14.

the words in the *Doctrine and Covenants,* section 76:38-39. President George Q. Cannon, years ago, corrected this erroneous interpretation, as follows:

"In many minds there has been a great misapprehension on the question of the resurrection. Some have had the idea and have taught it, that the sons of perdition will not be resurrected at all. They base this idea, and draw this conclusion from the 38th and 39th verses of section 76, of the book of *Doctrine and Covenants,* where the Lord says:

" 'Yea, verily, the only ones who shall not be redeemed in the due time of the Lord, after the sufferings of his wrath. For all the rest shall be brought forth by the resurrection of the dead, through the triumph and the glory of the Lamb, who was slain, who was in the bosom of the Father before the worlds were made.'

"A careful reading of these verses, however, and especially of the preceding paragraphs, will show that the Lord does *not,* in this language, exclude even the sons of perdition from the resurrection. It is plain that the intention is to refer to them explicitly as *the only ones on whom the second death shall have any power* 'For all the rest shall be brought forth by the resurrection of the dead, through the triumph and the glory of the Lamb.' This excluded class are the only ones on whom the second death shall have any power, and 'the only ones who *shall not be redeemed* in the due time of the Lord, after the suffering of his wrath.'

"This is by no means to say that they are to have no resurrection. *Jesus our Lord and Savior died for all, and all will be resurrected*—good, bad, white and black, people of every race, whether sinners or not; and no matter how great their sins may be, the resurrection of their bodies is sure. Jesus has died for them, and they all will be redeemed from the grave through the atonement which he has made."[53]

---

[53]*Era,* vol. 45, pp. 827-829; *Instructor,*
    vol. 35, p. 123.

No DEATH AFTER RESURRECTION. Will any after receiving the resurrection ever die, or have the dissolution of the spirit and body? The answer to this is obviously, *no!* What reason could there be in calling them forth and uniting their spirits and bodies only to cause death to intervene the second time and dissolve their souls? The words of the Prophet already quoted are to the effect that the sons of perdition, who concocted scenes of bloodshed, shall dwell in hell "worlds without end."[54] According to the word of the Lord—and that we must accept as final, no matter what may have been, or what may be now the opinions of men—we are told:

"And they who remain shall *also be quickened;* nevertheless, *they shall return again to their own place,* to enjoy that which they are willing to receive, because they were not willing to enjoy that which they might have received."[55]

"They who remain" must refer to *those who are not included in any of the three kingdoms,* and in another place, section 76:33, the Lord has said: "For they are vessels of wrath, doomed to suffer the wrath of God, with the devil and his angels in eternity." These are they who remain "filthy still."[56]

No CORRUPTION AFTER RESURRECTION. Amulek said: "Now, this restoration shall come to all, both old and young, both bond and free, both male and female, *both the wicked and the righteous;* and even there shall not so much as a hair of their heads be lost; but every thing shall be restored to its perfect frame, as it is now, or in the body, and shall be brought and be arraigned before the bar of Christ the Son, and God the Father, and the Holy Spirit, which is one Eternal God, to be judged according to their works, whether they be good or whether they be evil.

"Now, behold, I have spoken unto you concerning

[54]Smith, *op. cit.,* p. 361.   [56]*D. & C.* 88:35, 102.
[55]*D. & C.* 88:32.

the death of the mortal body, and also concerning the resurrection of the mortal body. I say unto you that this mortal body is raised to an immortal body, that is from death, even from the first death unto life, that *they can die no more; their spirits uniting with their bodies, never to be divided; thus the whole becoming spiritual and immortal, that they can no more see corruption."*[57]

In this statement it is shown that Amulek is speaking of the dead, both good and bad, and in the next, or 12th chapter, Alma confirms this doctrine in relation to the wicked who are cast out in the following words: "I say unto you, *they shall be as though there had been no redemption made; for they cannot be redeemed according to God's justice; and they cannot die, seeing there is no more corruption."*[58]

Unless every soul is raised, our Savior will not win the victory over death. His victory must be, and will be, complete, as Paul clearly declared.[59] In the resurrection the spirit and the body become inseparably connected, that they can never again be divided, and thus they become immortal.[60]

CAIN TO RULE OVER SATAN. Sons of perdition will have an ascendency over Satan himself, because he has no body. But who is Perdition? The Lord said to Cain: "If thou doest well, thou shalt be accepted. And if thou doest not well, sin lieth at the door, and *Satan desireth to have thee;* and except thou shalt hearken unto my commandments, I will deliver thee up, and it shall be unto thee according to his desire. And *thou shalt rule over him;* For from this time forth *thou shalt be the father of his lies; thou shalt be called Perdition; for thou wast also before the world."*[61]

Satan wanted him because Cain had a body. He wanted more power. A man with a body of course will have greater power than just a spirit without a body.

---

[57]Alma 11:44-45.
[58]Alma 12:18.
[59]I Cor. 15:53-57.

[60]*Era,* vol. 45, p. 829.
[61]Moses 5:23-24.

Cain sinned with his eyes open, so he became Perdition, the father of lies.[62]

STILLBORN CHILDREN

STILLBORN CHILDREN RESURRECTED. There is no information given by revelation in regard to the status of stillborn children. However, I will express my personal opinion that we should have hope that *these little ones will receive a resurrection and then belong to us.* I cannot help feeling that this will be the case.

When a couple have a stillborn child, we give them all the comfort we can. We have good reasons to hope. Funeral services may be held for such children, if the parents so desire. Stillborn children should not be reported nor recorded as births and deaths on the records of the Church, but it is suggested that parents record in their own family records a name for each such stillborn child.

WHEN THE SPIRIT ENTERS THE BODY. The time of quickening is when the mother feels the life of her unborn infant.[63] President Brigham Young has left us this explanation of the time when the spirit enters the body: "When the spirit leaves them [mortal bodies] they are lifeless; and *when the mother feels life come to her infant, it is the spirit entering the body preparatory to the immortal existence.* But suppose an accident occurs and the spirit has to leave this body prematurely, what then? All that the physician says is— 'It is a still birth,' and that is all they know about it; but whether the spirit remains in the body [i.e. in its own body] a minute, an hour, a day, a year, or lives there until the body has reached a good old age, it is certain that the time will come when they will be separated, and the body will return to mother earth, there to sleep upon that mother's bosom. That is all there is about death."

---

[62]*Church News,* Mar. 30, 1935, p. 6.   [63]Luke 1:39-41.

On other occasions, also, President Young taught that we should have hope for the resurrection of stillborn children. "They are all right," he said, and nothing in the way of sealings or ordinances need be done for them.[64]

RESURRECTION OF ALL THINGS

EARTH AND ALL LIFE RESURRECTED. Every creature on the earth, whether it be man, *animal, fish, fowl,* or *other creature,* that the Lord has created, is *redeemed from death* on the *same terms* that man is redeemed. These creatures are not responsible for death coming into the world any more than we were, and since they have been created by the Father, they are entitled to their *redemption and eternal duration.*

The *earth itself* shall be changed from its mortal body, for it too is a living thing now, under the curse of death, and it "abideth the law of a celestial kingdom, for it filleth the measure of its creation, and transgresseth not the law—Wherefore, it shall be sanctified; yea, notwithstanding *it shall die, it shall be quickened again,* and shall abide the power by which it is quickened, and the righteous shall inherit it."[65]

ALL LIVING THINGS RESURRECTED. "I know that, whatsoever God doeth," we read in the scriptures, "it shall be for ever: nothing can be put to it, nor anything taken from it."[66] We know that all these creatures are animated by the spirit which is in them, just as man is. The Lord declared through the Prophet that "the spirit of man [is] in the likeness of his person, also *the spirit of the beast, and every other creature which God has created.*"[67] Is there any living creature that God has not made? If so, the power of creation has gone out of his hands. He is supreme, and all life is from him, his gift to every creature.

---

[64]Pers. Corresp.; *Journal of Discourses,* vol. 17, p. 143.
[65]*D. & C.* 88:25-26.

[66]Eccles. 3:14.
[67]*D. & C.* 77:2.

The purified body will be the same body which shall rise in its "perfect form," and so we read: "And the end shall come, and the heaven and the earth shall be consumed and pass away, and there shall be a new heaven and a new earth. For all old things shall pass away, and all things shall become new, even the heaven and the earth, and *all the fulness thereof, both men and beasts, the fowls of the air, and the fishes of the sea;* And not one hair, neither mote, shall be lost, for it is the workmanship of mine hand."[68]

[68]*Era,* vol. 45, pp. 829-831; *D. & C.* 29:23-25.

CHAPTER 15

SALVATION AND RESURRECTION

BLESSINGS RECEIVED THROUGH RESURRECTION

RESURRECTION SAVES MAN FROM DEVIL. Immortality of the soul is the gift of God through the death and resurrection of his Son Jesus Christ. If the Savior had not died for the world, man would have remained in his sins. There could have been no resurrection from the dead and the physical body would have gone down into the grave without redemption, while the spirit would have become subject to the devil and his angels eternally.[1]

FULNESS OF JOY COMES THROUGH RESURRECTION. The spirit and the body in this mortal life are not inseparably connected. Hence man cannot in the mortal life receive a fulness of joy. It is only through the resurrection and the spirit and the body being united inseparably that immortality and eternal life can come.[2]

No man can receive the inseparable connection of the spirit and body until he dies. Therefore, *death is just as important, so far as life is concerned, as birth.* The reason is that in this life the spirit and the body are not inseparably connected. When mortal sickness comes, or old age, then dissolution comes, the spirit leaves the body, and the body goes into the grave to await the resurrection. When the spirit and the body unite again in the resurrection from the dead, they are joined together in such a way that they cannot be separated, and there shall be no more death.

Then man may receive a fulness of joy. While he is in this temporal state of spirit and body, he cannot re-

---

[1]*Era,* vol. 19, p. 199; 2 Ne. 9:7-9.   [2]*Church News,* Apr. 22, 1939, p. 3; D. & C. 88:14-16; 93:33-34.

ceive a fulness of joy. *No man in mortal life can receive the fulness of joy which the Lord has in store for him.* Only after the resurrection from the dead, only when the spirit and the body are inseparably connected—when through the resurrection the spirit and the body are welded together inseparably—can that fulness come. That is the *beauty* of the resurrection, that is the *objective* of the resurrection from the dead.

MORTALITY GIVEN TO PREPARE MEN FOR RESURRECTION. And so it is necessary that every man must die. It is necessary to bring to pass the greater blessing which cannot come unless we die. *No man wants to be cursed with mortal life and live forever. No, that would be a calamity.*[3] Mortal life is all right for the little space of time that we spend here in this world. It is necessary. It is a mighty important part of our existence, because it is here that we prove ourselves. It is here that we prepare ourselves for that which is to come. That is how important mortality is, and yet we treat it lightly, many of us. We look upon it as meaning little. "We are here today; we will be gone tomorrow. Tomorrow can take care of itself. We will have a good time here." That is the way many of us look on life. Now is the time, this is the day, Alma says, for repentance. Do not procrastinate the day of your repentance. The time may come when it is too late.[4]

NATURE OF RESURRECTED BODIES

SPIRITUAL BODIES IN THE RESURRECTION. In the resurrection from the dead, the bodies which were laid down *natural bodies* shall come forth *spiritual bodies.* That is to say, in *mortality* the life of the body is in the *blood,*[5] but the body when raised to *immortality* shall be *quickened by the spirit* and not the blood. Hence, *it be-*

---

[3]2 Ne. 9:6.   [5]Lev. 17:11.
[4]*Rel. Soc. Mag.,* vol. 7, pp. 13-14;
    Alma 34:31-35.

comes spiritual, but it will be *composed of flesh and bones, just as the body of* Jesus was, who is the prototype.[6]

TANGIBLE NATURE OF SPIRITUAL BODIES. These modern blind teachers of the blind who deny the literal resurrection have a very false understanding of what is meant by a *spiritual body.* They have based their conclusion on the statement that Paul makes that the body is raised a spiritual body and that flesh and blood cannot inherit the kingdom of God.[7] They cannot conceive in their minds of a body raised from the dead, being composed of flesh and bones, quickened by spirit and not by blood.

When Paul spoke of the *spiritual* body, he had no reference at all to the *spirit* body, and there they have made their mistake. They have confused the spiritual body, or, in other words, the body quickened by the spirit, with the body of the spirit alone. They think that those who believe in the resurrection of the literal body believe that it shall be raised again, quickened by blood, which is not the case. . . .

After the resurrection from the dead our bodies will be spiritual bodies, but they will be bodies that are tangible, bodies that have been purified, but they will nevertheless be bodies of flesh and bones. They will not be *blood bodies.* They will no longer be quickened by blood but quickened by the spirit which is eternal, and they shall become immortal and shall never die.[8]

BLOOD BODIES AND SPIRITUAL BODIES COMPARED. Now if our good friends understood this, they would not fall into this error of thinking that Paul's doctrine was in conflict with that of the Lord and Savior Jesus Christ, when Paul declared that the body that would be raised would be a spiritual body. You read in the Book of Genesis, where the Lord said to Noah after the flood, that the blood was the life of the body; the blood is the life

---

[6]*Era,* vol. 19, p. 430; Luke 24:36-43.   [8]*D. & C.* 88:15-32.
[7]1 Cor. 15:42-57.

thereof, he says. Therefore, "Whoso sheddeth man's blood, by man shall his blood be shed," because blood is the life of the mortal body.[9]

But with the body brought forth in the resurrection, which is the *immortal body,* that is not the case. In it blood does not exist, but the spirit is the life giving power. Hence, they are no longer bodies quickened by blood but bodies quickened by spirit, and hence they are *spiritual bodies,* but *tangible bodies of flesh and bones,* just as was the body of the Son of God. Now this is the doctrine of the Lord and Savior of the world.[10]

RESURRECTION IN INCORRUPTION. Now let us understand the meaning of that term *corruption.* Perhaps, because of the way that word is usually used, what you may have in mind is not exactly the meaning given by Paul in this passage of scripture.[11] *Corruption* here means *mortality.* It means to be in this world of change.

Our bodies are changing daily. They are throwing off the waste, taking on the new. They are so constituted that the food we eat, the water we drink, the air we breathe, build up and replace those parts which have decayed or have filled their mission of usefulness and have been discarded. So this is, as Paul put it, a corruptible body that we have now, and this prophet is speaking of the mortal body when he says corruption. This mortal body shall eventually, through the resurrection, become an incorruptible body, not subject to these changes, not subject to disease and decay.[12]

KINDS OF RESURRECTED BODIES. In the resurrection there will be different kinds of bodies; they will not all be alike. The body a man receives will determine his place hereafter. There will be celestial bodies, terrestrial bodies, and telestial bodies, and these bodies will differ as distinctly as do bodies here, for example, the white European, the Negro, the Philippino, the Indian.[13]

[9]Gen. 9:3-6.
[10]Conf. Rep., Apr., 1917, pp. 62-63.
[11]1 Cor. 15:42-57.
[12]*Church News,* Apr. 22, 1939, p. 3.
[13]D. & C. 76:50-113; 88:15-32; 1 Cor. 15:35-42.

Bodies will be quickened according to the kingdom which they are judged worthy to enter. Elder Orson Pratt many years ago in writing of the resurrection and the kind of bodies which would be raised in these kingdoms said:

"In every species of animals and plants, there are many resemblances in the general outlines and many specific differences characterizing the individuals of each species. So in the resurrection. There will be several classes of resurrected bodies; some celestial, some terrestrial, some telestial, and some sons of perdition. Each of these classes will *differ* from the others by *prominent* and *marked distinctions;* yet, in each, considered by itself, there will be found many resemblances as well as distinctions. *There will be some physical peculiarity by which each individual in every class can be identified."*

PROCREATION LIMITED TO CELESTIAL BODIES. *Some will gain celestial bodies with all the powers of exaltation and eternal increase.* These bodies will shine like the sun as our Savior's does, as described by John.[14] Those who enter the terrestrial kingdom will have terrestrial bodies, and they will not shine like the sun, but they will be more glorious than the bodies of those who receive the telestial glory.

In both of these kingdoms there will be changes in the bodies and limitations. They will not have the power of increase, neither the power or nature to live as husbands and wives, for this will be denied them and they cannot increase.

Those who receive the exaltation in the celestial kingdom will have the "continuation of the seeds forever."[15] *They will live in the family relationship.* In the terrestrial and in the telestial kingdoms there will be no marriage. Those who enter there will remain "separately and singly" forever.[16]

---

[14]Rev. 1:12-18; *D. & C.* 110:1-4; Ex. 24:9-10.   [15]*D. & C.* 132:19.   [16]*D. & C.* 132:15-32.

Some of the functions in the celestial body will not appear in the terrestrial body, neither in the telestial body, and *the power of procreation will be removed.* I take it that men and women will, in these kingdoms, be just what the so-called Christian world expects us all to be—neither man nor woman, merely immortal beings having received the resurrection.

RESURRECTED BODIES PASS THROUGH SOLID OBJECTS. *Resurrected bodies have control over the elements.* How do you think the bodies will get out of the graves at the resurrection? When the Angel Moroni appeared to the Prophet Joseph Smith, the Prophet saw him apparently come down and ascend through the solid walls, or ceiling of the building.[17] If the Prophet's account had been a fraud, he never would have stated such a story (as we may be sure he never would have thought of such a thing), but would have had the angel come in through the door. Why should it appear any more impossible for a resurrected being to pass through solid objects than for a spirit, for a spirit is also matter?[18]

It was just as easy for the Angel Moroni to come to the Prophet Joseph Smith down through the building as it was for our Savior to appear to his disciples after his resurrection in the room where they were assembled when the door was closed. "The same day at evening, being the first day of the week, *when the doors were shut* where the disciples were assembled for fear of the Jews, came Jesus and stood in the midst, and saith unto them, Peace be unto you."[19]

Here, you see that the door was shut, "for fear of the Jews," but this did not prevent Jesus from appearing to them in the room. How could he do it? He had power over the elements. This has been explained by some scientists by the statement that we are limited to three dimensions, but superior beings may have many dimen-

17Joseph Smith 2:30, 43-45.   19John 20:19.
18D. & C. 131:7-8.

sions of which we know nothing. One learned man, who does not believe in the resurrection, stated that a mortal being, if his body could vibrate in the proper manner, could pass through solid objects. Just how resurrected beings do it, we do not know, but that it has been done we do know, for the Savior and others have done it.[20]

PHYSICAL PERFECTION IN RESURRECTION

NO DEFORMITIES OR IMPERFECTIONS IN RESURRECTION. A little sound thinking will reveal to us that it would be inconsistent for our bodies to be raised with all kinds of imperfections. Some men have been burned at the stake for the sake of truth. Some have been beheaded, and others have had their bodies torn asunder; for example, John the Baptist was beheaded and received his resurrection at the time of the resurrection of our Redeemer. It is impossible for us to think of him coming forth from the dead holding his head in his hands; our reason says he was physically complete in the resurrection. He appeared to the Prophet Joseph Smith and Oliver Cowdery with a perfect resurrected body.

When we come forth from the dead, our spirits and bodies will be reunited inseparably, never again to be divided, and they will then be assigned to the kingdom to which they belong. *All deformities and imperfections will be removed, and the body will conform to the likeness of the spirit,* for the Lord revealed, "that which is spiritual being in the likeness of that which is temporal; and that which is temporal in the likeness of that which is spiritual; the spirit of man in the likeness of his person, as also the spirit of the beast, and every other creature which God has created."[21]

PERFECT AND PROPER FRAME IN RESURRECTION. The Prophet Amulek has stated the case very clearly in these words: "Now, there is a death which is called a temporal death; and the death of Christ shall loose the

---

[20]Pers. Corresp.   [21]D. & C. 77:2.

bands of this temporal death. . . . The spirit and the body
shall be reunited again in its *perfect form;* both limb and
joint shall be restored to its *proper frame,* even as we
now are at this time; and we shall be brought to stand
before God, knowing even as we know now, and have
a bright recollection of all our guilt.

"Now, this restoration shall come to all, both old
and young, both bond and free, both male and female,
both the wicked and the righteous; and even *there shall
not so much as a hair of their heads be lost;* but *every
thing shall be restored to its perfect frame,* as it is now,
or in the body, and shall be brought and be arraigned
before the bar of Christ the Son, and God the Father,
and the Holy Spirit, which is one Eternal God, to be
judged according to their works, whether they be good
or whether they be evil.

"Now, behold, I have spoken unto you concerning
the death of the mortal body, and also concerning the
resurrection of the mortal body. I say unto you that this
mortal body is *raised to an immortal body,* that is from
death, even from the first death unto life, that they can
die no more; their spirits uniting with their bodies, never
to be divided; thus the whole becoming *spiritual* and
immortal, that *they can no more see corruption."*[22]

Alma testifies to this same thing. Speaking of the
resurrection of our Lord which will give him power to
call forth all of the dead, he says: "Yea, this bringeth
about the restoration of those things of which has been
spoken by the mouths of the prophets. The soul shall
be restored to the body, and the body to the soul; yea,
and every limb and joint shall be restored to its body;
yea, *even a hair of the head shall not be lost; but all things
shall be restored to their proper and perfect frame."*[23]

WHY CHRIST RETAINED MARKS OF WOUNDS IN
HIS BODY. We must not judge the resurrection of others
by the resurrection of Jesus Christ. It is true that he

---

[22]Alma 11:42-45.   [23]Alma 40:22-23.

appeared to his disciples and invited them to examine the prints of the nails in his hands and in his feet, and the spear wound in his side, but this was a *special manifestation* to them.

We should know that the disciples had failed to understand that he was to rise again, and this manifestation was for their benefit. Thomas was absent, and it was with some difficulty that the other disciples could convince him that the Lord had risen. Thomas was not worse than any other one of the apostles. Perhaps they would have done just what he did had they been absent. The Lord said to them and later to him: "Behold my hands and my feet, that it is I myself: handle me, and see; for a spirit hath not flesh and bones, as ye see me have."[24]

CHRIST'S WOUNDS A WITNESS AT SECOND COMING. When the Savior comes to the Jews in the hour of their distress, as recorded in the *Doctrine and Covenants,* 45:51-53, he will show them the wounds in his hands and in his feet.

"And then shall the Jews look upon me and say: What are these wounds in thine hands and in thy feet? Then shall they know that I am the Lord; for I will say unto them: These wounds are the wounds with which I was wounded in the house of my friends. I am he who was lifted up. I am Jesus that was crucified. I am the Son of God. And then shall they weep because of their iniquities; then shall they lament because they persecuted their king."

The Prophet Zechariah has also prophesied of the Savior's Second Coming and his appearance to the Jews, when they will flee from their enemies and the Mount of Olives shall cleave in twain making a valley in which they shall seek refuge. At that particular time he will appear and they shall say: "What are these wounds in thine hands? Then he shall answer, Those with which I was wounded in the house of my friends."[25] Then will

---

[24]Luke 24:39; John 20:24-29.   [25]Zech. 12:9-14; 13:1-9; 14:1-21.

they mourn, each family apart, because they had rejected their Lord.

It is true that he also showed these wounds to the Nephites when he visited with them with the same purpose in view, to convince them of his identity, and give to them a witness of his suffering.[26] *It can hardly be accepted as a fact that these wounds have remained in his hands, side, and feet all through the centuries from the time of his crucifixion and will remain until his Second Coming.* But they will appear to the Jews as a witness against their fathers and their stubbornness in following the teachings of their fathers. After their weeping and mourning they shall be cleansed.[27]

NATURE OF HEALING POWER OF RESURRECTION. When a person rises in the resurrection, *his body will be perfect* but that does *not* mean that he will be perfect in faith.[28] There will be different kinds of bodies in the resurrection—celestial, terrestrial, and telestial—and they will not be alike any more than whites, browns, and blacks are alike in this life. Every man will receive according to his works.

Bodies will come up, of course, as they were laid down, but will be restored to their proper, perfect frame immediately. Old people will not look old when they come forth from the grave. Scars will be removed. No one will be bent or wrinkled. How foolish it would be for a man to come forth in the resurrection who had lost a leg and have to wait for it to grow again. Each body will come forth with its *perfect frame. If there has been some deformity or physical impairment in this life, it will be removed.*

The Lord is not impotent to heal and restore the dead to their perfect frame in the resurrection. If the Savior could restore withered hands, eyes that had *never* had sight, crooked bodies, in this mortal life, surely the

263 Ne. 11:10-17.
27*Era,* vol. 57, pp. 78-79.
282 Ne. 9:13-16; Mosiah 3:24-27; Alma 11:43; 12:14; 41:13-15; 42:22-25.

Father will not permit bodies that are not *physically perfect* to come forth in the resurrection.

No DISEASE IN RESURRECTION. If a man has gone through life with a club foot, or other deformity, will he be raised in the resurrection and have the club foot or deformity, and have to wait until the "restoration of all things," before this imperfection is corrected?

The answer to this is, No! Let us carry this a little farther. If a person through disease passes through the greater part of his life with some deformity—such as diabetes, tumors, consumption—will he have to be subject to such disease until the day of "restitution of all things?" Certainly not, and it is just as inconsistent to claim that the club foot would have to remain as to say that any of these other deformities or diseases would have to remain.

CHILDREN RESURRECTED AS CHILDREN. Of course, children who die do not grow in the grave. They will come forth with their bodies as they were laid down, and then they will grow to the full stature of manhood or womanhood after the resurrection, but *all* will have their bodies fully restored.[29]

RESTORATION TO PERFECTION THROUGH RESURRECTION. In speaking about the resurrection at the funeral of Sister Rachel Grant, President Joseph F. Smith said that the same person, in the same form and likeness, will come forth "even to the wounds in the flesh. Not that a person will always be marred by scars, wounds, deformities, defects or infirmities, for these will be removed in their course, in their proper time, according to the merciful providence of God."[30]

President Smith was in full accord with Amulek and Alma. He taught that the body will be restored as stated in Alma 11:42-45 and 40:22-23. While he expresses the thought that the body will come forth as it was laid

[29]Joseph F. Smith, *Gospel Doctrine,* 4th ed., p. 30.   [30]Smith, *op. cit.,* p. 30.

down, he also expresses the thought that it will take time
to adjust the body from the condition of imperfections.
This, of course, is reasonable, but at the same time the
length of time to make these adjustments will *not* cover
any appreciable extent of time.

President Smith never intended to convey the
thought that it would require weeks or months of time in
order for the defects to be removed. These changes will
come naturally, of course, but *almost instantly.* We cannot look upon it in any other way. For instance, a man
who has lost a leg in childhood will have his leg restored.
It does not grow in the grave, but will be restored naturally, but with the power of the Almighty it will not take
extended time for this to be accomplished.

RESTORATION TO PERFECTION ALMOST INSTAN-
TANEOUS. When President Smith declares that "the
body will come forth as it is laid to rest, for there is no
growth in the grave,"[31] he has in mind this: *Infants* and
children do not grow in the grave, but when they come
forth, they will come forth with the same body and in the
same size in which the body was when it was laid away.
After the resurrection the body will grow until it has
reached the full stature of manhood or womanhood. He
did not intend to teach that the *adult* who loses a leg will
come forth without that leg until it can be grafted on after
the resurrection. Rather, his body will come forth complete in every part. *Deformities and the like will be corrected, if not immediately at the time of the uniting of the
spirit and body, so soon thereafter that it will make no
difference.* We may be sure that every man will receive
his body in its *perfect frame* in the resurrection.[32]

FIRST AND SECOND RESURRECTIONS

A RESURRECTION OF LIFE AND OF DAMNATION. The
Lord meant literally just what he said when he declared
that the dead should hear his voice and should come forth,

---

[31]Smith, *op. cit.,* p. 566.   [32]Pers. Corresp.

they that had done good unto the *resurrection of life* and they that had done evil unto the *resurrection of damnation.*[33]

The resurrection shall come to *all* men, for they are not responsible for death. The Lord will not punish them for Adam's transgression.[34] Therefore, he took upon him the sins of all mankind and redeemed every creature from death and granted unto each one of us a resurrection, but not eternal life, not salvation, not an existence in the presence of his Father in the celestial kingdom. That comes through faithfulness, through diligence, through perseverance on our part and through our belief and acceptance and our keeping of the commandments of the Lord.[35]

FIRST RESURRECTION AT SECOND COMING. While there was a general resurrection of the righteous at the time Christ arose from the dead, it is customary for us to speak of the resurrection of the righteous at the Second Coming of Christ as the *first resurrection.* It is the first *to us,* for we have little thought or concern over that which is past. The Lord has promised that at the time of his Second Advent the graves will be opened, and the just shall come forth to reign with him on the earth for a thousand years.

John in the Book of Revelation writes of these: "And I saw thrones, and they sat upon them, and judgment was given unto them: and I saw the souls of them that were beheaded for the witness of Jesus, and for the word of God, and which had not worshipped the beast, neither his image, neither had received his mark upon their foreheads, or in their hands; and they lived and reigned with Christ a thousand years.

"But the rest of the dead lived not again until the thousand years were finished. This is the first resurrection. Blessed and holy is he that hath part in the first

33John 5:24-29.
341 Cor. 15:22.
35Conf. Rep., Apr., 1917, p. 64; D. & C. 18:10-12; 29:43-44.

resurrection: on such the second death hath no power, but they shall be priests of God and of Christ, and shall reign with him a thousand years."[36]

RESURRECTION OF CELESTIAL BODIES. In modern revelation given to the Church, the Lord has made known more in relation to this glorious event. There shall be at least *two classes* which shall have the privilege of the resurrection at this time: First, those who "shall dwell in the presence of God and his Christ forever and ever";[37] and second, honorable men, those who belong to the terrestrial kingdom as well as those of the celestial kingdom.

At the time of the coming of Christ, "They who have slept in their graves shall come forth, for their graves shall be opened; and they also shall be caught up to meet him in the midst of the pillar of heaven—They are Christ's, the first fruits, they who shall descend with him first, and they who are on the earth and in their graves, who are first caught up to meet him; and all this by the voice of the sounding of the trump of the angel of God."[38] These are the just, "whose names are written in heaven, where God and Christ are the judge of all. These are they who are just men made perfect through Jesus the mediator of the new covenant, who wrought out this perfect atonement through the shedding of his own blood."[39]

RESURRECTION OF TERRESTRIAL BODIES. Following this great event, and after the Lord and the righteous who are caught up to meet him have descended upon the earth, there will come to pass another resurrection. This may be considered as a part of the first, although it comes later. In this resurrection will come forth those of the *terrestrial order*, who were not worthy to be caught up to meet him, but who are worthy to come forth to enjoy the millennial reign.

---

[36]Rev. 20:4-6.
[37]D. & C. 76:62.
[38]D. & C. 88:97-98.

[39]*Church News*, Apr. 23, 1932, p. 6; D. & C. 76:68-69.

It is written that the second angel shall sound, which is the second trump, "and then cometh the redemption of those who are *Christ's at his coming;* who have received their part in the prison which is prepared for them, that they might receive the gospel, and be judged according to men in the flesh."[40]

This other class, which will also have right to the first resurrection, are those who are not members of the *Church of the Firstborn,* but who have led honorable lives, although they refused to accept the fulness of the gospel.

Also in this class will be numbered those who died without law and hence are not under condemnation for a violation of the commandments of the Lord. The promise is made to them of redemption from death in the following words: "And then shall the heathen nations be redeemed, and they that knew no law shall have part in the first resurrection; and it shall be tolerable for them."[41] These, too, shall partake of the mercies of the Lord and shall receive the reuniting of spirit and body inseparably, thus becoming immortal, but not with the fulness of the glory of God.

RESURRECTION OF TELESTIAL BODIES. All liars, and sorcerers, and adulterers and all who love and make a lie, shall not receive the resurrection at this time, but for a thousand years shall be thrust down into hell where they shall suffer the wrath of God until they pay the price of their sinning, if it is possible, by the things which they shall suffer.[42]

These are the "spirits of men who are to be judged, and are found under condemnation; And these are the rest of the dead; and they live not again until the thousand years are ended, neither again, until the end of the earth."[43]

---

[40]*Era,* vol. 45, p. 781; *D. & C.* 76:73-75; 88:89.
[41]*D. & C.* 45:54.
[42]*Church News,* Apr. 23, 1932, p. 6.
[43]*D. & C.* 88:100-101.

298 DOCTRINES OF SALVATION

These are the hosts of the *telestial world* who are condemned to "suffer the wrath of God on earth"; and who are "cast down to hell and suffer the wrath of Almighty God, *until* the fulness of times, when Christ shall have subdued all enemies under his feet, and shall have perfected his work."[44]

SUFFERINGS OF UNGODLY BEFORE RESURRECTION. These do not live during the millennial reign, but during that time are spending their time in torment, or anguish of soul, because of their transgressions. Christ has said that he suffered for all who will repent, but his wrath is kindled against all who will not repent, and they must suffer, "how exquisite you know not, yea, how hard to bear you know not. For behold, I, God, have suffered these things for all, that they might not suffer if they would repent; But if they would not repent they must suffer even as I; Which suffering caused myself, even God, the greatest of all, to tremble because of pain, and to bleed at every pore, and to suffer both body and spirit."[45]

This suffering will be a means of cleansing, or purifying, and through it the wicked shall be brought to a condition whereby they may, through the redemption of Jesus Christ, obtain immortality. Their spirits and bodies shall be again united, and they shall dwell in the telestial kingdom. But this resurrection will not come until the end of the world.

CHRIST DESTROYS DEATH THROUGH RESURRECTION. Paul says: "Then cometh the end, when he [Christ] shall have delivered up the kingdom to God, even the Father; when he shall have put down all rule and all authority and power. For he must reign, till he hath put all enemies under his feet. The last enemy that shall be destroyed is death."[46]

---

[44]*Era,* vol. 45, p. 781; *D. & C.* 76:104-106.

[45]*D. & C.* 19:15-18.
[46]1 Cor. 15:24-26.

The victory of Jesus Christ will not be complete until death is destroyed, and death will not be destroyed until every creature affected by the fall has been redeemed from death through the resurrection. This does not insure, however, a place in the kingdom of God for those who have lived lives of wickedness. While they pay the price of their sinning and obtain the resurrection, yet they shall go to "their own place, to enjoy that which they are willing to receive, because they were not willing to enjoy that which they might have received."[47]

They do not partake of eternal life, or salvation in the presence of God, but forever are shut out of his presence. Nevertheless, in his infinite goodness, our Eternal Father, will bless them as far as they may be blessed in accordance with the laws of justice and mercy.

This doctrine the Lord revealed to Joseph Smith. It is peculiar to the Latter-day Saints for even today the false idea persists that if a man is not saved in the kingdom of God, he is damned in the eternal torments of hell, without hope of relief from his sufferings.[48]

IS RESURRECTION GOING ON NOW? It is the opinion of some that the resurrection is going on all the time now, but this is purely *speculation without warrant in the scriptures.* It is true that the Lord has power to call forth any person or persons from the dead, as he may desire, especially if they have a mission to perform which would require their resurrection. For example, we have the cases of Peter, James, and Moroni.

We are given to understand that the *first* resurrection yet future, which means the coming forth of the righteous, will take place at *one particular time,* which is when our Savior shall appear in the clouds of heaven, when he shall return to reign. For us to speculate whether or not the Prophet Joseph Smith, Hyrum Smith, Brigham Young, and others have been called forth, without any revelation from the Lord, is merely supposition. When

---

[47]*D. & C.* 88:32.   [48]*Church News,* Apr. 30, 1932, p. 6.

the Lord wants any of these men, he has the power to
call them, but the first resurrection, with which we have
any future concern, will *commence* when Christ comes.[49]

ALMA'S "OPINION" ON RESURRECTION CLARIFIED.
Christ was the first fruits of the resurrection. He holds
the keys of the resurrection. The *first resurrection* took
place immediately following his resurrection. A misunderstanding has arisen in the minds of some because of
the words of Alma to his son Corianton.[50] They think
that Alma said all the dead, both good and bad, who lived
before the coming of our Lord, would receive the resurrection before any who should die after his coming. A
careful reading of Alma's words will show, however,
that he did not wish to convey any such thought. Abinadi
has made this matter very plain.[51]

Alma does not intend to say, although verse 19 of
chapter 40 implies it, that the wicked who lived before
Christ will be raised before the righteous who lived after
the coming of Christ; that may be implied by what he
says in verse 19, but in verse 20, he modifies this and says
it shall be the souls and bodies of the righteous who come
forth at the time of that resurrection.

We find Abinadi teaching that the wicked have no
part in the first resurrection, and the first resurrection
to Abinadi who lived before the days of Christ was the
time of our Savior's resurrection; so we conclude that
the wicked, no matter when they lived, will have to wait
until the final resurrection.[52]

TRANSLATED BEINGS STILL MORTAL. *Translated
beings are still mortal and will have to pass through the
experience of death, or the separation of the spirit and
the body, although this will be instantaneous.* The people
of the City of Enoch, Elijah, and others who received
this great blessing of translation in ancient times, *before*

---

[49]*Era,* vol. 45, pp. 781, 827.
[50]Alma 40:15-21.
[51]*Era,* vol. 45, p. 781; Mosiah 15:22-26.

[52]Pers. Corresp.; Matt. 27-52-53; 3 Ne.
3:9-10; Acts 2:29; Joseph Fielding
Smith, *Teachings of the Prophet
Joseph Smith,* pp. 188-189.

the coming of our Lord, could not have received the resurrection, or the change from mortality to immortality at that time, because our Lord had not paid the debt which frees us from mortality and grants to us the resurrection and immortal life.

Christ is the "resurrection and the life"[53] and the first fruits of them that slept.[54] Therefore, none could pass from mortality to immortality until our Savior completed his work for the redemption of man and had gained the keys of the resurrection, being the *first* to rise, having "life in himself" and the power to lay down his life and take it up again, thus freeing all men from the bondage which the fall had placed upon them.[55]

[53]John 11:25.
[54]1 Cor. 15:23.

[55]*Era,* vol. 56, p. 391; 3 Ne. 28:3-40; D. & C. 133:54-55.

CHAPTER 16

FAITH UNTO SALVATION

THE LAW OF FAITH

FAITH CENTERS IN CHRIST. Let it be uppermost in your minds, now and at all times, that Jesus is the Christ, the Son of the living God, who came into the world to lay down his life that we might live. That is the truth and is fundamental. *Upon that our faith is built.* It cannot be destroyed.

We must adhere to this teaching in spite of the teachings of the world and the notions of men, for this is paramount, this is essential to our salvation. The Lord redeemed us with his blood; he gave us salvation, provided—and there is this condition which we must not forget—that we will keep his commandments and always remember him. If we will do that, then we shall be saved, while the ideas and the foolishness of men shall perish from the earth. . . .

The reason that there is a lack of spirit and force in the religious teaching of the world is in part because they have tried to harmonize the Christian faith with the foolishness of men; and, of course, it will not harmonize with falsehood and with the doctrines of men. But we have received the light of the everlasting gospel. It is our salvation. Let us adhere to it and worship the Lord and keep his commandments, as we have been instructed to do, in the name of his Son.[1]

FAITH IN CHRIST AND JOSEPH SMITH GO TOGETHER. By faith we come to God. If we did not believe in the Lord Jesus Christ, if we had no faith in him or in his

[1]Conf. Rep., Oct., 1921, pp. 186-187.

atonement, we would not be inclined to pay any heed to his commandments. It is because we have that faith that we are brought into harmony with his truth and have a desire in our hearts to serve him. . . .

The first principle of the gospel is faith in the Lord Jesus Christ; and of course we are not going to have faith in the Lord Jesus Christ without having faith in his Father. Then if we have faith in God the Father and the Son and are guided, as we ought to be, by the Holy Ghost, we will have *faith in the servants of the Lord* through whom he has spoken.[2]

We must have faith in the mission of Joseph Smith. Because the world had lapsed into spiritual darkness, changed the ordinances and broken the everlasting covenant, the Church of Jesus Christ had to be brought again from the heavens. *Where there is no faith in these truths, there is no faith in Jesus Christ who sent the Prophet Joseph Smith.* This knowledge is vital to our eternal salvation.[3]

We are far ahead of any other people in the world. We have greater faith because we have a better understanding of the truth and because we are to a greater extent striving to keep the commandments of the Lord.[4]

JOSEPH SMITH PREPARED LECTURES ON FAITH. In the old *Doctrine and Covenants,* published before 1921, we have seven *Lectures on Faith.* I would like to make a correction of some thing that has gone forth. The statement has been made that Sidney Rigdon wrote these lectures. Sidney Rigdon did not have an analytical mind, I am told. He was considered to be the leading orator of the Church in his day, but he could not sit down and analyze his thoughts and arrange and correlate them, as we find them arranged and correlated here.

---

[2]*Church News,* Apr. 29, 1939, p. 3; 2 Ne. 9:21-24.

[3]*Church News,* June 12, 1949, p. 24; John 13:20; 15:1-10; Matt. 10:40-41; Luke 10:16; *D. & C.* 84:36-38.

[4]Conf. Rep., Apr., 1914, p. 92.

Furthermore, the only evidence we have as to where these *Lectures on Faith* come from is from the Prophet Joseph Smith. There was a committee appointed to prepare lessons for the School of the Prophets. I have here the statement from the *History of the Church,* December 1, 1834:

"Our school of the elders was now well attended, and with the lectures on theology [later called Lectures on Faith], which were regularly delivered, absorbed for the time being everything else of a temporal nature. The classes, being mostly elders gave the most studious attention to the all-important object of qualifying themselves as messengers of Jesus Christ, to be ready to do his will in carrying glad tidings to all that would open their eyes, ears, and hearts."[5]

Later the Prophet, in two different places, makes this statement: "January, 1835—During the month of January, I was engaged in the school of the elders, and in preparing the lectures on theology for publication in the book of *Doctrine and Covenants,* which the committee, appointed last September, were now compiling."[6]

These lectures are not now considered, and were not considered when they were placed in the *Doctrine and Covenants,* on a par with the revelations, but we must give the Prophet Joseph Smith credit for them. . . .

REVELATIONS WITHHELD FOR LACK OF FAITH. There is so much knowledge that is withheld from us. To many questions we have to postpone the answers. If we had the faith we could answer them. *The Lord is withholding knowledge from us because of our unworthiness.* Read what is written in the 27th chapter of 2nd Nephi, the 26th chapter of 3rd Nephi, the 3rd and 4th chapters of Ether. In these chapters the Lord tells us that he is withholding from the world and from the Church the greatest revelation that was ever written. It is the history of this world from the beginning thereof

---

[5]*History of the Church,* vol. 2, pp. 175-176.   [6]*History of the Church,* vol. 2, p. 180.

to the ending. The Lord says, in the 27th chapter of 2nd Nephi, that it shall not come forth in the days of wickedness.

When Mormon was about to write in the 26th chapter of 3rd Nephi, the things Christ had said to the disciples, the Lord stopped him, saying: *"I will try the faith of my people."*

"And when they shall have received this, which is expedient that they should have first, *to try their faith,* and if it shall so be that they shall believe these things then shall the greater things be made manifest unto them."[7]

ALL THINGS REVEALED BY FAITH. The brother of Jared went up into a mountain. He saw the finger of the Lord, and the Lord showed him his body. The scriptures tell us he could not be shut out, because of his great faith, and he beheld within the veil. The Lord told him to write it in a language that could not be read, gave him the interpreters by which in due time it would be read, and told him to seal up the interpreters also.

"And in that day that they shall exercise faith in me, saith the Lord, even as the brother of Jared did, that they may become sanctified in me, then will I manifest unto them the things which the brother of Jared saw, even to the unfolding unto them *all my revelations,* saith Jesus Christ, the Son of God, the Father of the heavens and of the earth, and all things that in them are."

"For the Lord said unto me: They shall not go forth unto the Gentiles until the day that they shall repent of their iniquity, and become clean before the Lord."[8]

I maintain that in this Church we are practicing the law of tithing, the Word of Wisdom, and many other things equally as well as we are practicing this first and fundamental foundation principle of the gospel. *We need more faith.*[9]

---

[7]3 Ne. 26:9-11.
[8]Ether 4:6-7.

[9]*Church News,* Mar. 16, 1935, pp. 3, 7.

FAITH, WORKS, AND GRACE

CHRIST TEACHES NEED FOR GOOD WORKS. "He that hath my commandments, and *keepeth them*, he it is that loveth me: and he that loveth me shall be loved of my Father, and I will love him, and will manifest myself to him."

These are the words of the Savior spoken to his disciples, and one of them, not fully comprehending his meaning, asked him a question. Jesus answered and said unto him: "If a man love me, he will keep my words: and my Father will love him, and we will come unto him, and make our abode with him. He that loveth me not keepeth not my sayings: and the word which ye hear is not mine, but the Father's which sent me."[10]

SECTARIAN CONTROVERSY OVER GRACE AND WORKS. There are throughout the Christian world various opinions regarding what is necessary to bring about the salvation of men. Some there are who have accepted very literally, but without comprehending the meaning of it, the expression that was uttered by Paul to the Ephesians: "For by grace are ye saved through faith; and that not of yourselves: it is the gift of God: Not of works, lest any man should boast."[11]

Those who accept that view as literally as it is recorded, without any reference to the context, disregard or reject the epistle of James which, apparently to them teaches a very different doctrine, for James says this: "Yea, a man may say, Thou hast faith, and I have works: shew me thy faith without thy works, and I will shew thee my faith by my works. Thou believest that there is one God; thou doest well: the devils also believe, and tremble. But wilt thou know, O vain man, that *faith without works is dead?*"[12]

And so the controversy has been going on since the days of the Reformation, if not before, in regard to these

[10]John 14:21-24; Matt. 7:21-23.   [12]Jas. 2:18-20.
[11]Eph. 2:8-9.

scriptures. Some men contending for the doctrine of James and some for the doctrine of Paul, both misunderstanding what Paul has written and what James has written, for in reality *there is no conflict.*

The world is full of good, honest people who believe that all that is necessary for one to do in order to be saved is to confess the name of Jesus Christ with their lips. A professed minister of the gospel once told me that if the entire *Bible* were lost with the exception of one passage, that one verse would be enough to save the world. It is as follows:

"If thou shalt confess with thy mouth the Lord Jesus, and shalt believe in thine heart that God hath raised him from the dead, thou shalt be saved."[13]

TEACHINGS OF PAUL AND JAMES IN HARMONY. Now, of course, this is a very extreme view. It would not be enough to save the world for the very good reason that the Lord has said unto us that we are to live by *every word* that proceedeth forth from the mouth of God,[14] and we are, as I have read to you, under the necessity of keeping his commandments.

I desire to point out wherein there is no conflict whatever in the teachings of these two apostles of old; that Paul taught the doctrine that was taught by James; and James was in full accord with the doctrine that was taught by Paul—the fact being that thy were approaching the subject from different angles.

Paul was dealing with the class of people who believed that a man could not be saved unless he subscribed to the *law of Moses,* that a man was under the necessity more or less of saving himself, and who *denied* the full power of the atonement of Jesus Christ.

James on the other hand was defending the necessity of works, counteracting the idea which prevailed among *others,* who professed faith in Christ, that if they had faith it was all-sufficient. Therefore they approached this

---

[13]Rom. 10:9.   [14]Matt. 4:4; Deut. 8:3.

subject from different viewpoints, and each of them
taught the truth.

GRACE AND WORKS: SAME DOCTRINE, TWO PER-
SPECTIVES. I might illustrate this. Many times I have
passed down the street and have looked in a store window
and have read a sign. As I have approached it from the
right, certain words appeared to be advertising certain
goods. As I have passed and come into full front view,
then something else has appeared; and as I have passed
on to the left and have looked back at that sign, other
words appeared, three different and distinct signs, but all
referring to the goods that are to be sold in that shop. I
might stand on the right side and say: "This sign says
so-and-so." You may stand on the left and say: "No,
you are wrong; I can see it, and it says so-and-so," and
we might contend over it, and we would both be wrong,
although we would both be partly right.

You have heard the story of the two knights who
contended over the shield that was on the arm of the
statue, one declaring that it was made of gold and the
other that it was of silver, and so they contended until
they came to blows and each received a mortal wound.
But as they fell to the earth and changed their positions
the one that was on the right saw that the gold shield was
silver, and the one that was on the left saw that the silver
shield was gold.

This is just the situation as we have it in regard
to the teaching of Paul and James. It is a doctrine of
the Church that is fully upheld and sustained by the
scriptures, and by the handdealings of God with the
children of men from the beginning, that he does not do
for us one thing that we can do for ourselves, but requires
of us that we do *everything* for ourselves that is within
our power for our salvation. I think that is logical and
reasonable. On the other hand, the Lord has done everything for us, for our salvation, that we could not do for
ourselves, and there were some things that we could not

do for ourselves, and we had to have help from an infinite source. . . .

ALL SALVATION COMES BY GRACE OF CHRIST. There is a difference between the Lord Jesus Christ and the rest of mankind. We have no life in ourselves, for no power has been given unto us, to lay down our lives and take them again.[15] That is beyond our power, and so, being subject to death, and being sinners—for we are all transgressors of the law to some extent, no matter how good we have tried to be—*we are therefore unable in and of ourselves to receive redemption from our sins by any act of our own.*

This is the *grace* that Paul was teaching. Therefore, *it is by the grace of Jesus Christ that we are saved.* And had he not come into the world, and laid down his life that he might take it again, or as he said in another place, to give us life that we may have it more abundantly[16]— we would still be *subject to death* and be *in our sins.*

BOTH IMMORTALITY AND ETERNAL LIFE COME BY GRACE. As it was pointed out by Isaiah and others of the prophets many hundreds of years before his birth, Christ took upon himself the transgressions of all men and suffered for them, that they might escape, on conditions of their repentance, and acceptance of his gospel, and their faithfulness to the end.[17] So we are saved by grace and that not of ourselves. It is the gift of God.[18]

If Jesus Christ had not died for us, there would have come to us no salvation, and we would have remained absolutely in our sins, without redemption, and would have become subject to Satan and his emissaries forever and ever.[19] But through the mercies of God, Christ came into the world and his blood was shed for the redemption of men, so that all who will believe and will acknowledge

---

[15]John 5:19-27.
[16]John 10:10-18.
[17]Isa. 53:1-12; 2 Ne. 9:17-27; 31:11-21.
[18]2 Ne. 9:8; 10:24-25; 25:23; Moro. 10:32-33.
[19]2 Ne. 9:6-9.

him and take upon them his commandments, enduring
to the end, shall receive eternal life.

So far as redemption from death is concerned, since
we were not responsible for it, we will be redeemed from
it. Therefore, *through the blood of Christ, every man
shall come forth from the dead in the resurrection,* and
the spirit and body shall be inseparably connected. Then
man, if he has been righteous, shall receive a fulness of
joy, and if unrighteous, he shall suffer, of course, for his
transgressions, but every man has been given immortality,
which means that he shall die again no more.

These are the doctrines that were taught by the Lord
Jesus Christ. This is the burden of the message which
we declare unto the world—Christ and him crucified
for the redemption of men.

GRACE AND WORKS UNITE TO BRING SALVATION.
So Paul taught these people—who thought that they
could be saved by some power that was within them, or
by observing the law of Moses—he pointed out to them
the fact that if it were not for the mission of Jesus Christ,
if it were not for this great atoning sacrifice, they could
not be redeemed. And therefore it was by the grace of
God that they are saved, not by any work on their part,
for they were absolutely helpless. Paul was absolutely
right.

And on the other hand, James taught just as the
Lord taught, just as Paul had taught in other scripture,
that it is our duty, of necessity, to labor, to strive in diligence, and faith, keeping the commandments of the Lord,
if we would obtain that inheritance which is promised
to the faithful, and which shall be given unto them
through their faithfulness to the end.[20] There is no conflict
in the doctrines of these two men. There is no need for
the world to be in conflict in regard to this question. It is

[20]Rom. 2:1-16; 6:1-5, 16-18, 23; 12:6-
21; 13:9-12; 1 Cor. 6:9-10; Gal.
5:19-26; 6:7-9; Eph. 6:10-18; Phil.
2:12; 4:8; 1 Thess. 5:16-22.

merely due to the fact that they cannot or do not comprehend the mission of Jesus Christ. They do not understand what salvation means. They do not know upon what it is based. . . .

SALVATION COMES BY GRACE, FAITH, AND WORKS. So it is easy to understand that we must accept the mission of Jesus Christ. *We must believe that it is through his grace that we are saved, that he performed for us that labor which we were unable to perform for ourselves, and did for us those things which were essential to our salvation, which were beyond our power; and also that we are under the commandment and the necessity of performing the labors that are required of us as set forth in the commandments known as the gospel of Jesus Christ.*

Unless a man will adhere to the doctrine and walk in faith, accepting the truth and observing the commandments as they have been given, it will be impossible for him to receive eternal life, no matter how much he may confess with his lips that Jesus is the Christ, or believe that his Father sent him into the world for the redemption of man. So James is right when he says the devils "believe and tremble," but they do not repent. So it is necessary, not merely that we believe, but that we repent, and in faith perform good works until the end; and then shall we receive the reward of the faithful and a place in the celestial kingdom of God.[21]

FAITH AND MIRACLES

FAITH COMES BY RIGHTEOUSNESS. *Miracles are not a permanent safeguard to faith.* Your faith may decrease, notwithstanding the fact that the Spirit has borne witness to you that Jesus Christ is the Son of God, that Joseph Smith is a Prophet of God, if you become *inactive.*

If we want to have a living, abiding faith, we must be active in the performance of every duty as members of this Church. I am as sure as I am that I am here that we would see more manifestations of the Spirit of God,

[21]*Era,* vol. 27, pp. 1145-1151.

for instance in the healing of the sick, if we would live just a little nearer to these fundamental truths. . . .

FOOLISH TO QUESTION BIBLE MIRACLES. I think it is not in good taste for any man today, within the Church or out of it, to scout the miracles of the *Bible*. It is certainly out of harmony in the Church. It is certainly not in keeping with the commission given to teachers in the Church to question the miracles in the scriptures and say, "I do not believe that Moses by the power of the Holy Spirit divided the Red Sea,[22] or that the walls of Jericho at the command of Joshua fell down,[23] or even that the sun and the moon stood still,[24] or that Jonah was cast into the sea and saved by being swallowed by a fish."[25] It is out of taste for us to say today that we do not believe these things, when we are living in a day when the greatest miracles the world has ever seen are right before us every day of our lives.[26]

MIRACLES OF BIBLE AND OF SCIENCE. I was talking with a man one day who said he could not accept the statements in the scriptures, about the fall of Adam and death being brought into the world. He could not believe in the miracles of the scriptures. He said to believe that Joshua commanded the sun and the moon to stand still and that Jonah was swallowed by a whale, or fish, was unscientific. "You cannot expect me to believe such things as these." He thought himself consistent with reason and that I was inconsistent.

All of you go back with me, in imagination, 100 years. Suppose we are living in the year 1830, when the Church was organized. Suppose I tell you—in 1830 —that within 100 years men will be able to travel from the Atlantic to the Pacific Ocean in one day? Will you accept that more quickly than the story of Joshua or of Jonah? In 1830, which story would you accept first?

[22]Ex. 14:13-22; 15:8; Hela. 8:11; D. & C. 8:3; Moses 1:25.
[23]Josh. 6:20; Heb. 11:30.
[24]Josh. 10:12-14; Isa. 38:1-8; 2 Kings 20:1-11; Hela. 12:3-17; Amos 8:9.
[25]Jonah 1:17; 2:1-10; Matt. 12:39-40.
[26]*Church News*, Mar. 16, 1935, p. 7.

If I should then say to you that a man could stand in New York, or Washington, and speak no more loudly than I am speaking to you now and he could be heard all over the world, which story would you believe first, this that I tell you or the story of Joshua? If you are honest with your thoughts, you will choose in preference what is written in the *Bible*.

These things I have mentioned are accomplished today. One of our own boys flew from the Atlantic to the Pacific in one day. I have listened over the radio to men speaking in Germany, Holland, England, and from various parts of the United States, yet I was sitting in my own home in Salt Lake City.

How the Sun Stood Still. But this man could not accept the story of Joshua because it is unscientific. He believes that the Lord could not hear Joshua's prayer and cause the earth to rotate less rapidly, for that is what took place. "Why, if this had happened," he said, "everything on the earth would have flown off into space."

Well, if the Lord can give to the earth its times and seasons, its revolutions, and so control all the heavenly bodies, are we going to deny him the power to regulate them, and say he could not slow up the earth and still keep the seas in their beds? I have traveled on a train going 60 miles an hour and have stood in the isle when the train was brought to a stop but was not thrown off my feet, because the train slowed up gradually. I think the Lord did this with the earth. He has the power to do it, has he not?

It seems to me so strange for a man to question the power of the Lord and yet acknowledge the wonderful achievements of man which are just as marvelous. But because he does not see what happens in one case, he rejects it, and because he sees with his eyes and hears with his ears in another, he believes it. . . .

We should have perfect confidence in the Lord and in his word. Some people would tie the hands of the

Lord. Some say that these miraculous events were added
in a day of superstition, many years after the time they
are said to have taken place; that the *Bible* is a book
written by men who had vivid imaginations and believed
in impossible, miraculous things. But these things are also
found in the *Book of Mormon* and in other revelations
coming from the Lord.

Nothing recorded in the scriptures is more miraculous or wonderful than the things we see demonstrated
around us every day. We, as Latter-day Saints, should
walk in righteousness and in the spirit of faith. We should
be willing and anxious to believe the words of the Lord
and have more confidence in what has come from him
than in what has come through the arm of flesh. *Let us
increase our faith and confidence in the Lord.*[27]

CHRIST BELIEVED STORY OF JONAH. Are we to reject
it as being an impossibility and say that the Lord could
not prepare a fish, or whale, to swallow Jonah? If Mr.
Robert Ripley and some of the others are to be believed,
a similar occurrence has taken place—perhaps more than
once—within the memory of man now living. Surely the
Lord sits in the heavens and laughs at the wisdom of the
scoffer, and then on a sudden answers his folly by a rep-
etition of the miracle in dispute, or by the presentation of
one still greater.

Is it more of a miracle for the Lord to prepare a fish
to carry Jonah to shore that he might fill the mission
assigned to him, than it is for the President of the United
States to speak in an ordinary tone and be heard, under
certain conditions, by all people in all parts of the earth?
Honestly, which is the greater miracle?

I believe, as did Mr. William J. Bryan, the story
of Jonah. My chief reason for so believing is not in the
fact that it is recorded in the *Bible,* or that the incident
has been duplicated in our day, but in the fact that *Jesus
Christ, our Lord, believed it.* The Jews sought him for a

[27]*Gen. & Hist. Mag.*, vol. 21, pp. 156-158.

sign of his divinity. He gave them one, but not what they expected. The scoffers of his day, notwithstanding his mighty works, were incapable, because of sin, of believing.

"He answered and said unto them, An evil and adulterous generation seeketh after a sign; and there shall no sign be given to it, but the sign of the Prophet Jonas: For as Jonas was three days and three nights in the whale's belly; so shall the Son of man be three days and three nights in the heart of the earth."[28]

FAITH AND DOCTORS. We should put our faith in the Lord and keep his commandments, but the Lord has also told us to exercise works with our faith, and there is wisdom in getting counsel to help us to take care of our bodies, and when sick, to find the best methods of restoring them to health. A physician has a proper place in the Church as well as in the days of the apostles of old. They had physicians, one of them being Luke, author of one of the gospels. We should live so that we will have faith, but the Lord has advised that we call in nurses or others to assist when the occasion requires.[29]

FAITH AND THE FLOOD

SO-CALLED SCIENTIFIC OBJECTIONS TO FLOOD. Most of our difficulties and doubts come from misunderstandings, and there is nothing, perhaps, which has been more misunderstood and ridiculed by the wise in their own learning, than the story of the flood. I am grateful that I was born with an understanding and believing heart and spirit. It is never hard for me to accept that which is written and affirmed by revelation. I am confident that the Lord is right, even where I am unable to understand the answers. In this case of the flood the answer is plain and simple.

Our brother, in denying the story of the flood, states, "There is not enough water existing in the earth

[28]*Church News,* Oct. 31, 1936, p. 8; Matt. 12:39-40.   [29]Pers. Corresp.; *D. & C.* 42:43; 59:16-20; 89:10-11; Alma 46:40.

and its atmosphere to flood the earth so that the mountains would all be covered."

Also, he says: "In the event of water being introduced from external space, the mass of the earth would be so altered that its astronomical constants would be altered, e.g., time taken to revolve in its orbit, distance from the sun, etc. Such an amount of water would not evaporate in the specified time of 150 days without boiling violently, when no life could possibly exist."

EARTH SURFACE TO BE RESTORED TO PRIMITIVE STATE. My answer to all of this is that it is mere *speculation*. The Lord, who created the earth, certainly controls it. Why try to deny him this power? Moreover, we are taught that portions of this earth have been taken from it, such as the city of Enoch, which included the land surface as well as the people. Yet the earth has maintained its steady course, and "abideth the law" which was given to it.[30]

Then, again, the surface of the earth was not the same at the time of the flood that it is today. We are living in the great day of the *restoration*. In this dispensation we are informed *the Lord will bring back all things to the condition in which they were before the curse came upon the earth*. The earth is to be *renewed* or *restored* to its primitive beauty and condition, and when that day comes the high mountains which are seen today will be *debased* and the valleys *exalted*. This is not merely a figure of speech, but a literal condition which will prevail. I commend to you the reading of the words of Elder Parley P. Pratt in the *Voice of Warning*, and of President John Taylor in his *Government of God*, in explanation of this point.[31]

PROPHETS FORETELL CHANGES IN EARTH'S SURFACE. Here are a few references from the scriptures:

[30]D. & C. 88:25.
[31]John Taylor, *Government of God*, pp. 106-115; Parley P. Pratt, *Voice of Warning*, ch. 5; Joseph Fielding Smith, *Man: His Origin and Destiny*, pp. 380-397.

"Every valley shall be *exalted*, and every mountain and hill shall be made *low:* and the crooked shall be made straight, and the rough places *plain.*"[32]

"For the *mountains shall depart*, and the *hills be removed;* but my kindness shall not depart from thee, neither shall the covenant of my peace be removed, saith the Lord that hath mercy on thee."[33]

"Oh that thou wouldest rend the heavens, that thou wouldest come down, that the *mountains might flow down at thy presence.*"[34]

"So that the fishes of the sea, and the fowls of the heaven, and the beasts of the field, and all creeping things that creep upon the earth, and all the men that are upon the face of the earth, shall shake at my presence, and the *mountains shall be thrown down*, and the steep places shall *fall*, and every wall shall fall to the ground."[35]

"And the heaven departed as a scroll when it is rolled together; and *every mountain and island were moved out of their places.*"[36]

LATTER-DAY REVELATION TELLS OF EARTH'S RESTORATION. I know it is customary to spiritualize these passages and to place upon them a figurative interpretation, but in our modern scriptures, as well as in the *Bible*, the literal meaning is clearly stated. I will give you a few references from the *Doctrine and Covenants*:

"Wherefore, be not deceived, but continue in steadfastness, looking forth for the heavens to be shaken, and the *earth to tremble* and to reel to and fro as a drunken man, and for the valleys to be exalted, and for the *mountains to be made low*, and for the *rough places to become smooth*—and all this when the angel shall sound his trumpet."[37]

"And he shall utter his voice out of Zion, and he shall speak from Jerusalem, and his voice shall be heard among

[32]Isa. 40:4.
[33]Isa. 54:10.
[34]Isa. 64:1.
[35]Ezek. 38:20.
[36]Rev. 6:14.
[37]*D. & C.* 49:23.

all people; And it shall be a voice as the voice of many
waters, and as the voice of a great thunder, which shall
*break down the mountains, and the valleys shall not be
found.*

"He shall command the great deep, and it shall be
driven back into the north countries, and the *islands shall
become one land;* And the land of Jerusalem and the land
of Zion shall be *turned back into their own place,* and the
earth shall be *like as it was in the days before it was
divided.*"[38]

MIGHTY CHANGES WROUGHT BY FLOOD. These
scriptural references teach us definitely that the day will
come when the mountains will be debased and naturally
the valleys will be exalted. This is part of the great restoration. The sea is to be driven back into the north, so
it must have been there once before. The land surface
of the earth will again be united, and the islands brought
back to the main land, as it was in the beginning.

Now why bring back the condition which was in the
beginning? Because in the beginning the Lord pronounced the earth *good.* Then after the fall a curse was
placed upon it, and many changes came. In this time of
restoration all things are to be brought back to their primitive condition. See the Tenth Article of Faith.

From the knowledge which has come to us through
revelation, we learn that the mountains in the days of
the flood were not the great and mighty peaks that we
see today. This makes a wonderful *difference* in the dis-
tribution of water over the face of the earth. We do not
know what the earth did by way of *change during the
flood.* Evidently there were great changes coming from
the surface being covered by water so suddenly.

AMOUNT OF WATER AVAILABLE FOR FLOOD. The
argument that there is not enough water in the earth and
its atmosphere to cover the earth with a coating under
certain conditions, I also say is pure speculation. Two-

[38]*D. & C.* 133:21-24.

thirds of the surface of the earth is water. This water
is as deep, or deeper, than the mountains *even today* are
high.

When the fountains of the great deep were broken
up and the floods from above came down, it seems that a
mighty wave could easily sweep over the face of the earth
without uncovering the ocean beds, and thus force a flood
of water sufficiently high to bury the land surface long
enough to meet the requirements of such an occasion. But
if someone wishes to contend that this could not furnish
enough water, then we also have the word of the Lord
which might indicate that water was brought from *elsewhere* and then *returned* again, the scientific theories of
men to the contrary notwithstanding.[39] The Lord holds
the earth in the "hollow of his hand." Surely he has
power to control it, to balance it and keep it in its orbit,
or do just what he pleases with it. How foolish and
impotent are the thoughts of men!

FLOOD COVERED WHOLE EARTH. Again, our
brother contends that the dove could not have found an
olive leaf when Noah sent it forth, because the entire
earth had been covered with water for five or more
months. I have seen trees covered with flood waters for
that length of time that again bore leaves when the
unfavorable condition was removed.

Then, it was not necessary for the entire face of the
earth to be covered, but for a very short time, and then
the waters could recede to their proper levels. There is
nothing in the scriptural account which contradicts this.
It is possible, and we may presume to state it as a fact,
that all the water did not remain on the face of the earth
for 150 days; but so far as Noah was concerned the land
had become dry in that length of time, at least the record
says the waters were "abated."

Another point that should be considered, if we are
willing to accept the revelations given to the Prophet

[39]Gen. 7:10-24; 8:1-14.

Joseph Smith, is that Noah built his ark somewhere in what we are pleased to call the Western Hemisphere, so far as we can discover. The ark rested on Mount Ararat a long distance from the place of starting, although at that time the earth had not been divided. So the flood could *not* have been a *local flood* as some wish us to believe.[40]

FLOOD WAS BAPTISM OF EARTH. Now a word as to the *reason* for the flood. *It was the baptism of the earth, and that had to be by immersion.* If the water did not cover the entire earth, then it was not baptized, for the baptism of the Lord is not pouring or sprinkling. These forms are strictly man made and not part of the gospel ordinances.

BRIGHAM YOUNG'S TEACHINGS ABOUT FLOOD. I will give a few quotations from the teachings of the leading brethren of the Church. President Brigham Young said of the earth: *"It has already been baptized.* You who have read the *Bible* must know that that is *Bible* doctrine. What does it matter if it is not in the same words that I use, it is not the less true that *it was baptized for the remission of sins.* The Lord said: 'I will deluge (or immerse) the earth in water for the remission of the sins of the people'; or if you will allow me to express myself in a familiar style, to kill all the vermin that were nitting, and breeding, and polluting its body; it was cleansed of its filthiness; and soaked in the water, as long as some of our people ought to soak. *The Lord baptized the earth for the remission of sins,* and it has been once cleansed from the filthiness that has gone out of it, which was in the inhabitants who dwelt upon its face."[41]

"Brethren and sisters, I wish you to continue in your ways of well doing; I desire that your minds may be opened more and more to see and understand things as they are. This earth, in its present condition and situa-

<hr>

[40]Smith, *op. cit.,* pp. 414-436; Ether   [41]*Journal of Discourses,* vol. 1, p. 274.
13:2.

tion, is not a fit habitation for the sanctified; but it abides the law of its creation, *has been baptized by water,* will be baptized by fire and the Holy Ghost, and by and by will be prepared for the faithful to dwell upon."[42]

"The earth, the Lord says, abides its creation; *it has been baptized with water,* and will, in the future, be baptized with fire and the Holy Ghost, to be prepared to go into the celestial presence of God, with all things that dwell upon it which have, like the earth, abided the law of their creation."[43]

ORSON PRATT'S TEACHINGS ABOUT FLOOD. Elder Orson Pratt taught: "Another great change happened nearly 2,000 years after the earth was made. *It was baptized by water.* A great flow of water came, the great deep was broken up, the windows of heaven were opened from on high, and the waters prevailed upon the face of the earth, sweeping away all wickedness and transgression—*a similitude of baptism for the remission of sins.* God requires the children of men to be baptized. What for? For the remission of sins. So he required our globe to be baptized by a flow of water, and all of its sins were washed away, not one sin remaining."[44]

"The heavens and the earth were thus polluted, that is, the material heavens, and everything connected with our globe all fell when man fell, and became subject to death when man became subject to it. Both man and the earth are redeemed from the original sin without ordinances; but soon we find new sins committed by the fallen sons of Adam, and the earth became corrupted before the Lord by their transgressions. It needs redeeming ordinances for these second transgressions The Lord ordained baptism or immersion of the earth in water as a justifying ordinance."[45]

TEACHINGS OF PRESIDENTS TAYLOR AND PENROSE ABOUT FLOOD. President John Taylor said: "The earth,

---

[42]*Journal of Discourses,* vol. 8, p. 83. [44]*Journal of Discourses,* vol, 21, p. 323.
[43]*Journal of Discourses,* vol. 10, p. 252. [45]*Journal of Discourses,* vol. 1, p. 291.

as a part of the creation of God, has fulfilled and will fulfil the measure of its creation. *It has been baptized by water,* it will be baptized by fire; it will be purified and become celestial, and be a fit place for celestial bodies to inhabit."[46]

President Charles W. Penrose has left us this: "Thus the inhabitants of the earth with the few exceptions that are beyond the power of redemption will eventually be saved. And the globe on which they passed their probation, having kept the law of its being, will come into remembrance before its Maker. It will die like its products. But it will be quickened again and resurrected in the celestial glory. *It has been born of the water,* it will also be born of the Spirit, purified by fire from all the corruptions that once defiled it, developed into its perfections as one of the family of worlds fitted for the Creator's presence, all its latent light awakened into scintillating action, it will move up into its place among the orbs governed by celestial time, and shining 'like a sea of glass mingled with fire,' every tint and color of the heavenly bow radiating from its surface, the ransomed of the Lord will dwell upon it."[47]

PHILOSOPHIES OF WORLD DESTROY FAITH. I have given quite a number of references. The great difficulty in the world today is unbelief, doubt, lack of faith. How much better it would be if we could keep ourselves in harmony with the Spirit so that we can feel and know the truth with the simple faith of Nephi. The guidance of the Holy Ghost is offered to every member of the Church so that they may not walk in darkness but be protected from error and know the truth. If we live as we should, we will be entitled to this guidance so that we will not be deceived. *The philosophies and doctrines of men today have a tendency to destroy faith in the Lord and cast doubt upon his revelations.*[48]

[46]*Times and Seasons,* vol. 5, pp. 408-409.
[47]*The Contributor,* vol. 2, p. 364.
[48]*Millennial Star,* vol. 106, pp. 590-592, 608.

CHAPTER 17

BAPTISM AND SALVATION

BAPTISM: A BIRTH AND RESURRECTION

BAPTISM IN OLD TESTAMENT TIMES. Baptism dates from the fall.[1] Without modern revelation this truth would have remained hidden from the world. The plan of salvation was declared before the foundation of the world was laid. God is unchangeable. The word of the Lord to Joseph Smith and through him, has cleared this doctrine and established it.[2] I believe there are passages in the Old Testament that we might term as having reference to baptism, although they are very indistinct, and without modern revelation we would not know it. *Baptism* is a Greek word, not a Hebrew word. The Jews had a font in the temple upon 12 oxen, and there are places where the word *washing* appears.[3]

WHY BAPTISM MUST BE BY IMMERSION. The mode of baptism is by immersion in water. Sprinkling or pouring did not come into vogue until two or three centuries after Christ, and such a practice was not universal until about the 13th century A.D. We have to go into history to find these particulars. Baptism cannot be by any other means than immersion of the entire body in water, for the following reasons:

1. *It is in the similitude of the death, burial, and resurrection of Jesus Christ,* and of all others who have received the resurrection.

2. *Baptism is also a birth and is performed in the similitude of the birth of a child into this world.*

---

[1]Moses 6:50-68; 8:24.
[2]D. & C. 20:21-28; 22:1-4.

[3]1 Kings 7:23-26, 39, 44; 2 Chron. 4:2-6; Psalm 51:7; Isa. 1:16; 48:1; 1 Ne. 20:1; Acts 22:16; Titus 3:5; Zech. 9:11.

3. Baptism is not only a figure of the resurrection, but also is literally a transplanting or resurrection from one life to another—from the life of sin to the life of spiritual life.

I want to take up the second reason: Baptism is also a birth and is performed in the similitude of the birth of a child into this world. When this earth was created, it came into existence the same way. (I am not speaking scientifically, and yet scientific doctrine tells us the same thing.) This earth was born in water. Before the land appeared the whole sphere was covered with water.

BIRTH COMES BY WATER, BLOOD, AND SPIRIT. In the Book of Moses we read: "Therefore I give unto you a commandment, to teach these things freely unto your children, saying: That by reason of transgression cometh the fall, which fall bringeth death, and inasmuch as ye were born into the world by water, and blood, and the spirit, which I have made, and so became of dust a living soul, even so ye must be born again into the kingdom of heaven, of water, and of the Spirit, and be cleansed by blood, even the blood of mine Only Begotten; that ye might be sanctified from all sin, and enjoy the words of eternal life in this world, and eternal life in the world to come, even immortal glory; For by the water ye keep the commandment; by the Spirit ye are justified, and by the blood ye are sanctified."[4]

That is one of the finest passages I know, and we find practically the same thing recorded by John.[5]

SAME ELEMENTS PRESENT IN FIRST AND SECOND BIRTHS. Every child that comes into this world is carried in water, is born of water, and of blood, and of the spirit. So when we are born into the kingdom of God, we must be born in the same way. By baptism, we are born of the water. Through the shedding of the blood of Christ, we are cleansed and sanctified; and we are

[4]Moses 6:58-60.   [5]1 John 5:3-9.

justified, through the Spirit of God, for baptism is not complete without the baptism of the Holy Ghost. You see the *parallel* between birth into the world and birth into the kingdom of God. How foolish it is to think for a moment that baptism could be accomplished by pouring water on a child's head. It does not meet the requirements.

I have heard some of our young elders preaching on baptism say that the Lord could have brought to pass the remission of sins in some other way. They reasoned he could have done it by sprinkling, or in this way or that way. The Lord could not consistently do it any other way, only by being buried in the water, born of water and of the Spirit, and cleansed by the blood of Christ, just as a child is born into this world of water, blood, and spirit. The comparison is very striking.

BAPTISM: A RESURRECTION TO LIFE. Coming now to the third reason: Baptism is not only a figure of the resurrection, but also is literally a transplanting or resurrection from one life to another—from the life of sin to the life of spiritual life. For proof of that, I am going to read first something the Lord said to Joseph Smith.

"Wherefore, I, the Lord God, caused that he [Adam] should be cast out from the Garden of Eden, from my presence, because of his transgression, wherein *he became spiritually dead,* which is the first death, even that same death which is the last death, which is spiritual, which shall be pronounced upon the wicked when I shall say: Depart, ye cursed."

Here we have two conditions, spiritual life and spiritual death. The condition of Adam in the Garden of Eden was spiritual life. He was in the presence of God. Through his transgression, *he was banished into spiritual death—a new life entirely.* He was no longer in the presence of God. He was shut out, separated, a veil drawn between him and the Lord.

Adam, after the fall, was in spiritual death, and not

only Adam but every man and woman upon the face of the earth who is accountable before God. We will not consider the last death more than to say it is also banishment from the presence of God.

"But, behold, I say unto you that I, the Lord God, gave unto Adam and unto his seed, that they should not die as to the temporal death, until I, the Lord God, should send forth angels to declare unto them repentance and redemption, through faith on the name of mine Only Begotten Son. And thus did I, the Lord God, appoint unto man the days of his probation—that by his natural death he might be raised in immortality unto eternal life, even as many as would believe; And they that believe not unto eternal damnation; for they cannot be redeemed from their *spiritual fall,* because they repent not."[6]

We find Adam, then, in spiritual death, and all his posterity, excepting little children. All men and women need repentance. Death is banishment. They are in spiritual *death.* How are they going to get back? By being *buried* in the water. *They are dead and are buried in the water and come forth in the resurrection of the Spirit back into spiritual life.* That is what baptism is.

WHY BAPTISM REMITS FUTURE SINS. I have heard some of our young men, and some not so young, when talking on baptism, say they do not know why it is, since baptism is for the remission of sins, that a man does not have to be baptized every time he commits a sin. Do you see the reason? *As long as a man sins and stays within spiritual life, he is alive, he can repent and be forgiven. He does not need to be baptized to be brought back to where he already is.* But there are sins, John says, "unto death," and if a man commits a sin *unto death,* he is banished *again* and comes *back into spiritual death.*[7]

Through this kind of transgression he loses the effect of baptism and is banished into spiritual death. When a man commits a sin unto death, he is *banished from spir-*

---

[6]*D. & C.* 29:41-44.   [7]1 John 4:14-15; 5:16-17.

itual life. The shedding of innocent blood is one such sin and blasphemy against the Holy Ghost another. The enemies of the Prophet Joseph Smith carried him off to Carthage and put him and his brother to death. Deliberately murdering the servants of God is the shedding of innocent blood.

If a man sins unto death, he goes back again to spiritual death, but as long as he stays within spiritual life, he does not have to be baptized again.

DEATH TO SIN BRINGS RESURRECTION TO LIFE. Paul had that very clearly in mind. He says, in writing to the Romans: "What shall we say then? Shall we continue in sin, that grace may abound? God forbid. How shall we, that are *dead to sin,* live any longer therein? Know ye not, that so many of us as were baptized into Jesus Christ were baptized into his death?

"Therefore we are *buried* with him by baptism into *death:* that like as Christ was raised up from the dead by the glory of the Father, even so we also should walk in newness of life. For if we have been planted together in the likeness of his death, we shall be also in the likeness of his resurrection: Knowing this, that *our old man is crucified with him, that the body of sin might be destroyed,* that henceforth we should not serve sin."[8]

Paul is speaking to members of the Church. We are dead to sin because we have left it. Banishment works one way as well as the other. In other words, when we are in spiritual life (or in the Church or in the kingdom of God), we ought not to sin. Through baptism we come back from the spiritual death which is upon all unbaptized men. Whether they are Roman Catholic or Protestant, if they are unrepentant and unbaptized they are in spiritual death. But we who have received the gospel, why should we live in sin when we have been baptized and are in spiritual life?

8Rom. 6:1-6.

How Saints Are in Presence of God. We are back in the presence of God. The question might naturally be raised: How do we come back into the presence of God if we do not see him? We do not see him now, but are we not in his presence when we have the gift of the Holy Ghost, one of the members of the Godhead, to lead and direct us in righteousness? *We are back in his presence, if we keep the commandments and do not longer live in sin; then we are in spiritual life.* That is an important thing in connection with baptism not generally understood.[9]

HOW BAPTISM BRINGS SALVATION

Nature of Covenant of Baptism. Every person baptized into this Church has made a covenant with the Lord to keep his commandments.[10] We are to serve the Lord with all the heart, and all the mind, and all the strength that we have, and that too in the name of Jesus Christ. Everything that we do should be done in the name of Jesus Christ.[11]

In the waters of baptism, we covenanted that we would keep these commandments; that we would serve the Lord; that we would keep this first and greatest of all commandments, and love the Lord our God; that we would keep the next great commandment, we would love our neighbor as ourselves; and with all the might that we have, with all the strength, with all our hearts, we would prove to him that we would "live by every word that proceedeth forth from the mouth of God";[12] that we would be obedient and humble, diligent in his service, willing to obey, to hearken to the counsels of those who preside over us and do all things with an eye single to the glory of God.

We should not forget these things, for this commandment is binding upon us as members of the Church.[13]

---

[9]*Church News*, Mar. 30, 1935, p. 8.
[10]Mosiah 18:8-13.
[11]*D. & C.* 59:5-7; Deut. 6:4-5; 10:12; 30:6; Matt. 22:37; Luke 10:27.

[12]*D. & C.* 84:44; 98:11; Deut. 8:3; Matt. 4:4.
[13]Conf. Rep., Apr., 1940, p. 95.

OBLIGATION TO KEEP COVENANT OF BAPTISM. Every soul baptized, truly baptized, has humbled himself; his heart is broken; his spirit is contrite; he has made a covenant before God that he will keep his commandments, and he has forsaken all his sins. Then after he gets into the Church, is it his privilege to sin after he is in? Can he let down? Can he indulge in some of the things which the Lord has said he should avoid? No. It is just as necessary that he have that contrite spirit, that broken heart, after he is baptized as it is before.[14]

GOSPEL ORDINANCES FOR CELESTIAL KINGDOM ONLY. Will those who enter the terrestrial and telestial kingdoms have to have the ordinance of baptism? No! Baptism is the door into the celestial kingdom. The Lord made this clear to Nicodemus.[15] We are not preaching a salvation for the inhabitants of the terrestrial or the telestial kingdoms. *All of the ordinances of the gospel pertain to the celestial kingdom, and what the Lord will require by way of ordinances, if any, in the other kingdoms he has not revealed.*

It seems to me to be so clear that the ordinances of the gospel are for those who are entitled to enter the celestial kingdom, based on obedience to the principles of the gospel, that there should be no question about it.

BAPTISM FOR CELESTIAL KINGDOM ONLY. If the Lord intended baptism and other ordinances for everyone, why did he say, "He that believeth not shall be damned"?[16]

Why should he say what he has said of those who enter the telestial kingdom: "And they shall be servants of the Most High; but where God and Christ dwell they cannot come, worlds without end"?[17]

Why did he say: "Verily, verily, I say unto you, except ye abide my law ye cannot attain to this glory.

[14]Conf. Rep., Oct., 1950, p. 12; *D. & C.* 20:37.
[15]John 3:3-5.
[16]Mark 16:16.
[17]*D. & C.* 76:112.

For strait is the gate, and narrow the way that leadeth unto the exaltation and continuation of the lives, and few there be that find it, because ye receive me not in the world neither do ye know me. . . . Broad is the gate, and wide the way that leadeth to the deaths; and many there are that go in thereat, because they received me not, neither do they abide in my law"?[18]

How can we explain this: "Verily, verily, I say unto you, they who believe not on your words, and are not baptized in water in my name, for the remission of their sins, that they may receive the Holy Ghost, shall be damned, and *shall not come into my Father's* kingdom where my Father and I am. And this revelation unto you, and commandment, is in force from this very hour upon all the world, and the gospel is unto all who have not received it"?[19]

And, again, this: "And he that endureth not unto the end, the same is he that is also hewn down and cast into the fire, from whence they can no more return, because of the justice of the Father"?[20]

We know that the great majority of men will be barred from the celestial kingdom forever. If this is not so, then the word of the Lord must be revised.[21]

BAPTISM *SAVES* MEN FROM LOWER KINGDOMS. The First Presidency have said in answer to a similar question: "We know of no ordinances pertaining to the terrestrial or the telestial kingdom. All of the ordinances of the gospel are given for the salvation of men in the celestial kingdom and pertain unto that kingdom."

The Lord has said positively that those who reject the gospel shall be "damned." Baptism and obedience are to save them from damnation. If we are to be baptized for *all* who are dead without regard to the glory which they receive, then logically we must say that they

---

[18]D. & C. 132:21, 25; Matt. 7:13-14; 3 Ne. 14:13-14; 27:33.
[19]D. & C. 84:74-75.
[20]3 Ne. 27:17.
[21]D. & C. 76:71-112; 88:22-24; 132:16-17.

are not to be damned, and such a thing is a contradiction of the word of the Lord.

This doctrine, that baptism is to be required of *all* men, is doing a great deal of harm in that it tends to encourage men in the procrastination of their repentance and holds out to them the false hope that they shall eventually, notwithstanding their unfaithfulness and disobedience, receive the blessings of the celestial kingdom of God. The doctrine is entirely foreign to the gospel plan which has been given to men to prepare them for celestial glory.

REPENTANCE MUST PRECEDE BAPTISM. Consider the instruction the Lord gave to candidates for baptism, *Doctrine and Covenants,* section 20, verse 37. Did he not mean it? I read in this verse that the candidate should have a broken heart, and a contrite spirit, and give witness before the Church that he has truly repented of *all* his sins and that he has a determination to serve the Lord to the end.

I ask, how can a man do all of this and still be addicted to tobacco or liquor? How can he do it if he is living in violation of any other commandment?

Again: "And we know that all men must repent and believe on the name of Jesus Christ, and worship the Father in his name, and *endure in faith on his name to the end,* or they cannot be saved in the kingdom of God."[22]

Again: "And he commandeth all men that they must repent, and be baptized in his name, having *perfect faith in the Holy One of Israel, or they cannot be saved in the kingdom of God.*"[23] How can a man have perfect faith when he is violating a commandment?

"And no unclean thing can enter into his kingdom; therefore nothing entereth into his rest save it be those who have washed their garments in my blood, because of their faith, and the repentance of all their sins, and

---

[22]*D. & C.* 20:29.   [23]2 Ne. 9:23.

their faithfulness unto the end."[24] How can a man obtain the remission of *all* his sins, if he has not repented of *all* his sins? The trouble with many of us is that we do not take the word of the Lord seriously; we do not think he means what he says.

REPENTANCE REMOVES SCAR OF SIN. It appears to me the most extreme folly to believe, much less to teach, that the atonement of Jesus Christ merely *paved the way* for the remission and forgiveness of the sins of those who truly repent; and after one has truly repented and been baptized, he still must pay the price to some extent for his transgressions. This means that the man has not been truly forgiven, but is placed on probation with a penalty attached. This idea, which has so often been taught by saying that the holes remain after the nails are withdrawn, is a *false doctrine* when applied to the atonement for the truly repentant sinner.[25]

REBAPTISM

TWOFOLD PURPOSE OF BAPTISM. The question has been asked why rebaptism was established in the day of the Prophet Joseph Smith, why it was continued for a number of years in Utah under the direction of President Brigham Young, and why it is now abandoned?

There is really in the Church no such thing as *rebaptism*. Baptism, as we understand it, is one of the cardinal principles of the gospel, commanded primarily *for the remission of sins,* and, secondarily, as *the door by which we enter into the Church.* It was first made known and taught, as one of the ordinances of the gospel, to Adam who was commanded to instruct his children and call upon them to be baptized for the remission of sins.

The ordinance of baptism was known and practiced in ancient Israel, and in all ages of the world, as one of the essential ordinances of the gospel where the gospel

---

[24]3 Ne. 27:19.   [25]Pers. Corresp.; *D. & C.* 19:4, 15-19; Alma 7:14; Acts 22:14-16; 1 Pet. 2:24; Isa. 53:5.

has been found on the earth. It is just as necessary today as at any other period in the history of the world, for without it the sinner cannot receive a remission of his sins and be admitted into the kingdom of God.

PIONEERS AND OTHERS REBAPTIZED. It is true that during the administration of the Prophet Joseph Smith some members of the Church who were in transgression were again baptized, without first having lost their membership by excommunication. And so it has been from that day down to the present, where the repentant transgressor has desired that the ordinance be performed *for the remission of sins.* Frederick G. Williams was rebaptized and on August 5, 1838, was confirmed at Far West, Missouri, although he was then a member of the Church.[26]

After the arrival of the Pioneers in the Salt Lake Valley, and subsequently for a considerable period, all those who entered the valley were baptized anew at the request of President Brigham Young who, with the Council of the Twelve, set the example to the people who were gathering from all parts of the world.

PIONEERS RENEWED COVENANTS BY BAPTISM. There were various reasons for this action on the part of President Young and the leading brethren. They stated that it was for the "renewal of their covenants." They came into the valley rejoicing after many trials and untold hardships from a land where they had been subject to mob violence and dictation on the part of enemies who denied to them the privilege guaranteed in the Constitution of our land, to worship God according to the dictates of conscience.

After their arrival in this western land, they were free from molestation, and in humility they approached the Lord, *not because of transgression,* but because of *thankfulness for their deliverance* from wicked enemies,

---

[26]*History of the Church,* vol. 3, p. 55.

and knowing no better way to express their gratitude decided to make *covenant* with the Lord that from that time forward they would serve him and keep his commandments. As a *token of this covenant* they entered the water and were baptized and confirmed, renewing their covenants and obligations as members of the Church.

LOST RECORDS LED TO REBAPTISM. Another reason that caused these brethren to take such a step and make the renewal of the covenant general, applying to all who came into the valley, was the fact that during their drivings, mobbings, persecutions, and final exodus, many branch and ward records had been lost. When the people entered the Salt Lake Valley and sought a standing in the communities of the saints, many of them were without certificates of baptism and were unable to point to the records from whence they came to show their proper claim to full fellowship among the saints. As it is essential that a record of the members be kept, it was thought well to have all such do their first works over again, that the record might be made, and thus no question could be raised in later years regarding their standing in the Church. To make the matter fair and avoid feelings that otherwise might have arisen, the requirement was made of all.

SOME WAYWARD SAINTS REBAPTIZED. Another reason was the fact that following the martyrdom of Joseph and Hyrum Smith some members of the Church had actually strayed away and in their darkness had followed after false shepherds such as James J. Strang, William Smith, Zenas H. Gurley, and Jason W. Briggs, not knowing what to do and not being firmly founded in the faith by which they could recognize the true Shepherd. After their repentance and return to the fold, they desired to renew their covenants and be again established in their full standing in the Church. For these reasons and others of lesser import the practice of *rebaptizing* all who entered the Valley of Salt Lake prevailed at that early day.

REBAPTISM NOT ESSENTIAL TO SALVATION. As already stated, baptism is for the remission of sins on the part of those who have not come into the Church and the door by which they enter. *Those who have been baptized and confirmed members of the Church, who transgress, may receive the remission of their sins through the atonement of our Savior on conditions of their humility and repentance, without again entering the waters of baptism.*

Should a person sin to that degree that it would be necessary to deprive him of his membership in the Church, it would be necessary, of course, for him after repenting again to enter the Church through baptism. *Rebaptism* as understood in the question has not been done away, for even today where persons feel that they have transgressed to such a degree that they cannot conscientiously claim membership in the Church, and request baptism, even as new members, in order to be restored to fellowship among the saints, their request may be granted.

It is unnecessary, however, to rebaptize persons merely as a renewal of their covenants every time they transgress in order that they may obtain forgiveness, for this would greatly cheapen this sacred ordinance and weaken its effectiveness. *One baptism by water for the remission of sins should be enough,* and there are *other* means by which sins may be forgiven for those who have made covenant with the Lord, provided they do not sin away their right to a standing in the Church.

The rebaptism spoken of in section 22 of the *Doctrine and Covenants* applied to those who had been baptized into some other organization, without authority from the Lord and who afterwards desired to unite with the Church and be accepted on their unauthorized baptism, which had been performed by one without the priesthood and power to officiate in gospel ordinances.[27]

REBAPTISM AMONG NEPHITES. When Christ appeared to the Nephites on this continent, he commanded them to be baptized, although they had been baptized previously for the remission of their sins. We read how Nephi beheld angels who came and ministered to him daily; how he baptized all who came to be baptized for the remission of sins; how he organized the Church; and how he even raised his brother from the dead, since he held the priesthood.[28] Then we read that the Savior commanded Nephi and the people to be baptized again, *because he had organized anew the Church under the gospel.*[29] *Before that it had been organized under the law.*[30]

REBAPTISM OF JOSEPH SMITH. For the same reason Joseph Smith and those who had been baptized prior to April 6, 1830, were again baptized on the day of the organization of the Church. Joseph Smith and Oliver Cowdery were baptized on the 15th day of May, 1829, Samuel Smith a few days later, Hyrum Smith a little later, and a few others, before the Church was organized. *That baptism was for the remission of sins.*

When the Church was organized, each of the brethren who organized the Church, and the others who had been baptized, were baptized again. *They had to be in order to come into the Church by the door.* Suppose Joseph Smith had overlooked that. It is just a little thing, but how vital it is. You will find all through the ministry of Joseph Smith that all these little things are there; not a thing is overlooked that is vital to the story.[31]

WHY ALMA IMMERSED HIMSELF. Alma was baptized and held the priesthood before the coming of

[27]*Era,* vol. 20, pp. 916-918.
[28]3 Ne. 7:18-26.
[29]3 Ne. 19:7-15.
[30]3 Ne. 9:15-22; 11:10-40; 12:18-19; 15:4-10.
[31]*Church News,* Mar. 30, 1935, pp. 6, 8.

Abinadi, but he became involved with other priests under the reign of the wicked King Noah, and when he baptized Helem, he felt he needed a cleansing himself so he buried himself in the water as a token of full repentance.[32]

---

[32]Pers. Corresp.; Mosiah 17:1-4; 18:1-29.

CHAPTER 18

THE SACRAMENT AND SALVATION

LAW OF THE SACRAMENT

SAINTS COMMANDED TO PARTAKE OF SACRAMENT.
In the present dispensation, at the time of the organization
of the Church, the Lord said: "It is expedient that the
church meet together *often* to partake of bread and wine
in the remembrance of the Lord Jesus." Then follow
the exact words which are to be used in blessing the bread
and the wine, or water, which by revelation has been
substituted for wine.[1]

To meet together *often* for this purpose is a requirement made of members of the Church, which is just as
binding upon them in its observance as the requirement
in relation to any other principle or ordinance of the gospel. *No member of the Church who refuses to observe
this sacred ordinance can retain the inspiration and
guidance of the Holy Ghost.*

It is as true today as it was in the days of Paul, that
many members of the Church are weak and sickly, *in
spirit and body,* and many sleep, because they have failed
to show their love for, and obedience to, the Lord Jesus
Christ in the keeping of this commandment.[2]

SACRAMENT BEARS RECORD OF ATONING SACRIFICE.
Ingratitude is the most prevalent of all sins; it is also one
of the greatest. Jesus Christ came into the world, not
to do the will of man, but to do the will of his Father,
and he said, "For God so loved the world, that he gave
his only begotten Son, that whosoever believeth in him
should not perish, but have everlasting life."[3] The love

---

[1]*D. & C.* 20:75-79; 27:1-4.   [3]John 3:16.
[2]1 Cor. 11:20-34.

of our Savior was equally as great, and because of it he was willing to suffer and die, that he might bring to all men the resurrection, and eternal life to those who were willing to believe and obey his gospel.[4]

In remembrance of this great act of infinite love, which has been the means of redeeming a fallen world, those who profess his name show their *gratitude* and likewise "the Lord's death till he come,"[5] by observing this holy ordinance.

SAINTS GAIN SPIRIT THROUGH SACRAMENT. But the ordinance means more than this. When we eat the bread and drink the water, we covenant that we will eat and drink in remembrance of the sacrifice which he made for us in the breaking of his body and the shedding of his blood; that we are willing to take upon us the name of the Son; that we will always remember him; that we will always keep his commandments which he has given us. In this act we witness to the Father, by solemn covenant in the name of the Son, that we will do all of these things. Through our faithfulness to these covenants, we are promised that we will always have the Spirit of the Lord to be with us to guide us in all truth and righteousness.[6]

How can a man who refuses to meet *often* with his fellow worshippers to keep this commandment have a claim upon the guidance and the blessings of the Lord? Yet, strange to say, there are those who seemingly have this false understanding.[7]

SACRAMENT REPLACES SACRIFICE. The partaking of these emblems constitutes one of the most holy and sacred ordinances in the Church, an ordinance which has replaced the slaying and eating of the paschal lamb which was typical of the sacrifice upon the cross of our Redeemer, an ordinance given to Israel in Egypt in

[4]D. & C. 34:1-3.   [6]D. & C. 20:77-79; Moro. 4:1-2; 5:1-2.
[5]1 Cor. 11:26.   [7]Era, vol. 40, p. 171.

remembrance of the great sacrifice which was, to them, future.

From the time of the exodus from Egypt to the crucifixion of our Redeemer, the Israelites were commanded to observe the passover at a certain time each year.[8] On the solemn night before the crucifixion, the Lord changed this ordinance and gave in its stead the sacrament.[9] We have been commanded to meet often, not merely once each year, and go to the house of prayer and there remember our Redeemer and make covenant with him in partaking oft of his holy ordinance.[10]

SACRAMENT NOT A SUPPER. This ordinance was not intended merely for the apostles, but for all the members of the Church, and it was the custom of the ancient saints to meet *often* for this purpose, as they were commanded. Then came the days of apostasy when this simple and holy ordinance was turned into a feast which brought from Paul a rebuke because the sacrament had been turned into a supper of revelry and drunkenness. The sacrament is not a "supper," although it has become the custom to refer to it as such.[11]

SACRAMENT MEETING

THE FIRST SACRAMENT MEETING. In my judgment the sacrament meeting is the *most sacred,* the *most holy,* of all the meetings of the Church. When I reflect upon the gathering of the Savior and his apostles on that memorable night when he introduced the sacrament, when I think of that solemn occasion, my heart is filled with wonderment and my feelings are touched. I consider that gathering one of the most solemn and wonderful since the beginning of time.

There the Savior taught them of his coming sacrifice, which in their bewilderment they could not understand. He plainly told them of his death and that his

8Ex. 12:3-30.   11*Rel. Soc. Mag.,* vol. 30, pp. 589-590;
9Luke 22:15-20.   1 Cor. 11:23-34.
10*D. & C.* 59:7-14.

blood should be shed, and this was said in the very hour of his agony for the sins of the world. It was a very solemn occasion; there the sacrament was instituted, and the disciples were commanded to meet together often and commemorate the death and sufferings of Jesus Christ, for his sacrifice was for the redemption of the world.[12]

He was about to take upon him the responsibility of paying the debt brought upon the world through the fall, that men might be redeemed from death and from hell. He had taught the people that he was to be lifted up that he might draw all men unto him, and that all who would repent and believe in him, keeping his commandments, should not suffer for he would take upon himself their sins.[13]

RENEW COVENANTS IN SACRAMENT MEETING. We have been called upon to commemorate this great event and to keep it in mind constantly. For this purpose we are called together once each week to partake of these emblems, witnessing that we do remember our Lord, that we are willing to take upon us his name, and that we will keep his commandments. This covenant we are called upon to *renew* each week, and we cannot retain the Spirit of the Lord if we do not consistently comply with this commandment. If we love the Lord, we will be present at these meetings in the spirit of worship and prayer, remembering the Lord and the covenant we are to renew each week through this sacrament as he has required it of us.

STANDARDS FOR SACRAMENT MEETINGS. I do not believe that the Lord is pleased with us when we turn this sacred meeting into a concert. I do not believe that he is pleased with us if we assemble in this meeting in a spirit of levity and not solemnity. I am sure he is not pleased when men are called to speak in these services whose hearts are not touched by the principles of the

---

[12]Matt. 26:26-29; Mark 14:22-25; Luke 22:14-20.   [13]John 3:14-15; 8:28; 12:32-34; *D. & C.* 18:10-11; 19:15-20.

gospel, and when they have no faith in the mission of Jesus Christ, and when they cast doubts upon the efficacy of his atonement and the sacrifice he made for the sins of the world. I am sure he is not pleased when we meet on such occasions to be amused, to be entertained, rather than to be instructed and to obtain spiritual education and thought and reflection.

I do not believe it is necessary, very frequently at least, for presiding officers to go outside of their wards and stakes to find speakers; not that this is something they should never do, but I think we many times ignore worthy men living in our wards, who are filled with the spirit of the gospel. I know it is not pleasing to me when I attend a service and someone is called upon to speak who stands before the people and presents, though it be in a pleasing way, some platitudes, some philosophy of men—the ideas of those who today mould the thought of the world, but who in their own hearts have no faith in or love for Jesus Christ—or who discuss questions at variance with the fundamental principles of the gospel.

SOLEMN NATURE OF SACRAMENT MEETINGS. I think this is an occasion when *the gospel should be presented, when we should be called upon to exercise faith, and to reflect on the mission of our Redeemer, and to spend time in the consideration of the saving principles of the gospel,* and not for other purposes. Amusement, laughter, light-mindedness, are all out of place in the sacrament meetings of the Latter-day Saints. We should assemble in the spirit of prayer, of meekness, with devotion in our hearts. I know of no other place where we can gather where we should be more reflective and solemn and where more of the spirit of worship should be maintained.[14]

REVERENCE NEEDED IN SACRAMENT MEETINGS. Members of the Church are under obligation and commandment to "live by every word that proceedeth forth

[14]Conf. Rep., Oct., 1929, pp. 60-62.

from the mouth of God," and through their study and faith, worship the Father and the Son in Spirit and in truth.[15] Too frequently Latter-day Saints indulge in conduct foreign to these definite instructions.

In our sacrament meetings, and other solemn gatherings, there occasionally enters a spirit of levity and noisy conduct before the meeting is called to order. And, then, at times, there are exercises which are permitted to enter into the worship which are not in harmony with the spirit of the meeting. We are commanded to cast away "idle thoughts," and "excess of laughter," and to "cease from all your light speeches, from all laughter, from all your lustful desires, from all your pride and light-mindedness, and from all your wicked doings."[16]

Undue levity in a sacred meeting hampers the free expression of the Holy Spirit. All our singing as well as our speaking should be in full accord with the nature of these sacred services. Missionary farewells, conducted in the sacrament meetings, frequently partake of a spirit detrimental to the nature of those services. All such detractions from sacred worship, the Lord directs we should avoid.[17]

PARTAKING OF SACRAMENT UNWORTHILY. The sacrament meeting is the most sacred and the most important meeting required of all the members of the Church. If any of the members are not in good standing; if they have in their hearts any feeling of hatred, envy, or sin of any kind, they should not partake of these emblems. If there are any differences or feelings existing between brethren, these differences should be adjusted before the guilty parties partake; otherwise they will eat and drink unworthily and bring upon them the condemnation spoken of by Paul.[18] We should all see that our hearts and hands are clean and pure.

---

[15]D. & C. 84:43-47; John 4:22-23.
[16]D. & C. 59:13-15; 88:69, 121.
[17]Era, vol. 44, p. 525.

[18]1 Cor. 11:20-24; 3 Ne. 18:28-32; 20:8; Morm. 9:29.

Those members of the Church who habitually absent themselves from the sacrament meeting and who do not enter into the covenants which the sacrament requires of them, are guilty of grievous sin and are under grave condemnation. The Spirit of the Lord cannot dwell in them, and they deny to themselves the guidance of that Spirit.

Willful and protracted absence is a sign of apostasy, and if persisted in will lead to faultfinding, disagreement with authorities, and misunderstanding and criticism of the doctrines of the Church. If such a course is continued, it will lead those who are guilty out of the Church, for the Spirit of the Lord cannot be their companion when they show indifference to this sacred commandment.[19]

COVENANT OF THE SACRAMENT

NATURE OF THE COVENANT OF SACRAMENT. I have often wondered if we fully realize the significance and importance of the covenants we make in partaking of these emblems in remembrance of the body and blood of Jesus Christ. It is our duty carefully and thoughtfully to consider the nature of these prayers, when we hear them offered in our meetings. There are four very important things we covenant to do each time we partake of these emblems, and in partaking, there is the token that we subscribe fully to the obligations, and thus they become binding upon us. These are as follows:

1. We eat in remembrance of the body of Jesus Christ, promising that we will always remember his wounded body slain upon the cross.

2. We drink in remembrance of the blood which was shed for the sins of the world, which atoned for the transgression of Adam, and which frees us from our own sins on condition of our true repentance.

3. We covenant that we will be willing to take upon us the *name* of the Son and always remember him. In keeping this covenant we promise that we will be called

---

[19]*Rel. Soc. Mag.*, vol. 30, p. 590.

by his name and never do anything that would bring shame or reproach upon that name.

4. We covenant that we will keep his commandments which he has given us, not one commandment, but that we will be willing to "live by every word that proceedeth forth from the mouth of God."[20]

If we will do these things, then we are promised the continual guidance of the Holy Ghost, and if we will not do these things, we will not have that guidance.[21]

VIOLATION OF COVENANT OF SACRAMENT. Again, I have wondered how members of the Church can go to the sacrament service and partake of these emblems, and make these solemn covenants, and then immediately after the close of the meeting go out to some place of amusement, to attend a picture show, a baseball game, or some resort, or to gather at some home to play cards.

When any of these things is done, the guilty person violates this sacred covenant so recently made or renewed. Do they who do this pay so little attention to their obligations that they really do not sense their significance? Or do they think that the Lord in his abundant goodness and mercy will overlook their shortcomings, and do they look upon it as being not a very great sin after all to violate covenants made in this manner? Of course, only those who are guilty are able to answer these questions.

The fact remains, however, that when we indulge in habits of this kind we are *covenant breakers* guilty of offenses, as taught by Paul, of the most serious kind. Because of these breaches of the commandments, and the violation of covenants thus solemnly taken, many among us are in the same condition as they were in the days of Paul; they are *spiritually sick, weak in the faith, and they sleep the spiritual sleep that leads to death.*[22] . . .

SACRAMENT AN INCENTIVE TO RIGHTEOUSNESS. *The primary and outstanding reason why we should at-*

---

[20]*D. & C.* 84:44 .
[21]*D. & C.* 20:77-79; John 6:48-57.

[22]1 Cor. 11:20-34; *D. & C.* 82:3-4.

*tend these services is that we may renew our covenants
by partaking of the sacrament.* The question, who will
speak, is of secondary importance, although it is too frequently considered the first. Our faith is always meas-
ured by our works. If we fully appreciated the many
blessings which are ours through the redemption made
for us, there is nothing that the Lord could ask of us that
we would not anxiously and willingly do.[23]

*Do you think a man who comes into the sacrament
service in the spirit of prayer, humility, and worship, and
who partakes of these emblems representing the body and
blood of Jesus Christ, will knowingly break the commandments of the Lord?*

If a man fully realized what it means when he partakes of the sacrament, that he covenants to take upon
him the name of Jesus Christ and to always remember
him and keep his commandments, and this vow is renewed week by week—do you think such a man will fail
to pay his tithing? Do you think such a man will break
the Sabbath day or disregard the Word of Wisdom?
Do you think he will fail to be prayerful, and that he will
not attend his quorum duties and other duties in the
Church? It seems to me that such a thing as a violation
of these sacred principles and duties is impossible when
a man knows what it means to make such vows week by
week unto the Lord and before the saints.

If we have the right understanding, we will live in
full accord with the principles of truth and walk in righteousness before the Lord. How can we receive his Spirit
otherwise? I can see the significance in the commandment
the Lord has given us to assemble frequently and partake
of these emblems in commemoration of his death. It is
our duty to assemble and renew our covenants and take
upon us fresh obligations to serve the Lord and keep
his sayings.

[23]*Rel. Soc. Mag.,* vol. 30, p. 591-592.

REMEMBER CHRIST'S SUFFERINGS DURING SACRA-
MENT. How can a man go forth after making such covenants and cheat his neighbor? Or rob the Lord? Or
violate any other commandment and refuse to walk in
the light of truth? I am sure if we could picture before
us (as I have tried many times to do), the solemn occasion when the Savior met with his apostles, if we could
see them there assembled—the Lord in his sadness,
sorrowing for the sins of the world, sorrowing for one
of his apostles who was to betray him, yet teaching
these 11 men who loved him and making covenant with
them—I am sure we would feel in our hearts that we
would never forsake him.

If we could see them there assembled and could
realize the weight of the burden which was upon our
Lord, and after their supper and the singing of an hymn,
their going forth, the Lord to be betrayed, mocked and
scorned, the disciples to forsake him in the deepest hour
of his trial—if we could understand all this (feebly
though it be, and feebly it must be, I am sure, my brethren and sisters), we would forever more want to walk
in the light of truth. If we could see the Savior of men
suffering in the garden and upon the cross and could
fully realize all that it meant to us, we would desire to
keep his commandments and we would love the Lord
our God with all our heart, with all our might, mind and
strength, and in the name of Jesus Christ would serve
him.[24]

CHILDREN AND THE SACRAMENT

ALL SAINTS TO ATTEND SACRAMENT MEETING.
This requirement is made of *all* members of the Church.
None are exempt or excused, except it be on account
of disability due to sickness or disease. Neither is there
any age limit. Many years ago the privilege of admin-
istering the sacrament in the Sunday School was
granted, as it was thought that here the children would

[24]Conf. Rep., Oct., 1929, pp. 62-63.

be taught reverence for this sacred ordinance. This in-
novation, however, does not excuse or exempt, and was
never intended so to do, any members of the Church
from attendance at the regularly appointed sacramental
service. This commandment is for all members of the
Church, both old and young, the halt, the blind, the
deaf and all who are physically able to attend.

The fact that this ordinance has been granted to
the Sunday Schools has caused the feeling to grow up
among some members of the Church that the children
are excused from the regular sacrament service, but this
is not the case. "Remember now thy Creator," we read
in the scriptures, *"in the days of thy youth,* while the
evil days come not, nor the years draw nigh, when thou
shalt say, I have no pleasure in them."[25]

And Malachi declares: "Then they that feared the
Lord spake often one to another: and the Lord hearkened, and heard it, and a book of remembrance was
written before him for them that feared the Lord, and
that thought upon his name."[26] So it shall be today, a
book of remembrance shall be kept for all those who
honor the Lord in the covenants required of us in the
ordinance of the sacrament.

CHILDREN TO BE TAUGHT IN SACRAMENT MEET-
ING. Among the Nephites, at the time their souls had
been fully charged with faith due to the personal visit
of the Lord, it is written that they found pleasure in
walking after the commandments which they had received, "continuing in fasting and prayer, and in meeting
together oft both to pray and to hear the word of the
Lord."[27] Moreover, their small children were blessed
with remarkable manifestations.

The Lord has set the age of accountability at eight
years. At this age children are to be baptized and thus
become entitled to all blessings as members of the

25Eccles. 12:1.   27 4 Ne. 12.
26Mal. 3:16.

Church. A child who has become a member of the Church through baptism is under the same commandment—for it is to all members of the Church—to attend the regularly established sacramental meetings.

Any man who thinks himself to be devout and who is faithful in his own personal attendance at these meetings, but who neglects this duty in behalf of his children, permitting them to run the streets, or otherwise occupy their time contrary to the way the Lord has commanded, is guilty of a transgression. Has not the Lord emphatically declared that it is the duty of parents in Zion or any of her stakes to teach their children the doctrines of the kingdom, and if they neglect this important duty, the sin shall be upon the heads of the parents?[28]

In what better way can parents teach their children than by example? Where can the children be instructed in the ways of the Lord any better than in their attendance at these sacred meetings? Yet it is too frequently the case that the younger members of the Church are absent from the sacramental meetings.

CHILDREN TO ATTEND SACRAMENT MEETING. We are not justified in thinking that if the children attend the Sunday School, and there partake of the bread and water in remembrance of the body and blood of our Redeemer, that they have fulfilled their duty. The Lord has required them—as members of the Church—to be in attendance at the constituted meeting which he has himself ordained and appointed for the benefit and salvation of all members of his Church.

There is nothing complicated in the plan of salvation that little children cannot understand. Some churches have clouded their doctrines with mysteries and symbolic ceremonies which even adults cannot comprehend, but this is all foreign to the gospel of Jesus Christ. Otherwise our Savior would have placed the year of accountability at the age of 21 or some other

[28]D. & C. 68:25-29.

period when the mind is mature and not at eight years of age. Brethren and sisters—parents in Zion—it is your solemn duty to be in attendance regularly at the sacramental service of the Church, and the obligation is also upon you to see that your children, who are given into your charge by their Heavenly Father, are also there.[29]

CHILDREN TO PARTAKE OF SACRAMENT. All little children virtually belong to the Church until they are eight years of age. Should they die before that age, they would enter the celestial kingdom. The Savior said, "Of such is the kingdom of heaven."[30] Then why should they be deprived of the sacrament?

NON-MEMBERS AND THE SACRAMENT. Non-members cannot comply with the covenants embodied in the blessings of the sacrament and, therefore, should not partake of it. They are old enough to reason and should understand that the sacrament, so far as adults are concerned, is for those who have repented of their sins in the waters of baptism.

It would be proper in a meeting to say, "The sacrament will now be administered to the members of the Church," in cases where there are non-members present; otherwise nothing need be said of this nature. If non-members are present and partake of the sacrament, we would not do anything to prevent it, for evidently they would take it in good faith, notwithstanding the nature of the covenant.

DENYING SACRAMENT TO UNWORTHY. The Lord has said that we should not permit anyone to partake of the sacrament unworthily. This means, as I understand it, anyone in the Church who has been in transgression of some kind and who has not repented. It would also apply to the apostate.[31]

[29]*Era*, vol. 40, pp. 171, 182.   [31]Pers. Corresp.; 3 Ne. 18:28-30.
[30]Matt. 19:14.

[END OF VOLUME II]

INDEX

A

Abraham, parable relative to, 157-158.

Adam, Book of Remembrance kept by, 200-201; celestial marriage of, 69-71; everlasting nature of marriage of, 70; genealogical records kept by, 200-201; God officiated at marriage of, 71; immortal creation of, 69-70; patriarchal family chain headed by, 67-68; spiritual death passed upon, 6-7; temporal death passed upon, 6-7; written language had by, 200-201.

Adam-ondi-Ahman, Adam worshipped at, 232.

Adultery, death penalty for, 94, 97; penalty for, 93-94; repentance for, 93-94.

Advancement, limitations on, 31-34.

Age of Accountability, Lord's setting of, 53.

Agency, conditional redemption governed by, 10; salvation cannot be gained without, 2.

Ahab, Elijah ministered in day of, 101; Elijah's warning to, 104; Naboth murdered by, 106; search of, for Elijah, 103-104.

Alma, quoted—physical perfection in resurrection, 290; resurrection "opinion" of, 300; self-immersion of, 336-337.

All Things, exalted beings attain unto, 35-37.

Amulek, quoted—now is day of our salvation, 181; quoted — physical perfection in resurrection, 289-290; resurrection taught by, 267.

Ancestors, responsibility to do temple work for, 150.

Angels, plan of salvation taught by, 6-7; unmarried have status of, 32-33, 61-65.

Animals, resurrection of, 281-282.

Annihilation, no such thing as, 64, 227-228.

Antiochus Epephanes, temple desecrated by, 235.

Apocrypha, Elijah's deeds recited in, 107-108.

Apostate Factions, temple work unknown to, 246-247.

Apostates, no salvation for dead for, 188.

Apostles, resurrection testimony of, 269-270.

Asteroth, false worship of, 104.

Atonement, children saved by 50-52; original sin doctrine denies power of, 50-51; sacrament bears record of, 338-339; salvation based on, 3; universal resurrection because of, 25; vicarious nature of, 141-142.

Auxiliary Organizations, genealogical society not one of, 211-212.

B

Baal, Elijah challenges priests of, 104-106; false worship of, 104-106; worship of, as fire god, 105.

Babies: See Children.

Banishment, receipt of, by sons of perdition, 220-221; spiritual death known as, 227-228.

Baptism, antiquity of, 323; children have no need of, 49-53; celestial salvation only involved in, 329-330; covenant of, 17-18; earth subject to, 320-322; elements of, 323-325; future sins remitted by, 326-327; keeping of record of, 205; men saved from lower kingdoms by, 330-331; mentally deficient have no need of, 55-56; mode of, 323-325; nature of, as birth and resurrection 323-328; nature of covenant of, 328-329; no salvation without, 3, 161; obligation to keep covenant of, 329; performance of, in Old Testament times, 323; repentance required for, 331-332; resurrection nature of, 325; salvation comes because of, 323-337; similitude of, 323-325; twofold purpose of, 332-333.

Baptism for Dead, Catholic suppression of, 163; Elijah did not participate in, 114, 116; Elijah's keys enable performance of, 118-119; first modern performance of, 169; keys of, 111-112; laws and conditions of, 161-164; meridian saints' practice of, 163; Nauvoo Temple performance of, 170; Paul's teaching of, 163; suggested schedule for, 151; youth participation in, 162-163.

Baptist, John: See John the Baptist.
Barefooted Carmelites, Elijah legendary founder of, 100.
Barrel of Meal, Elijah's blessing of, 103.
Beasts, resurrection of, 281-282.
Beatific Vision, false doctrine of, 51-52.
Beersheba, Elijah flees to, 106.
Beth-el, Jacob's temple at, 231-232.
Bible, improper to question miracles of, 312-313.
Birth: See Birth Control.
Birth, immortality and eternal life result from, 85-86; importance of, 85-86; righteous parentage important in, 88-92; spirit enters body before, 280-281.
Birth Control, damnation result of, 88-89; gospel laws relative to, 85-89; loss of salvation through, 88; wickedness of, 87-89.
Birth Under Covenant, blessings of, 89-92.
Blasphemy against Holy Ghost, sealing up against, 46-47; unpardonable sin known as, 221.
Blessing, keeping of record of, 205.
Blood, element of, in baptism, 323-325.
Blood Bodies, nature of, 285-286.
Blood of Dead, responsibility of Church for, 144-145.
Bodies, kinds of, in resurrection, 33-34.
Book of Mormon, resurrection testimony of, 271.
Book of Remembrance, Adam's keeping of, 200-201.
Brass Plates, genealogical data recorded on, 198.
Broken Homes, tragedy of, 80-81.
Brother, raising up seed unto, 78-79.
Brunson, Seymour, salvation for dead first taught at funeral of, 169.
Buffetings of Satan, wicked turned over to, 96-97.

C

Cahoon, Reynolds, Kirtland Temple work of, 239.
Cain, Satan subject to, 279-280.
Calling and Election Sure, attaining status of, 46-47.
Candles, burning of, for dead by Catholics, 136.
Cannon, George Q., quoted—resurrection of sons of perdition, 276-277.
Carnality, fallen man in state of, 30.
Carter, Jared, Kirtland Temple work of, 239.
Carthage, council of, 163.

Catholic Church, apostate teachings of, 51, 54; baptism for dead suppressed by, 163; false salvation for dead teachings of, 136-137, 188-189.
Celestial Beings, limitations on progression of, 32-33.
Celestial Bodies, procreation limited to, 287-288; resurrection of, 33-34, 296; some resurrected with, 286-287.
Celestial Earth, meek gain inheritance on, 26.
Celestial Earths, many have status of, 26-27.
Celestial Kingdom, all children saved in, 52-55, baptism required for, 329-330, exaltation within, 24-25; family unit continues in, 67; gospel ordinances apply only to, 190-191; laws and conditions pertaining to, 23-27; only the sanctified attain unto, 98; temple ordinances pertain to, 40-41.
Celestial Marriage, Adam lived order of, 69-71; apostate denial of, 71-72; becoming sons of God through, 64-65; blessings of, for unmarried women, 76-78; care in entering into, 77-78; children heirs of, 54-55; children to be taught laws of, 75-76; conditional nature of blessings of, 46-47; crowning gospel blessings come through, 58-59; Elijah's keys enable performance of, 118-119; eternal life results from, 58; exaltation gained through, 43-44, 58-65; first performance of, by God, 71; fulness of Father gained through, 62-63; godhood attained through, 62-63; keys required for performance of, 73-74; laws and conditions of, 58-59; laws governing order of, 73-79; nature of, 21; no exaltation without, 32-33, 65; obligation to enter into, 74-75; perfection comes through, 84; restrictions relative to, 72-73; Saducees' denial of, 71-73; unrighteous denied status of, in heaven, 72-73.
Children, baptism not needed by, 49-53; birth of, under covenant, 88-92; celestial kingdom inherited by, 52-55; celestial marriage taught to, 75-76; divorce annuls rights of, 80-82; enduring family right of, 82-83; eventual marriage of, 54-55; exaltation of, 54-55; hearts of, turn to fathers, 123-128; no blessing denied to, 54-55; no temptation for, 56-57; parental claim on, 90-92; patriarchal status of, 79; primeval innocence of, 49-50; reclaiming of, 90-92; re-

Daughters of God, eternal life inherited by, 8-9; exaltation attained by, 37-41.

Dead: See Death; Salvation for Dead.

Dead, baptism for, 161-164; damnation of, 131-132; gospel taught to, 132-135; no perfection without, 175; no salvation without, 173-176; prayers for, by Catholic Church, 136; saints work for salvation of, 147-153; salvation of, 131-132; salvation cannot be forced on, 185-190; temple proxies representatives of, 142-143.

Death: See Spiritual Death.

Death, Adam lived before day of, 69-70; Christ's destruction of, 261-262; civil marriage ended by, 59-60; destruction of, through resurrection, 298-299; meaning of, 64; nature of, 216; resurrection puts end to, 278; sins unto, 96; subjection of, to Christ's power, 259-260; temporary status of, 216-217; time of performance of vicarious ordinances following, 178-179; unmarried recieve inheritance of, 64.

Deformities, resurrection without, 289.

Degrees of Glory: See Celestial Kingdom; Terrestrial Kingdom; Telestial Kingdom.

Degrees of Glory, Church members can attain any of, 28; laws and conditions pertaining to, 20-34; reasonable to believe in, 20; restrictions on progression in, 31-34.

Desires, judgment according to, 76-77.

Destruction, divorce brings nations to, 84-85.

Destruction in Flesh, certain subject to, 96-97.

Destruction of Soul, meaning of, 227-228.

Devil: See Satan.

Devil, angels to, 260; resurrection saves man from, 283.

Devils, curse of denial of bodies to, 85-86; sons of perdition status of, 219-220.

Dispensation of Fulness of Times, mighty work reserved for, 147-148.

Disobedience, divorces come because of, 80-82; children's rights destroyed by, 80-82; disobedience brings about, 82; gospel laws pertaining to, 80-85; gospel plan leaves no room for, 80-81; justification of, in some cases, 82; keys embrace loosing power of, 84; Lord's penalty for, 83-84; nations destroyed because of evil of, 84-85; promises of exaltation lost through, 83; salvation lost through, 81-82; tragedy of, 80-81.

Disease, resurrected beings not subject to, 293.

Doctors, faith goes with, 315.

Dominion, exalted beings attain fulness of, 35-37.

E

Earth, celestial destiny of, 26; changes in surface of, foretold, 316-318; covering of, by flood, 318-322; death and resurrection of, 26-27; Elijah's coming prevents cursing of, 120-122; flood wrought changes on, 318; latter-day revelation tells restoration of, 317-318; restoration of, 316-318; resurrection of, 281.

Earths, celestial destiny of, 26-27.

Ecclesiasticus, Elijah's deeds recited by, 107-108.

Eddy, Robert Henry, genealogical interests of, 126.

Edersheim, quoted—Jewish belief in coming of Elijah, 100-101.

Election, doctrine of, 46-47.

Elias: See Elijah.

Elias, Elijah known as, 107-108; John the Baptist not same as, 108-109; New Testament teachings about, 108-110.

Elijah, Ahab's search for, 103-104; Ahab warned by, 104; ancient ministry of, 100-112; ancient mission of, 116-117; Apocrypha recites deeds of, 107-108; appearance of, at transfiguration, 109-110; appearance of, to Joseph Smith and Oliver Cowdery, 122-123; coming of, 112-114; dead raised by, 103; earth cursed except for coming of, 120-122; Elisha called by, 106; family unit preserved through keys of, 120-122; fire called down from heaven by, 105-107; flight of, to Beersheba, 106; genealogical research proves coming of, 124-128; Jews have belief in coming of, 100-101; John the Baptist not same as, 108-109; justice and mercy of God shown by, 115; keys restored by, 111 - 112; kings and prophets anointed by, 106; latter-day coming of, 112-113; latter-day mission of, 117; legends about, 100-102; Malachi foretells coming of, 115; meeting of Obadiah with, 103-104; miracles of, 102-108; mission and sealing power of, 115-128; Moroni foretells coming of, 115-116, 118;

mortal ministry of, 102-108; no baptism for dead in days of, 114, 116; New Testament teachings about, 108-110; oil and meal blessed by, 103; priests of Baal challenged by, 104-106; proof of coming of, 122-128; prophecies about, 112-114; power of, had in meridian of time, 164; publication of family histories follows coming of, 126-127; reason for translation of, 110-111; restoration of all things by, 110; resurrection of, 119; revelation needed to comprehend coming of, 115-116; salvation comes through sealing power of, 122; sealing of heavens by, 102; sealing power held by, 116-120; spirits participate in work of, 119-120; traditions about, 100-101; translation of, 106-107; world proves coming of, 123-128.

Elisha, Elijah's call of, 106-107.

El-Khudr, Mohammedan tradition about, 100.

End, enduring to, 4, 13-19, 25-26, 95-96.

Endless Life: See Eternal Life.

Endless Punishment, nature of, 8; meaning of, 228.

Endowment House, temple status of, 245.

Endowments, Ensign Peak site of, 165; exaltation gained through, 45-46; giving of, on Mount of Transfiguration, 165; keeping of covenants incident to, 255-257; missionaries given blessings of, 255-256; nature of, in Kirtland Temple, 241-242; necessity for, for genealogical workers, 213; no exaltation without, 253; promise given of, 238; protective nature of, 252-253; regulations incident to, 252-257; righteousness to precede receipt of, 254-255; sonship obtained through, 40-41; 55-56; youth should seek receipt of, 253-254.

Endure to End: See Obedience.

Enduring to End, necessity for, 193-194; relationship of salvation for dead to, 192-196.

Enoch, salvation for dead promises of, 156-157.

Ensign Peak, endowments given on, 165.

Ephraim, Israel to receive blessings from, 250-251.

Eternal Damnation: See Damnation.
Eternal Damnation, nature of, 224-225.
Eternal Father: See God.
Eternal Fire, nature of, 224-225.

Eternal Increase, celestial marriage leads to, 43-44; exalted beings attain unto, 47-48; 68-69.

Eternal Life: See Exaltation; Salvation.

Eternal Life, definition of, 4-9; exaltation reward of attaining unto, 217-218; grace basis of, 309-310; nature of, 4-9, 24, 217-218; obedience essential to gaining of, 6; sealed up unto, 46-47; spiritual death opposite of, 218.

Eternal Lives: See Eternal Life.

Eternal Lives, exalted beings attain unto, 63.

Eternal Marriage: See Celestial Marriage.

Eternal Progression, celestial marriage essential to, 58, kinds of, 31-34; limitations on, 31-34; terrestrial and telestial limits on, 22.

Eternal Punishment, meaning of, 228; nature of, 8; repentance brings end to, 160.

Eternal Suffering, repentance brings end to, 160.

Eternal Torment, nature of, 224-225.
Ethbaal, Jezebel daughter of, 104.
Eve, creation and marriage of, 69-71.
Everlasting Life: See Eternal Life.
Exaltation: See Eternal Life; Salvation.

Exaltation, all things embraced within, 35-37; celestial marriage essential to, 43-44, 65; celestial status of, 24-25; children heirs of, 54-55; covenant of, 58-59; definition of, 8-9; disobedient spouse cannot deprive worthy of, 65; divorce breaks promise of, 83; eligibility for gaining of, 43; endowments and sealings essential to, 40-41, 45-46, 253; family continues in state of, 65-69; fulness of Father part of, 44-45; God's attainment of, 47-48; marriage essential to, 32-33; meaning of, 11-13; membership in Church of Firstborn part of, 41-42; nature of, 35-57; overcoming all things required for, 25-26; patriarchal order exists in state of, 67-68; requirements for attaining of, 43-49; some attain celestial kingdom without, 32-33; spirit children born in state of, 68-69; unmarried women may attain unto, 76-78.

Ezekiel, resurrection taught by, 266.

F

Faith, all things revealed by, 305; Christ center of, 302; doctors go with, 315; flood accepted by, 315-322; Joseph Smith recipient of, 302-303; law of, 302-311; laws and conditions of, 302-322; miracles flow from, 311-322; need for, 305; no salvation without, 3, 15-16, 138-139; revelations withheld for lack of, 304-305; righteousness basis of, 311-312; worldly philosophies destructive of, 322.

"Faith Alone" Doctrine, false sectarian views on, 138-141; justice of God denied by, 140-141; man damned for belief in, 139-140.

Faithful, no blessing denied to, 176-177.

Fallen Man: See Man.

Fall of Adam, first marriage performed before, 69-71; man not accountable for, 50-51; resurrection necessary because of, 258-259.

Families, patriarchal joining of, 67-69.

Family, celestial continuance of, 67; children's right to perpetuity of, 82-83; eternity of, 65-69; exalted beings enjoy continuation of, 65-69.

Family of God, membership in, 66-67, 173-174; sealings essential to membership in, 174.

Family Histories, Elijah's coming presages publication of, 126-127.

Family Unit: See Family.

Family Unit, Elijah's keys provide for preservation of, 120-122; no perfection without, 175; sealing power enables continuation of, 173.

Father: See God.

Fathers, hearts of, turn to children, 123-128; our duty to seek knowledge of, 128; promise of salvation made to, 154-157.

Father's House, many mansions in, 20-34.

Fellowship with God, resurrection essential to, 260-261.

Fire, Elijah calls down, from heaven, 105-107.

Fire God, Baal worshipped as, 105.

First Death: See Spiritual Death.

First Presidency, quoted—baptism for celestial kingdom only, 330.

First Resurrection: See Resurrection.

Fishes, resurrection of, 281-282.

Flood, changes wrought by, 318; earth baptized by, 320-322; objections to, 315-316; faith causes acceptance of, 315-322; water available for, 318-319.

Forgiveness, repentance and punishment sometimes required for, 97-98.

Fowls, resurrection of, 281-282.

Free Agency: See Agency.

Friends, limitations on doing temple work for, 208.

Frisian Chief, false doctrine taught to, 136-137.

Fulness of Father, celestial marriage leads to, 62-63; exalted beings attain unto, 24, 44-45.

G

Genealogical Data, early preparation of, 209-210; furnishing of, by resurrected beings, 149-150.

Genealogical "Link-Men," beware of, 212.

Genealogical Records, Adam's keeping of, 200-201; importance of, 210; millennial revelation of, 167-168.

Genealogical Research, Elijah's coming proved by, 124-128; fascinating nature of, 125-126; limitations on, 206-208; policies and procedures concerning, 206-215; purpose of, 206-207.

Genealogical Research Consultants, choosing of, 214.

Genealogical Researchers, accuracy needed by, 208-210.

Genealogical Societies, Elijah's coming foreshadows coming of, 124-128.

Genealogical Society, non-auxiliary organization status of, 211-212; purpose of, 210-212.

Genealogical Workers, capable persons needed as, 213-214; endowments essential for, 213; qualifications of, 212-215; responsibility of, 152-153.

Gentiles, temple building work of, 250.

Gift of Holy Ghost: See Holy Ghost.

Glory: See Degrees of Glory; Kingdoms of Glory.

Glory, degrees of, 20-34; kingdoms of, 20-23.

God, family of, 66-67; first marriage performed by, 71; justice of, 129-135; life eternal gained by knowledge of, 7; membership in family of, 173-174; mortal probation of, 47-48; perfection of, 35; saints in presence of, 328.

Godhood, exalted beings attain status of, 35-49; sons of God attain unto, 39.

Gods, attaining status of, 32; exalted beings attain status of, 35-49; status of, attained through marriage, 62-65.

Ordinances: See Gospel Ordinances.

Ordinances, admission to celestial kingdom gained by, 329; celestial nature of, 190-191; Elijah's keys enable performance of, 118-119; performance of, for dead, 143; reservation of, for latter-days, 154-155; sealing power needed for performance of, 116-117; vicarious nature of, 141-143.

Original Sin, damnable nature of doctrine of, 50-51; false doctrine of, 49-53.

Overcoming All Things, process of, brings exaltation, 25-26.

P

Paradise, nature of, 228-230; righteous go to, 229-230.

Parents, children subject to claim of, 89-92; false tradition that Elijah and Melchizedek were without, 101-102.

Passover, feast of, 339-340.

Patriarchal Chain, families joined in, 67-69.

Patriarchal Order, children born in, 79.

Patriarchal Records, keeping and custody of, 206.

Paul, quoted—baptism a resurrection, 327; quoted—Christ destroys death through resurrection, 298 - 299; quoted — family in heaven, 66; quoted—joint-heirs with Christ, 24, 218; quoted—kinds of bodies in resurrection, 33-34; quoted—salvation by grace, 306-307; teachings of, concernnig grace and works, 306-311.

Penalty, divorce subject to, 83-84; imposition of severe, for certain sins, 96-97.

Penrose, Charles W., quoted—baptism of earth by flood, 322.

Pentecostal Manifestations, Kirtland Temple locale of, 240-241.

Perdition: See Sons of Perdition.

Perdition, status of Cain as, 279-280; status of Lucifer as, 225.

Perfection, attainment of, 18; celestial marriage lays foundation for, 84; dead essential to, 175; exalted beings attain unto, 35-37; family organization brings, 175.

Personal Record Keeping, law of, 204-206.

Peter, endowments given to, 165, 170; keys received by, on Mount of Transfiguration, 109-111; quoted—Christ visits spirits in prison, 159;

quoted—making our calling and election sure, 46-47.

Philosophies, faith destroyed by, 322; resurrection denied by, 265-266.

Phoenician Fire God, status of Baal as, 105.

Physical Death: See Death.

Physical Imperfections, resurrection without, 289.

Pioneers, rebaptism of, 333-335.

Plan of Salvation, Adam received knowledge of, 6-7; ingratitude for, 4; terms and conditions of, 3-4.

Plan of Redemption: See Plan of Salvation; Redemption.

Poverty, Kirtland Temple built in time of, 239.

Power, exalted beings gain fulness of, 35-37.

Pratt, Orson, quoted—baptism of earth by flood, 321; quoted—conditional and unconditional salvation, 9-10; quoted—kinds of resurrected bodies, 287.

Prayers for Dead, apostate church performance of, 136.

Pre-existence, labors toward salvation in, 1-2; rebellion of Lucifer in, 218-219.

Preparatory Temple, Kirtland Temple known as, 242.

Presidency, quoted—baptism for celestial kingdom only, 330.

Priesthood, Elijah to bring restoration of, 118-119; patriarchal family chain part of, 67-68; sonship attained through, 37-38.

Priesthood Bearers, performance of ordinances by, 179-180; temple work responsibility of, 145-146.

Priests, exalted beings attain status of, 24; membership in Church of Firstborn attained by, 42.

Priests of Baal, Elijah's challenge to, 104-105.

Prison: See Spirit Prison.

Prison, saints open doors to, 135.

Prisoners, coming forth of, 155-165.

Procreation, celestial bodies only have power of, 287-288; man commanded to comply with law of, 85-89.

Progress, history an aid to, 197.

Progression: See Eternal Progression.

Progression, limitations on, 31-34.

Promises Made to Fathers, nature of, 154-157.

Prophecies, Elijah's mission foretold in, 112-114.

Prophecy, more sure word of, 46-47.

Proxies: See Temple Proxies.

bodies in, 284-285; stillborn children come forth in, 280-281; sufferings of ungodly prior to, 298; telestial bodies in, 296-297; terrestrial bodies in, 296-297; time of, 299-300; universal extent of, 25, 273-280.

Revelation, coming of Elijah known only by, 115-116; lack of faith causes withholding of, 304-305; laws of salvation come by, 2-3; piecemeal nature of, 168.

Reverence, sacrament meetings deserving of, 342-343.

Rigdon, Sidney, Lectures on Faith not written by, 303-304; resurrection testimony of, 271-273.

Righteousness, faith comes because of, 311-312; sacrament leads to, 345-346; salvation for dead based on, 191-192; salvation predicated upon, 13-19.

Ripley, Robert, quoted—fish swallowing man, 314.

S

Sacrament, children to partake of, 347-350; covenant of, 344-347; laws and conditions pertaining to, 338-350; non-members should not partake of, 350; record of atonement borne by, 338-339; remember Christ's sufferings during, 347; righteousness results from partaking of, 345-346; sacrifice replaced by, 339-340; saints commanded to partake of 338; Spirit gained through, 339; unworthy partaking of, 343-344, 350; violation of covenants of, 345.

Sacrament Meeting, attendance of all saints required at, 347-348; attendance of children at, 349-350; children taught in, 348-349; Christ's institution of, 340-341; covenants renewed in, 341; instructions relative to, 340-344; reverence needed in, 342-343; solemn nature of, 342; standards for, 341-342.

Sacred Grove, temple status of, 234.

Sacrifice, exaltation gained through, 48-49; sacrament replaces offering of, 339-340.

Sadducees, denial of celestial marriage by, 71-73.

Sainthood, attainment of, 19.

Saints, celestial marriage commanded for, 60; doors to spirit prison opened by, 135; keys and endowments promised to, 238; making of, 19; salvation not gained by half of, 13-19.

Salvation: See Eternal Life; Exaltation; Plan of Salvation; Redemption; Salvation Universal.

Salvation, acceptance of available light leads to, 192-193; all but sons of perdition attain unto, 20-21; all receive offer of, 129-135; all to hear truths of, 182-183; angels give knowledge of, 6-7; baptism essential to, 323-337; baptism leads to, 328-332; baptism needed for, 161-162; birth control causes loss of, 88; celestial kind of, 24-25; celestial, terrestrial, and telestial nature of, 21-22; conditional, definition of, 9-10; children attain unto, 49-57; Church members have no guarantee of, 14-19; discussion of, 1-19; divorce causes loss of, 81-82; enduring to end essential to attainment of, 193-194; extent those without gospel law attain unto, 29; faith and obedience required for, 138-141; faith leads to, 302-322; faith unto, 302-322; faithful to attain unto, 176-177; false limitations on, 129-130; first obligation with reference to, 145; free agency essential to, 2; future day of, 181-182; general, definition of, 9-10; gospel acceptance required for, 134-135; grace basis of, 309; grace and works unite to bring, 310-311; importance of, 1; individual, definition of, 9-10; individual nature of, 91; kinds of, 9-13; kinds Church members may attain unto, 28-29; little sins keep us from, 16-17; mentally deficient gaining of, 55-56; no second chance for, 181-196; now is day of, 181; place of history in plan of, 197-200; post-mortal search for, 18-19; pre-existent labors toward, 1-2; promises of, made to fathers, 154-157; rebaptism not essential to, 335-336; rebellious cannot gain reward of, 194-197; repentance a requisite for, 194-197; resurrection determines degree of, 283-301; revealed nature of, 2-3; sacrament essential to, 338-350; sealing power of Elijah essential to, 122; sins keep us from, 14-17; special meaning of, 11-13; spirit world teachings of, 182-183; telestial kind of, 22-23; those who die without a knowledge of, 181-182; those who overcome attain unto, 25-26; truths of, easily understood, 1; unclean have no promise of, 99; unconditional, definition of, 9-10; understanding truths of, 1;

unfaithful never to attain unto, 193-194; universal offer of, 139-141; unworthy denied status of, 185-190; usual meaning of, 11; valiance essential to gaining of, 28-29; vicarious atonement basis of, 141-142; vicarious law of, 141-143; works required for gaining of, 13-19; worthy dead essential to, 176.

Salvation of Children: See Children; Salvation.

Salvation for Dead, ancient prophets taught doctrine of, 154-157; apostates cannot attain unto, 188; beginning of revelation of, 168; divinity of Church shown by teachings of, 135-138; false Catholic practice relative to, 136-137; false Catholic teachings about, 135-138; false "faith alone" doctrine compared with, 138-141; false notions about, 184-185; grandeur of doctrine of, 143; importance of, 143-147; Isaiah's promises relative to, 155-156; laws and conditions pertaining to, 154-180; millennial era of, 166-168; none exempt from work of, 148-149; no practice of, before Christ, 164-165; obligatory nature of, 149; relationship of enduring to end to, 192-196; reservation of, for final dispensation, 147-148; restoration of doctrine of, 168-173; revelation of fulness of doctrine of, 168-169; righteousness basis of, 191-192; those eligible for, 181-185; trend toward apostate concept of, 189-190; unselfish nature of, 144; unworthy have no promise of, 185-190; vision of, 168; work of, reserved for latter-days, 166; worthy persons only subject to, 190-192.

Salvation Universal: See Salvation; Salvation for Dead.

Salvation Universal, doctrine of, 129-153.

Sanctuaries: See Temples.

Satan, Cain to rule over, 279-280; children not tempted by, 56-57; sons of perdition servants of, 220-221.

Saviors, gaining status of, 143.

Scape Goat, use of, 141-142.

Scars, removal of, in resurrection, 292.

Science, foolish to question miracles of, 312-313.

Scriptures, rule of interpretation, 95.

Sea, return of, to north countries, 318.

Sealing Power, all authority embraced in, 117; conditional effect of, 98-99; Elijah had mission and keys of, 116-117; family unit in eternity

because of, 173; restoration of, 118-120.

Sealings: See Temple Sealings.

Sealings, exaltation gained through, 45-46; membership in family of God gained through, 174; millennial adjustment of, 177-178; policies governing performance of, 176-180; sonship obtained through, 40-41.

Second Chance for Salvation: See Salvation; Salvation for Dead.

Second Coming of Christ, Elijah's return shows nearness of, 112-113; first resurrection at time of, 295-296.

Second Death: See Spiritual Death.

Second Death, nature of, 131.

Second Marriages, disapproval of, out of temple, 78.

Second Resurrection: See Resurrection.

Second Resurrection, telestial bodies come forth in, 22.

Section 132:26, interpretation of, 94-99.

Seed, raising up, unto one's brother, 78-79.

Seeds: See Continuation of Seeds.

Seeds, exalted beings have continuation, of, 9.

Servants, civil marriage leads to classification as, 61-65; exaltation not obtained by, 41; unmarried left in status of, 59.

Servants of Lord, faith in, 302-303.

Sex Sin, enormity of, 92-94.

Shelem, temple status of, 233.

Sin, actual forgiveness of, by repentance, 332; death to, by baptism, 327; original and personal, comparison of, 9-10.

Sinai, temple status of, 233.

Sins, attainment of kingdom of God prevented by, 195-196; salvation not gained in event of, 14-17; spirit world forgiveness of, 160-161.

Sins Unto Death, no repentance for, 96.

Smith, George A., Kirtland Temple work of, 239.

Smith, Hyrum, Kirtland Temple work of, 239.

Smith, Joseph, coming of Elijah to, 122-123; faith in, 302-303; Lectures on Faith prepared by, 303-304; quoted—baptism applies to celestial kingdom, 25-26; quoted—greatest individual responsibility, 145-146; quoted—how God attained exaltation, 47-48; quoted—keys given on Mount of Transfiguration, 110;

Telestial Beings, celestial status never attained by, 31-32.

Telestial Bodies, procreative power denied to, 287-288; resurrection of, 33-34, 297-298; some resurrected with, 286-287.

Telestial Damnation, nature of, 22-23.

Telestial Kingdom, celestial presence denied to, 5-6; laws and conditions pertaining to, 27-31; no marriage in, 73; some Church members attain unto, 28; terrestrial beings minister to, 5-6.

Telestial Salvation, most men to attain unto, 22; nature of, 22.

Temple, ordinances greater than, 172-173; vicarious ordinances performed in, 171-173.

Temple Blessings, indifference leads to loss of, 193; regulations as to receipt of, 252-257.

Temple Building, commandment of, 237-238; Lamanite participation in, 247-251; law of, 231-257.

Temple Covenants, condemnation for breaking of, 256-257; obligation for keeping of, 255-257; regulations pertaining to, 252-257.

Temple Marriage: See Celestial Marriage.

Temple Ordinances: See Vicarious Ordinances.

Temple Ordinances, exaltation gained by, 40-41, 45-46; membership in Church of Firstborn attained through, 41-43; mortals only to engage in, 178; performance of, not for all, 176; restrictions on immediate performance of, 178-179.

Temple Proxies, dead represented by, 142-143; vicarious service of, 142-143.

Temple Recommends, foresight in applying for, 179.

Temple Records, early preparation of, 209-210; orderly preparation of, 208-209.

Temples, admission to, 243; definition of, 231; divinity of Church established by, 235-236; groves and mountains used as, 232-234; keys revealed in, 40-41; latter-day building of, 243-246; nature and antiquity of, 231-237; prophecies foretell latter-day building of, 244; purpose of, 243-244; unworthy not to go in, 61.

Temple Sealings: See Sealings.

Temple Sealings, policies governing performance of, 176-180.

Temple Work, blessings flow from,

180; celestial exaltation only involved in, 176; conversion needed for, 152; millennium a period of, 251-252; old and young to participate in, 150-151; orderly performance of, 208-209; performance of, by priesthood brethren, 179-180; rebellious not entitled to blessings of, 185-190; rejection of Church if no performance of, 171; rendering assistance to others in, 151-152; responsibility of Church for, 145-153; restrictions on performance of, 208; suggested schedule for, 151.

Temporal Death: See Death.

Temporal Death, Adam subject to, 6-7.

Terrestrial Beings, limitations on progression of, 31-34.

Terrestrial Bodies, procreative power denied to, 287-288; resurrection of, 33-34, 296-297; some resurrected with, 286-287.

Terrestrial Kingdom, celestial beings minister to, 5; laws and conditions pertaining to, 27-31; no marriage in, 73; non-valiant attain unto, 28-29; second chance for salvation leads to, 183-184; some Church members attain unto, 28; status of those who attain unto, 28-29.

Terrestrial Salvation, nature of, 21-22.

Testimony, cannot do genealogical work without, 212.

Thompson, T. B., catalogue of British family histories published by, 126-127.

Tishbite, Elijah known as, 101.

Transfiguration, appearances on Mount of, 109-111.

Translated Beings, mortal status of, 300-301.

Translation, Elijah taken to heaven by, 106-107; Moses and Elijah attained status of, 110-111; reason for, 107.

Truth, exalted beings gain fulness of, 35-37; teachings of, in all degrees of glory, 23.

U

Ulai River Bank, temple status of, 234.

Unchaste, damnation of, 92-93.

Unchastity, offense of, 92-94.

Unclean, damnation promised to, 99; no salvation for, 19.

Uncleanliness, no salvation in event of, 193-194.

Unfaithful, salvation forever withheld from, 193-194.

Ungodly, sufferings of, before resurrection, 298.
Unpardonable Sin, covenant broken by, 90; spiritual death result of, 221.
Unvirtuous, damnation of, 92-93.
Unworthy, sacrament denied to, 350; temple blessings denied to, 61.

V

Valiance, no salvation without, 28-29.
Valleys, exaltation of, 316-318.
Vicarious Ordinances: See Temple Ordinances.
Vicarious Ordinances, denial of, to murderers, 192; duty to engage in, 214-215; meridian of time performance of, 165; performance of, 161-162; performance of, not required for all, 191; provision for, 141-143; purpose of, 143; rebellious not benefited by, 187-188; suggested schedule for, 151; temples place for, 171-172.
Vicarious Salvation: See Salvation.
Vicarious Salvation, some not eligible for, 183.

W

Water, baptism of, 323-325.
Whitmer, David, resurrection testimony of, 271-273.
Whitmer, John, position of, as Church historian and recorder, 201.
Wife, care in choice of, 77-78.
Williams, Frederick G., rebaptism of, 333.
Wisdom, exalted beings gain fulness of, 35-37.
Witnesses, Elijah's coming testified to by, 124; testimony about salvation by, 1.
Wolfran, denial of salvation for dead by, 136-137.

Women (unmarried), exaltation for, 76-78.
Works, attainment of salvation through, 13-19; Christ taught need for, 306; grace unites with, 310-311; law of, 306-311; men judged by, 27; sectarian controversy over, 306-307.
World, marriage of, 72-73.
Worthiness, salvation for dead based on, 190-192.
Wounds, resurrection without, 289-292.
Writing, Adam had knowledge of, 200-201.

Y

Young, Brigham, Nauvoo Temple font dedicated by, 170; quoted—baptism of earth by flood, 320; quoted—birth control, 88; quoted—heirs of covenant, 90-91; quoted—rebellious fight truth after death, 195; quoted—spirit entering body, 280-281; quoted—spirit participation in work of Elijah, 119-120; quoted—virtue, 93; rebaptism of, 333.
Youth, endowments should be sought by, 252-254; ordinances performed by, 162-163.

Z

Zacharias, responsibility for blood of, 144-145.
Zarepath, Elijah's ministry in, 102-103.
Zechariah, quoted—wounds of Christ, 291-292.
Zerubbabel, temple of, 235.
Zidon, Elijah's ministry in, 103.
Zidonians, nation of, 104.
Zion, gentiles to assist in building of, 250.